LIGHT & EASY
BAKING

Other Outstanding Cookbooks from Random House Value Publishing:

SPECIAL OCCASIONS by John Hadamuscin

MENNONITE COUNTRY-STYLE RECIPES by Esther H. Shank

AMISH COOKING

MARION CUNNINGHAM'S GOOD EATING

THE FRUGAL GOURMET by Jeff Smith

FROM JULIA CHILD'S KITCHEN by Julia Child

THE WAY I COOK by Lee Bailey

THE FANNIE FARMER BAKING BOOK by Marion Cunningham

LIGHT & EASY
BAKING

BEATRICE OJAKANGAS

Gramercy Books
New York

To those for whom baking is first and light is best

This 2000 edition is published by Gramercy Books™, an imprint of Random House Value Publishing, Inc., 280 Park Avenue, New York, NY 10017, by arrangement with Clarkson N. Potter/Publishers, a member of the Crown Publishing Group, a division of Random House, Inc.

Gramercy Books™ and design are trademarks of Random House Value Publishing, Inc.

Design by Margaret Hinders

Printed in the United States of America

Random House
New York • Toronto • London • Sydney • Auckland
http://www.randomhouse.com/

Library of Congress Cataloging-in-Publication Data

Ojakangas, Beatrice A.
   Light & easy baking / Beatrice Ojakangas.
      p. cm.
   Includes index.
   ISBN 0-517-20962-4
      1. Baking. 2. Low-fat diet—Recipes. 1. Title.

 TX763 .O3323 2000
 641.8'15—dc21

                                                          00-042994

ISBN 0-517-20962-4

9 8 7 6 5 4 3 2

Acknowledgments

So many people have been a source of inspiration, ideas, and information. I would like to start by thanking Arlene Wanderman, who, a few years ago, asked me to develop "low-calorie" dessert recipes using cake flour. This project got me going. Since then, new and natural products have proliferated on the market, all of which make it much easier and more possible to create tender and tasty baked goods. Product nutrition labels, which we take for granted today, were not always there and are wonderfully helpful. In addition, it helps that the public is actually interested in and willing to accept foods that are more healthful and have less fat.

I would like to thank Elise Simon Goodman, my agent, for pursuing the topic of light baking, and for encouraging me to go ahead with it. I am also grateful to my editor, Katie Workman, who, after reading the manuscript, recognized that not only is this book about "Light Baking" but it is also about "Light and Easy Baking." Thanks also go to Erica Youngren and the willing staff at Clarkson Potter, who have been a pleasure to work with.

Finally, thanks to Zojirushi, Oster, West Bend, Regal, Toastmaster, Welbilt, Hitachi, and American Harvest who all allowed me to use their machines for testing recipes.

Contents

Introduction

The Essentials of Light and Easy Baking

We have in our attic a box labeled "Mom's diets," which my husband cleared out of his mother's house a few years ago. Some of them date back to the early 1930s. There was the "three-day diet," the "seven-day diet," the "water diet," and the "banana diet," among others. Over the years, our culture has been continually interested in, if not obsessed with, keeping trim. Dietary guidelines have changed again and again. Each fad diet seems to be nothing more than that: a fad, a gimmick that has temporary results at best. Basically, we need to remember that our bodies work just like a checking account: If you put more in than you take out, the balance goes up. If you spend more than you put in, it goes down. But, today, it is more than just weight we're concerned about, it is the relationship between high-fat diets and heart disease, as well as our health in general.

Light and Easy Baking is not a book about diets. It's a book about delicious, sensible reduced-fat baking. It can be a real challenge to produce tasty low-fat cakes, cookies, pies, pastries, desserts, and breads. It simply is not possible to duplicate the real richness and flavor of a fudge brownie, or of buttercream frosting, with substitute ingredients. These indulgences are best left unadulterated, served for very special occasions with their full and glorious fat content intact. Healthful baking and healthful food habits go hand in hand, and one healthful habit is that of moderation, eating well most of the time so you can indulge once in a while.

Instead of trying to make substitutions for chocolate, butter, and whipping cream in rich and gooey favorites, this book includes baked goods that are already relatively low in fat or that started off not too far above the 30-percent-calories-from-fat guidelines. I don't believe in torturing recipes. Many, if not most, of the recipes included here required only a slight reduction in fat.

For instance, my original recipe for cakelike cocoa brownies checks out at 40 percent of calories from fat, with 8 grams of fat per bar. By reducing the butter by 25 percent and by using one egg instead of two, these brownies drop down to 27 percent calories from fat, 4 grams of fat per brownie, and the calorie count drops from 180 to 138. This is without adding any odd ingredients to the formula. The flavor is just as delicious, the brownies are just as tender and cakelike; in fact, I wonder why it needed the extra fat in the first place. There are many other baked items that are naturally low in fat, too, and they are included within the pages of this book, with just a little extra trimming. Wonderfully light, as well as grainy and rich tasting, yeast breads and yeast-raised coffee cakes are among the choices. There are pies (such as meringue-crusted angel pies), cakes (such as applesauce, zucchini, and some carrot cakes), desserts (such as cobblers and puddings), and cookies that clock in at 30 percent of calories from fat or less, without any sacrifice of taste or texture.

Some recipes needed a little more work to reach the 30 percent goal, so I used alternatives for part of the shortening that would add, along with the lost volume, moistness, flavor, and tenderness to the baked product. In some recipes nonfat dairy products or fruit purées replace part of the shortening in a recipe. I have also used a variety of ingredients, such as fruit purées; applesauce; nonfat sour cream, yogurt, cottage cheese, cream cheese; and corn syrup. Products such as "light butter" or "light margarine" do not work well for baking because they have water added, which changes the basic formula and affects the outcome of the recipe. Sugar substitutes are artificial and have no place in quality baked goods.

All of my recipes are developed using natural ingredients and are absolutely doable. I get tired just reading about having to brown two tablespoons of butter, then mix with two tablespoons of flour, then freeze it, then work it into a pastry dough along with other ingredients. I avoid such tedious steps, and I'm sure you do, too.

Baking is fun and rewarding when the final product is irresistible and something you, the baker, can be proud to serve. The American Heart Association recommends that a daily diet derive no more than 30 percent of its calories from fat; in fact, this is a recommended *average,* but each and every one of the well-tested recipes in this book adheres to this percentage, so you can enjoy these treats without worrying about how they are affecting your daily fat intake. Most of the recipes in this book are very simple, and the majority are also quick to make. Some baked goods, most notably yeast-raised breads and sweets, necessarily take more time, but usually the additional steps are not hands-on, and you can do something else while the bread is rising, for instance, and not be trapped in the kitchen. There is a nutritional analysis at the end of each recipe, including calories, percentage of calories from fat, grams of fat and cholesterol, sodium, and dietary fiber contents. (The program I use is *The Food Processor II, Nutrition and Diet Analysis System* by Elizabeth S. Hands.)

You can use the recipes in this book, along with the introductory material, as a guideline to re-create and adapt your own favorite recipes. Low-fat eating and baking is not a punishment! There are lots of choices for wonderful, light cakes, cookies, pies, breads, and desserts here. I hope they will send you directly to the kitchen!

THE ROLE OF INGREDIENTS

Baking is an art that is also a science because it depends on a scientific balance of ingredients. A cook can make a wonderful salad, soup, or entrée without ever having to measure anything. Not so with baking. Even when Grandma threw in a handful of this and a handful of that into her bread or cookie dough, she knew what she was doing as she measured by handfuls. She knew that balance of ingredients was critical, however unscientific her method appeared to be.

Reducing the fat in baked products also engages art and science. There are limits to how much the fat-to-flour ratio can be "stretched."

The structure of all baked goods is similar. Whether you are making a dough or a batter, the critical ingredients are the same: flour, fat, and liquid. The proportion of these basic ingredients plus additional ingredients, such as leavening, sweeteners, flavorings, and eggs, are what distinguish one baked product from another. There is flexibility to make some, but not all, recipes healthier without compromising flavor and quality. Those that could not be adjusted were simply left out of this book.

FLOUR

Flour provides the basic structure in baked goods. Flour is made by grinding grain, usually wheat. Nonwheat flours, such as corn, rye, oats, barley, and rice, add special qualities to baked goods, and are usually used in combination with wheat flours, since they don't have leavening qualities. In some recipes flour particles are blended with fat so that the flour doesn't absorb the liquid ingredients, as in pastries and some cookies. Pastries and cookies require a high proportion of fat to make a tender dough and are a challenge to the low-fat baker. Flour in yeast breads, on the other hand, absorbs liquid, which when leavened provides a tender structure for the final product. Thus, yeast breads need little fat or can get by with no fat at all in the recipe.

All-purpose flour is made from wheat. Either bleached or unbleached can be used interchangeably and both are a blend of both hard and soft wheat flours. All-purpose flour can be used in all types of baking; however, when baking some yeast breads, it might be too "soft" (have insufficient gluten) to produce a quality product.

Cake flour is milled to a fine texture out of soft winter-wheat flour and contains much less gluten than all-purpose or bread flour, so it does not develop the gluten in the dough. This makes a more tender cake because cake flour holds more moisture and allows for better distribution of fat. In some recipes, cake flour makes it easier to reduce the total amount of fat without toughening the product.

Bread flour is ground from hard wheat, which has a higher gluten (protein) content, and is used mainly for yeast breads.

Whole wheat flour contains the entire wheat kernel and has nearly five times the fiber of all-purpose flour, but less leavening capacity.

Other grains that add texture, color, and flavor to baked products are cornmeal, either white or yellow, old-fashioned or quick-cooking oats, oat bran, rye flour, and barley flour.

FATS

Fats play an important role in baking. They tenderize, add flavor, and help to bind ingredients together. The main fats used in baking are butter, shortening, and oil. While butter and shortening have 100 calories per tablespoon, and derive 80 percent of their calories from fat, the oils have 120 calories per tablespoon, and are 100 percent fat. Butter melts at 92°F, while hydrogenated shortening melts at a higher temperature, about 110°F. The fat-to-flour ratio in a recipe is important in each type of baked product.

TIPS AND TECHNIQUES FOR REDUCING FAT IN BAKED GOODS

While fats do have good qualities, too much fat in a diet is associated with increased risk of heart disease. So where does one start in reducing fat in a favorite recipe? Well, first of all, look for the ingredients in the recipe that add fat. Butter, shortening, and oil are obvious, but egg yolks, sour cream, whole milk, cottage cheese, nuts, and chocolate add fat, too.

BUTTER AND SHORTENING

Fat, whether butter, vegetable shortening, or oil, has an important role to play in baking. It makes food taste rich, smooth, and creamy. Fats tend to blend the flavors of all ingredients together. They absorb and carry flavors and aromas. Many ingredients are fat-soluble, meaning their flavors are carried by fats, so removing the fats entirely will make flavors disappear, creating an "empty" taste. In baked goods, fats and shortenings both moisturize and tenderize the crumb and crust. Fats need to be reduced with care when developing low-fat baked goods.

> ❧ Use butter where the flavor of butter is important, but use less of it. When oils are hardened to make a butter substitute, they are made into saturated fat. That's why margarine, an oil-based fat, stays solid. These fabricated (hydrogenated) fats are called *trans* fats; they do not taste good and are not good for you.

> ❧ Reduce the amount of fat (butter, shortening, or oil) called for in a recipe by 25 percent, but replace that fat in volume by adding a liquid ingredient, such as nonfat sour cream, applesauce, apple butter, corn syrup, puréed fruits, or water, depending on the recipe. Substituting puréed prunes or applesauce for all of the fat in baked goods may or may not always be successful. I found cookies and brownies made with 100 percent puréed prunes in place of shortening or butter to be sticky and heavy.

EGGS

Eggs provide flavor, structure, and volume and help to bind together ingredients. The egg yolk contains fat and provides most of the calories in an egg. To reduce the fat from eggs in baked goods, you can:

> ❧ Substitute ¼ cup liquid egg product for 1 whole egg.

> ❧ Substitute egg whites for whole eggs in a recipe. One large egg measures ¼ cup, and only about 1 tablespoon of it can be credited to the egg yolk. In most recipes that call for one egg, you can simply eliminate the egg yolk and it will not make much of a difference in the final product. Also note that one egg yolk only contains 5 grams of fat, so it is worth keeping some yolks in a recipe if possible. Using a lot of egg whites in place of whole eggs can produce a tough texture in cookies, muffins, and cakes. It is better to use a combination: 2 whole whites and one whole egg in place of 2 whole eggs, for example.

MILK AND DAIRY PRODUCTS

Milk and dairy products moisten ingredients, tenderize the crumb in yeast breads, provide flavor, and help in the browning of most baked goods.

- ❧ Substitute skim or 1 percent milk for whole milk to reduce fat without much, if any, difference in flavor while retaining the same nutritional value.

- ❧ Use a lower-fat version of a cultured dairy product, such as nonfat or low-fat sour cream for regular sour cream, nonfat or low-fat yogurt in place of regular yogurt, nonfat or low-fat cottage cheese in place of regular cottage cheese, and reduced-fat versions of brick or hard cheeses.

- ❧ Evaporated skimmed milk and fat-free half-and-half are excellent replacements for light cream in many recipes.

- ❧ Light sweetened condensed milk can be used instead of regular sweetened condensed milk.

- ❧ Vanilla- or lemon-flavored nonfat and low-fat yogurt make excellent substitutes for whipped cream as a topping.

- ❧ Softened nonfat and low-fat ice milk or frozen yogurt make excellent low-fat toppings for desserts in place of whipped cream.

NUTS

Nuts provide distinctive flavor, aroma, and texture to all kinds of baked products. They are high in fat, but they also are good sources of protein and other nutrients.

- ❧ When a recipe calls for nuts, use fewer and replace the volume with dried fruits, such as raisins, dried cherries, dates, dried cranberries, or chopped mixed dried fruits. Sometimes I use a nuggetlike dry breakfast cereal (Grape-Nuts) to replace a "nutty" texture in a topping, such as a streusel on coffee cakes and muffins.

- ❧ To toast nuts, place them in a single layer and bake them in a 350°F oven for 4–5 minutes, stirring occasionally so that they toast evenly and do not burn. For nuts such as hazelnuts or filberts, rub the warm nuts in a clean towel to remove the skins.

꩜ When the nutty flavor is important, use a high-quality nut oil for part of the shortening oil and top the cake, muffin, cookie, or other baked good with just a few chopped nuts for appearance and texture.

CHOCOLATE

Cocoa can usually be substituted for melted chocolate. To give the product a flavor boost, add a little powdered espresso coffee or additional vanilla to the recipe.

STORING LOW-FAT BAKED GOODS

Generally, low-fat baked goods have a high moisture content and no preservatives. Fat in baked goods tends to hold in moisture. Without fat, baked goods allow the moisture to evaporate quickly. Most are best eaten the day they are baked. What isn't eaten should be stored as soon as possible to retain freshness.

To keep cookies, place them in an airtight container, arranged in single layers separated by sheets of wax paper, and freeze them. Cakes, muffins, quick breads, yeast breads, pies, and pastries should be wrapped carefully in plastic wrap, placed in an airtight container or wrapped in foil, and then frozen.

Often, I will cut baked goods into serving-size pieces so that I can remove just what I need from the freezer—a few cookies, a slice or two of bread, or a piece of cake. If, however, I have thawed a whole cake, bread, or pastry, and it is not all used, I can still safely refreeze the remaining amount, provided it hasn't dried out. Refreezing will never improve the quality of an item, but it will keep it from deteriorating any further. Keep in mind that it is always better to freeze than to refrigerate baked goods. It's a funny thing, but refrigerated cakes, cookies, and breads become dry and stale more quickly than they do at room temperature.

COOKIES

Cookies depend on fat for flavor and texture, making them a special challenge in light baking. Once I had entered all of my favorite cookie recipes into the computer's nutritional program, I was able to determine how much fat to cut out of each recipe.

After that, I baked hundreds of batches of cookies, from simple drop cookies to bars, to shaped and rolled-out cookies, to twice-baked cookies, experimenting with ratios of ingredients. I tried recipes that substituted prune purée or apple butter for all of the fat versus only part. However, the cookies baked into doughy lumps, not at all crisp and tender as I had expected. The most challenging were rolled-out cookies and those cookies with fewest ingredients. If I had tried every possible variation and still failed to produce a cookie that was tender and delicious, I simply discarded that recipe.

The standard fat-to-flour proportion in drop cookies is one measure of butter (for example, $\frac{1}{2}$ cup) and three measures each of flour and sugar ($1\frac{1}{2}$ cups each). This ratio produces a cookie that is rather high in the percentage of calories from fat (about 40 percent) even though the cookies might have only 70 calories each. When you reduce the fat, the resulting cookie can be too sweet. Reducing the sugar, however, not only changes the balance of fat in the recipe, it also decreases the total volume of the mixture. I have balanced these recipes with additional ingredients that add volume, moistness, and flavor. Nonfat and low-fat sour cream, applesauce and other puréed fruits, corn syrup, and even additional skim-milk powder or water are ingredients that I've used, depending on the recipe.

Because butter melts at a low temperature (92°F), butter cookies spread out in the oven before the cookie sets up. Cookies made with hydrogenated shortening begin to set up before the shortening is melted. Sometimes a combination of butter and vegetable shortening produces the best cookies. Some margarines melt at an even lower temperature, especially those that are spreadable at refrigerator temperature. This makes it difficult to bake cookies with margarine. I did not use margarine in any of my testing. Oil works well in some cookies, too, but it cannot be directly substituted for butter or shortening in most recipes since it is liquid at the start.

I hope you enjoy the recipes in this chapter. They are modifications of cookie recipes from my fifty-some years of baking. (Don't kids usually start out baking cookies? I did.) Use these recipes as a guide to reduce the fat in your own favorite recipes. To do that, compare the ingredients and the amounts. Check the amount of shortening or fat in each recipe, the amount of sugar, the number of other ingredients, and the type of cookie that it is. A drop cookie's standard of excellence might be how soft and tender it is. A rolled-out cookie needs to be crisp as well as tender, and to accomplish crispness, it may need to be rolled out *very* thinly. Bar cookies can be cakelike, or they might be moist and chewy.

After completing this book, I have a big file of "impossibles," recipes that could never be modified to a low-fat version. In the file are some of my favorites, like buttery spritz, a fudgelike brownie, sand cookies, chocolate madeleines, brandy snaps, deep-fried rosettes, and most Scandinavian specialties. I would rather leave them as they are and enjoy them in moderation!

TIPS FOR BAKING COOKIES

1. Preheat the oven for at least ten minutes before baking.

2. Use shiny, thin aluminum cookie sheets without sides for the best air circulation around the cookie as it bakes. If you do not have rimless cookie sheets, you can bake cookies on an inverted jelly roll pan or other pans that have sides.

3. Cover baking sheets with parchment paper rather than greasing them for convenience and to make cleanup easy.

4. Put unbaked cookie dough on cool cookie sheets so that the dough will not melt and spread before baking. Space the cookies well apart so they will not run together in the oven.

5. For best results bake only one sheet of cookies at a time in the oven.

6. When baking bar cookies, use the designated-size pan. A pan that is too large will cause bars to be dry and overbaked, while in one that is too small, the bars will be too soft and underbaked.

7. Use a small (#70 or smaller) ice cream scoop to shape drop cookies so that they will be uniform.

8. Refrigerate cookie dough before shaping and baking, especially in the summertime, or when the kitchen is very warm.

9. Cookie dough can be refrigerated up to two days before shaping and baking. For longer storage, place it in a heavy-duty plastic bag and freeze.

10. Bake cookies until they are just firm to the touch. When overbaked, reduced-fat cookies can become hard and dry.

11. Cool the cookies on a wire rack, or right on the parchment paper they were baked on directly on the countertop. Place in airtight containers as soon as possible. Freeze cookies that are to be kept longer than a day.

12. Store different kinds of cookies in separate containers. Heavy-duty plastic bags work well, if you have just a few cookies of a kind. Seal and place them together in a rigid container to prevent damage to the cookies.

13. If crisp cookies have softened during storage, re-crisp them on a cookie sheet in a 350°F oven for a few minutes.

DROP COOKIES

Cherry–Golden Raisin Cookies

Among the wide variety of dried berries and fruits being produced today, dried tart cherries are one of my favorites.

½ cup dried cherries

½ cup golden raisins

½ cup water

6 tablespoons (¾ stick) unsalted butter, at room temperature

1 cup sugar

1 large egg, lightly beaten

1¼ cups all-purpose flour

½ cup whole wheat flour

½ cup wheat germ

1 teaspoon ground cinnamon

¼ teaspoon ground nutmeg

½ teaspoon baking powder

½ teaspoon baking soda

⅛ teaspoon ground allspice

1 teaspoon salt

1 teaspoon vanilla

Preheat the oven to 375°F Cover two cookie sheets with parchment paper or spray the cookie sheets with nonstick spray.

In a saucepan, combine the cherries, raisins, and water and heat to boiling; lower the heat, simmer 1 minute, then cool the mixture. In a large mixing bowl, cream the butter and sugar, then add the egg and mix well. In a small bowl, stir the flours, wheat germ, cinnamon, nutmeg, baking powder, baking soda, allspice, and salt together until well mixed. Add the dry ingredients to the creamed ingredients, mixing well. Stir in the vanilla.

Drop the dough by rounded teaspoons about 2 inches apart on the prepared cookie sheets. Bake for 12 to 15 minutes, until lightly browned. Cool on a wire rack.

MAKES 48 COOKIES

PER COOKIE: *60.3 calories, 27% calories from fat, 1.74 g fat, 8.32 mg cholesterol, 61.8 mg sodium, 0.5 g dietary fiber*

Brown Sugar—Sour Cream Drop Cookies

When I reduced the fat by one third and removed the egg yolk to lower the fat content of this recipe, the cookies were too dry. Then I added nonfat sour cream to the creamed mixture, resulting in cookies that were soft and moist with an appealing hint of tartness.

- 6 tablespoons (¾ stick) unsalted butter, at room temperature
- ½ cup sugar
- ½ cup packed brown sugar
- 1 large egg white
- ⅓ cup nonfat sour cream
- 1 teaspoon vanilla
- 1½ cups all-purpose flour
- ½ teaspoon baking soda
- ½ teaspoon salt
- ½ cup dried currants

Preheat the oven to 375°F. Lightly grease or cover with parchment paper two or three cookie sheets.

In a large mixing bowl, cream the butter with the sugars, egg white, sour cream, and vanilla and beat until light and fluffy. In another bowl, combine the flour, baking soda, and salt. Blend the flour mixture into the creamed mixture until the dough is smooth. Stir in the currants.

Drop teaspoonfuls of the dough on the cookie sheets, about 2 inches apart. Bake for 8 to 10 minutes or until lightly browned. Cool on a wire rack.

MAKES 48 COOKIES

PER COOKIE: 50 calories, 26% calories from fat, 1.48 g fat, 3.88 mg cholesterol, 33.4 mg sodium, 0.2 g dietary fiber

Chewy Raisin-Oatmeal Cookies

These are the best moist and flavorful oatmeal cookies, perfect for late-night snacking. They're quick to stir up, too. To make them both dairy-free and egg-free, you can substitute 2 tablespoons of water for the egg.

- 1½ cups all-purpose flour
- 1½ cups packed brown sugar
- ½ teaspoon salt
- ½ teaspoon baking soda
- ½ teaspoon ground cinnamon
- 2 cups quick-cooking rolled oats
- 1 large egg, lightly beaten
- ½ cup corn oil
- ½ cup skim milk
- 1 cup light or dark raisins

Preheat the oven to 375°F. Lightly grease three cookie sheets or cover them with parchment paper.

In a large mixing bowl, stir the flour, brown sugar, salt, baking soda, cinnamon, and rolled oats together until the sugar is completely incorporated into the mixture. In a small bowl, combine the egg, oil, and skim milk. Stir the liquid mixture into the dry ingredients until the batter is thoroughly mixed. Stir in the raisins.

6

Drop the dough by teaspoonfuls onto the cookie sheets, spacing them 1½ to 2 inches apart. Bake for 8 to 10 minutes until the cookies feel firm when touched and are lightly browned. Remove the cookies from the cookie sheet and cool on a wire rack.

MAKES 60 COOKIES

PER COOKIE: *67.8 calories, 26% calories from fat, 2.03 g fat, 0.03 mg cholesterol, 5.8 mg sodium, 0.54 g dietary fiber*

Carrot-Raisin Cookies

These are chewy, slightly soft cookies that are perfect for snacks or the lunchbox.

1 cup quick-cooking rolled oats

1½ cups all-purpose flour

2½ teaspoons baking powder

½ teaspoon salt

½ teaspoon ground cinnamon

⅛ teaspoon ground cloves

1 cup packed brown sugar

6 tablespoons (¾ stick) unsalted butter, at room temperature

1 large egg, lightly beaten

1 cup shredded carrot, loosely packed (about 1 large carrot)

1 teaspoon vanilla

½ cup raisins

GLAZE

½ cup confectioners' sugar

2 teaspoons warm coffee

Preheat the oven to 375°F. Cover two cookie sheets with parchment paper.

Put the rolled oats into a food processor with the steel blade in place and process until the oats are ground fine. In a small bowl, mix the oats with the flour, baking powder, salt, cinnamon, and cloves.

In a large mixing bowl, cream the brown sugar and butter until smooth. Add the egg and beat until light. Stir in the dry ingredients, carrots, vanilla, and raisins until well mixed.

Drop dough by teaspoonfuls onto the prepared cookie sheets. Bake for 10 to 12 minutes, or until the cookies are lightly browned around the edges. Remove the cookies on the parchment paper onto a wire rack to cool.

While the cookies are baking, stir together the confectioners' sugar and coffee to make a thin glaze. With a pastry brush, paint the cookies while they are warm to give them a thin coating.

MAKES 48 COOKIES

PER COOKIE: *61.4 calories, 24% calories from fat, 1.7 g fat, 8.32 mg cholesterol, 44 mg sodium, 0.46 g dietary fiber*

Chocolate Chip and Raisin Cookies

I have reduced the fat by half in these cookies, but they retain their texture and moistness thanks to a secret ingredient: water!

1½ cups all-purpose flour

¾ teaspoon baking soda

½ teaspoon salt

¾ cup packed brown sugar

¼ cup sugar

4 tablespoons (½ stick) unsalted butter, at room temperature

½ teaspoon vanilla

1 large egg white

3 tablespoons water

½ cup miniature semisweet chocolate chips

½ cup raisins

Preheat the oven to 350°F. Cover two cookie sheets with parchment paper or lightly grease or coat with nonstick spray.

Combine the flour, baking soda, and salt in a small bowl. In a mixing bowl, cream the sugars and butter until smooth. Stir in the vanilla, egg white, and water. Add the dry ingredients, chocolate chips, and raisins and stir until well blended.

Drop the dough by rounded teaspoonfuls onto the prepared cookie sheets. Bake for 10 to 12 minutes until just set. Slide the cookies on the parchment paper onto a countertop to cool, or remove the cookies from the cookie sheets and cool on a wire rack.

MAKES 36 COOKIES

PER COOKIE: *70 calories, 27% calories from fat, 2.23 g fat, 3.45 mg cholesterol, 51.3 mg sodium, 0.84 g dietary fiber*

Chocolate Chip Meringues

Because there is no other fat in these cookies, it's possible to add up to 3 ounces of chocolate chips and still enjoy a fancy little cookie without losing ground in the battle against fat. There's less than 1 gram of fat in each cookie, but they are sweet and definitely to be considered a treat.

3 large egg whites

Pinch of salt

1 cup sugar

½ cup (3 ounces) miniature semisweet chocolate chips

2 tablespoons unsweetened cocoa powder

½ teaspoon vanilla

Preheat the oven to 275°F. Line two cookie sheets with foil or brown paper. In a large bowl, with an electric mixer, beat the egg whites with the salt until stiff. Gradually beat in the sugar. Stir in the chocolate chips, cocoa powder, and vanilla. Drop the batter by walnut-size spoonfuls onto the prepared sheets. Bake for 30 minutes. Transfer the entire foil sheet to a rack and allow the cookies to cool. Store in an airtight container.

MAKES 36 COOKIES

PER COOKIE: *35.5 calories, 21% calories from fat, 0.92 g fat, 0 mg cholesterol, 5.11 mg sodium, 0.16 g dietary fiber*

Cinnamon-Honey Cookies

I cut the amount of sugar and butter in these cookies by half, and I actually found I like them better when they're not as sweet and rich.

> 1¾ cups all-purpose flour
>
> 2 teaspoons baking powder
>
> ½ teaspoon salt
>
> 1½ teaspoons ground cinnamon
>
> 6 tablespoons (¾ stick) unsalted butter, at room temperature
>
> ½ cup packed brown sugar
>
> ½ cup honey
>
> 1 large egg, lightly beaten

Preheat the oven to 350°F. Cover two large cookie sheets with parchment paper.

Measure the flour, baking powder, salt, and cinnamon into a medium bowl. Stir with a whisk until well mixed. In a large mixing bowl, with an electric mixer, cream the butter with the brown sugar. Mix in the honey and egg. Stir in the flour mixture to make a smooth, stiff dough. Chill for 1 hour, covered, until the dough is firm.

Drop the dough by rounded teaspoonfuls onto the prepared cookie sheets. Bake for 8 to 10 minutes, or until the cookies are lightly browned and feel firm to the touch. Slide the cookies, paper and all, onto the countertop, or onto a wire rack to cool.

MAKES 36 COOKIES

PER COOKIE: *65.4 calories, 28% calories from fat, 2.11 g fat, 11 mg cholesterol, 51.5 mg sodium, 0.15 g of dietary fiber*

Cinnamon-Raisin Cookies

Molasses in the mixture keeps these old-fashioned cookies soft and chewy. Because they are something like a soft cake, they're best when not overbaked.

> 4 tablespoons (½ stick) unsalted butter, at room temperature
>
> ¾ cup sugar
>
> 1 large egg plus 1 large egg white, lightly beaten
>
> ¼ cup light or dark molasses
>
> 1½ cups all-purpose flour
>
> ½ teaspoon baking soda
>
> ¼ teaspoon salt
>
> 1 teaspoon ground cinnamon
>
> ½ cup light or dark raisins

Preheat the oven to 375°F. Cover one large cookie sheet with parchment paper or grease lightly.

In a mixing bowl, mix the butter and sugar together until creamy. Add the egg, egg white, and molasses and blend well.

Stir the flour, baking soda, salt, and cinnamon together in another bowl and slowly stir into the creamed mixture. Stir in the raisins until well mixed.

Drop rounded teaspoonfuls of the cookie dough onto the cookie sheet, about 1 inch apart. Bake for 8 to 10 minutes, until golden. Cool on a wire rack.

MAKES 36 COOKIES

PER COOKIE: *60.2 calories, 22% calories from fat, 1.48 g fat, 9.37 mg cholesterol, 43.7 mg sodium, 0.29 g dietary fiber*

Coconut Macaroons

The only fat in these cookies comes from the coconut, which is also the main flavoring ingredient. Made into tiny cookies, they're a moderate indulgence, but a nice addition to any holiday cookie tray.

>   4 large egg whites
>   Pinch of salt
>   ¾ cup sugar
>   1 teaspoon vanilla
>   1 cup flaked sweetened coconut

Preheat the oven to 300°F. Cover two or three cookie sheets with parchment paper and dust lightly with flour.

In a large bowl, with an electric mixer, beat the egg whites with the salt until foamy. Gradually add the sugar and beat until stiff and glossy, but not dry. Add the vanilla and mix in well. Fold in the coconut. Drop the batter by rounded teaspoonfuls onto the prepared cookie sheets, 2 inches apart. Bake 25 to 30 minutes, or until the macaroons feel firm when touched in the center. Cool on the parchment paper, then remove and store in an airtight container.

MAKES 60 COOKIES

PER COOKIE: *18.5 calories, 26% calories from fat, 0.5 g fat, 0 mg cholesterol, 7.8 mg sodium, 0.15 g dietary fiber*

Date and Nut Confections

More like a crisp and chewy confection than a buttery cookie, these are a great addition to any holiday dessert tray. They keep well in an airtight tin in the freezer or in a cool place. Frozen, they keep several months; otherwise, count on keeping them up to a month. The pecans are the only ingredient in this cookie with any fat.

>   1 cup dates, chopped
>   ½ cup pecans, chopped
>   1 cup sifted confectioners' sugar
>   ½ teaspoon ground cinnamon
>   1 large egg white

Preheat the oven to 350°F. Coat a cookie sheet with nonstick spray and dust with flour.

In a medium bowl, combine the dates, pecans, confectioners' sugar, and cinnamon. Stir in the egg white; mix well. Drop by teaspoonfuls onto the prepared cookie sheet, about 2 inches apart. Bake until lightly browned, about 12 minutes. Cool on a wire rack. Store in an airtight container.

MAKES 30 COOKIES

PER COOKIE: *42.9 calories, 27% calories from fat, 1.37 g fat, 0 mg cholesterol, 2.1 mg sodium, 0.61 g dietary fiber*

Glazed Apple Drop Cookies

Chopped tart apple and raisins make these cookies moist and chewy, and walnuts add a crunchy bite. I added whole wheat flour to emphasize the nutty flavor, even though I cut the nuts by one third from my original recipe to save on fat calories. I buy whole wheat pastry flour at the whole-foods co-op.

- **6 tablespoons (¾ stick) unsalted butter, at room temperature**
- **1 cup packed brown sugar**
- **1 large egg, lightly beaten**
- **1 large tart apple, peeled, cored, and finely chopped**
- **1 cup raisins**
- **½ cup walnuts, finely chopped**
- **1 teaspoon grated lemon zest**
- **1 cup unbleached all-purpose flour**
- **1 cup whole wheat pastry flour**
- **1 teaspoon baking soda**
- **½ teaspoon salt**
- **1 teaspoon ground cinnamon**
- **1 teaspoon freshly grated nutmeg**

GLAZE

- **½ cup confectioners' sugar**
- **2 teaspoons strong coffee, apple juice, or water**

Preheat the oven to 375°F. Cover two cookie sheets with parchment paper. In a large bowl, cream the butter and sugar until light and fluffy. Stir in the egg, apple, raisins, walnuts, and lemon zest. Mix in the flours, baking soda, salt, cinnamon, and nutmeg until well blended.

Drop the dough by tablespoonfuls onto the prepared sheets, about 2 inches apart. Bake for 10 to 12 minutes, or until the cookies feel firm to the touch.

Remove the cookies from the oven. Let cool slightly on a wire rack. For the glaze, stir the confectioners' sugar with enough liquid to make a thin mixture. With a pastry brush, paint the warm cookies with the glaze.

MAKES 60 COOKIES

PER COOKIE: *61.7 calories, 27% calories from fat, 1.95 g fat, 6.66 mg cholesterol, 17 mg sodium, 0.61 g dietary fiber*

Hazelnut Cocoa Cookies

This is a wonderfully crunchy, chewy, and tasty cookie—perfect for the "after-dinner cookie tray." Hazelnuts are the European name for filberts, although the European nut is generally found in the wild, while filberts are grown in the United States in orchards. It's amazing to be able to get by with as much as ¾ cup hazelnuts in any cookie recipe, but that's because the remainder of the ingredients have little or no fat.

3 large egg whites, at room temperature

1½ cups sugar

1 cup unsweetened cocoa powder

¾ cup hazelnuts or filberts, toasted, husked, and chopped (see page xiii)

Preheat the oven to 300°F. Line a cookie sheet with parchment paper.

With an electric mixer, beat the egg whites in a large bowl, until soft peaks form. Gradually add the sugar and beat until stiff and shiny, but not dry. Put the cocoa powder into a sieve and stir with a spoon until it is sifted onto the egg whites. Fold the cocoa into the whites until fully mixed. Fold in the hazelnuts.

Transfer the mixture to a large, heavy saucepan. Set over medium heat and stir with a wooden spoon until the mixture is shiny and pulls away from the bottom and sides of the pan, about 6 minutes. Drop batter by teaspoonfuls onto the prepared cookie sheet, about 2 inches apart. Bake until firm, about 25 minutes.

MAKES 24 COOKIES

PER COOKIE: *82.3 calories, 29% calories from fat, 2.93 g fat, 0 mg cholesterol, 8 mg sodium, 1.3 g dietary fiber*

Honey and Fruit Cookies

Honey and fruit are a "natural" blend in these soft and chewy cookies.

¼ cup honey

2 tablespoons brown sugar

3 tablespoons unsalted butter, at room temperature

1 large egg, lightly beaten

1 cup all-purpose flour

¼ cup whole wheat flour

¼ teaspoon salt

¼ teaspoon baking soda

½ teaspoon ground cinnamon

⅛ teaspoon ground cloves

½ cup dried blueberries, cranberries, chopped dried fruit, or raisins

Preheat the oven to 375°F. Line a cookie sheet with parchment paper or lightly grease or spray with nonstick spray and dust with flour.

Mix the honey, brown sugar, and butter in a large mixing bowl. Add the egg and mix well. In a small bowl, mix the flours, salt, baking soda, cinnamon, and cloves together. Add the dry ingredients to the honey mixture and mix well. Stir in the dried fruit.

Drop the dough by rounded half-teaspoonfuls to make small mounds no larger than 1 inch in diameter onto the prepared cookie sheet, about 2 inches apart. Bake for 8 to 10 minutes, until the cookies are just firm to the touch. Remove from the oven and cool on the parchment paper on a wire rack.

MAKES 48 COOKIES

PER COOKIE: *31.5 calories, 24% calories from fat, 0.8 g fat, 6.38 mg cholesterol, 13.1 mg sodium, 0.25 g dietary fiber*

Hermits

These spicy cookies, which are tender and light but not very sweet, were named "Hermits" because they keep a long time. They tend to mellow and improve with a bit of aging, that is, if your cookie monsters don't get them first! In 1918 the Conservation Division of the Food Administration in Washington, D.C., was recommending that people use "coarse flours," such as oat, barley, or rye flour, in place of wheat, which was needed for export. Sugar and butter were in scarce supply, and that's when recipes such as this were being circulated among the American public. Interesting that now, nearly eighty years later, we're doing the same thing, but for a different reason! Traditionally, hermits are full of raisins and nuts. Without the nuts, the basic cookie is respectably low in fat.

½ **cup (1 stick) unsalted butter, at room temperature**

1 **cup packed brown sugar**

1 **large egg**

½ **cup nonfat sour cream**

1½ **cups all-purpose flour**

½ **teaspoon baking soda**

¼ **teaspoon salt**

½ **teaspoon ground cinnamon**

½ **teaspoon ground nutmeg**

¼ **teaspoon ground cloves**

¼ **teaspoon ground allspice**

1¼ **cups light or dark raisins**

GLAZE
½ **cup confectioners' sugar**

1 **to 2 tablespoons skim milk**

Preheat the oven to 400°F. Lightly grease two cookie sheets or cover with parchment paper.

In a large mixing bowl, cream the butter and sugar until smooth, then add the egg and beat until light. Mix in the sour cream. In a medium bowl, combine the flour, baking soda, salt, cinnamon, nutmeg, cloves, and allspice and add to the creamed mixture, mixing until the dough is smooth. Stir in the raisins.

Drop the dough onto the prepared cookie sheets by rounded teaspoonfuls about 2 inches apart. Bake for 8 to 10 minutes, or until the cookies feel firm when touched in the center; do not overbake.

To make the glaze, mix the confectioners' sugar and milk in a small bowl. Brush the glaze over the hot cookies. Slide the cookies on the parchment paper onto the countertop to cool, or lift with a spatula onto a wire rack.

MAKES 48 COOKIES

PER COOKIE: *68.2 calories, 27% calories from fat, 2.08 g fat, 9.61 mg cholesterol, 23.8 mg sodium, 0.36 g dietary fiber*

Lemon Oatmeal Cookies

The tang of fresh lemon distinguishes these delicious little cookies. They're especially wonderful hot out of the oven.

6 tablespoons (¾ stick) unsalted butter, at room temperature

1 cup sugar

1 large egg

3 tablespoons fresh lemon juice

2 teaspoons grated lemon zest

1¾ cups all-purpose flour

2 teaspoons baking powder

¼ teaspoon salt

1 cup quick-cooking rolled oats

Preheat the oven to 375°F. Cover two large cookie sheets with parchment paper or grease lightly.

In a large mixing bowl, mix the butter and sugar together until creamy. Add the egg, lemon juice, and lemon zest and blend well.

Stir the flour, baking powder, and salt together in another bowl and slowly stir into the creamed mixture. Stir in the rolled oats until well mixed.

Drop rounded teaspoonfuls of the cookie dough onto the cookie sheets, about 1 inch apart. Bake for 13 to 15 minutes or just until the cookies begin to brown. Remove from the cookie sheets and cool the cookies on a rack.

MAKES 42 COOKIES

PER COOKIE: *61.5 calories, 28% calories from fat, 1.94 g fat, 9.5 mg cholesterol, 30.3 mg sodium, 0.35 g dietary fiber*

Old-Fashioned Sugar Drop Cookies

Here's a recipe for a basic drop cookie that is simple and delicious. Soft, moist cookies such as this are often even better than before when the fat is reduced. To restore some of the volume, and to keep the cookies tender and tasty, I added nonfat sour cream.

6 tablespoons (¾ stick) unsalted butter, at room temperature

1 cup sugar

1 large egg white, beaten

½ cup nonfat sour cream

1 teaspoon vanilla

Pinch of ground nutmeg

1½ cups all-purpose flour

1 teaspoon baking powder

¼ teaspoon salt

Preheat the oven to 375°F. Cover one large cookie sheet with parchment paper or grease lightly.

In a large mixing bowl, mix the butter and sugar together until creamy. Add the egg white, sour cream, vanilla, and nutmeg and mix until smooth. In a small bowl, stir the flour, baking powder, and salt together. Stir into the creamed mixture until well blended.

Drop teaspoonfuls of the cookie dough onto the cookie sheet, 1 inch apart. Bake for 8 to 10 minutes, until the tops of the cookies are firm to the touch and pale golden around the edges. Cool on a wire rack.

MAKES 40 COOKIES

PER COOKIE: *53.8 calories, 29% calories from fat, 1.77 g fat, 4.66 mg cholesterol, 23.4 mg sodium, 0.12 g dietary fiber*

Moist and Chewy Pineapple Cookies

These moist pineapple-studded cookies have been a favorite of mine ever since I received the recipe from a neighbor many years ago. The original recipe contained twice the butter and eggs and a whole cup of fat-filled walnuts.

- **6 tablespoons (¾ stick) unsalted butter, at room temperature**
- **1 cup packed brown sugar**
- **1 large egg, lightly beaten**
- **1 (8-ounce) can juice-packed crushed pineapple, drained, juice reserved**
- **2 cups all-purpose flour**
- **1 teaspoon baking powder**
- **½ teaspoon baking soda**
- **½ teaspoon salt**
- **1 teaspoon vanilla**

PINEAPPLE GLAZE

- **1½ cups confectioners' sugar**
- **4 to 5 tablespoons juice reserved from drained pineapple**
- **1 teaspoon vanilla**

Preheat the oven to 350°F. Cover two cookie sheets with parchment paper or coat lightly with nonstick spray.

In a large mixing bowl, cream the butter and sugar until blended, add the egg, and beat until light. Stir in the drained pineapple.

Place a wire sieve over the mixing bowl and measure in the flour, baking powder, baking soda, and salt. Stir the flour mixture until it is sifted into the creamed mixture. Add the vanilla and mix until cookie dough is stiff.

Using rounded teaspoonfuls of dough, shape 50 cookies, spaced about 2 inches apart, on the prepared cookie sheets. Bake for 12 minutes, until the cookies are browned and feel firm when touched in the center. Slide the parchment paper with the cookies on it onto a wire rack, or remove the cookies from the cookie sheet onto the rack.

In a small bowl, stir the confectioners' sugar, pineapple juice, and vanilla together to make a thin glaze. With a pastry brush, coat the top of each cookie while still warm. Cool completely.

MAKES 50 COOKIES

PER COOKIE: *61.9 calories, 22% calories from fat, 1.53 g fat, 7.99 mg cholesterol, 35.6 mg sodium, 0.17 g dietary fiber*

Sour Cream—Dried Fruit Cookies

Nonfat and low-fat sour cream are relatively new products on the market. They're easy to use because they have the same consistency as regular commercial sour cream, and add flavor and moistness to baked products, but they contain less fat. All kinds of interesting dried fruits are available now, too, such as dried cranberries and blueberries. Chopped fruit bits, which contain dried apples, apricots, and other fruits, are also delicious in baked goods. They all work well in this versatile cookie.

> **6 tablespoons (¾ stick) unsalted butter, at room temperature**
>
> **1 cup sugar**
>
> **1 large egg, lightly beaten**
>
> **½ cup nonfat or low-fat sour cream**
>
> **1 teaspoon vanilla**
>
> **1½ cups all-purpose flour**
>
> **1 teaspoon baking powder**
>
> **¼ teaspoon salt**
>
> **1 cup dried berries, chopped dried fruits, or light or dark raisins**

Preheat the oven to 375°F. Cover one large cookie sheet with parchment paper or grease lightly.

In a large mixing bowl, mix the butter and sugar together until creamy. Add the egg, sour cream, and vanilla and mix until smooth. In a small bowl, stir the flour, baking powder, and salt together. Stir into the creamed mixture until well blended. Stir in the dried fruit.

Drop teaspoonfuls of the cookie dough onto the cookie sheet, 1 inch apart. Bake for 8 to 10 minutes, until the tops of the cookies are firm to the touch and pale golden around the edges.

MAKES 36 COOKIES

PER COOKIE: *75 calories, 25% calories from fat, 2.12 g fat, 11 mg cholesterol, 26.7 mg sodium, 0.4 g dietary fiber*

Oatmeal Molasses Cookies

At 26 percent calories from fat, these are cookies that you don't have to feel guilty about serving the kids after school, or packing into their lunchboxes. My original recipe included a cup of walnuts, which has nothing to do with the tenderness of the cookie but has a lot to do with texture and crunch. A cupful of nuts adds a lot of fat to any cookie and will bring this one up to 35% of the calories from fats, which can still be part of an overall low-fat diet.

> **½ cup (1 stick) unsalted butter, at room temperature**
>
> **1 cup packed brown sugar**
>
> **1 large egg plus 1 large egg white, beaten**
>
> **1 tablespoon apple juice or water**
>
> **⅓ cup light or dark molasses**
>
> **1¾ cups all-purpose flour**
>
> **1 teaspoon baking soda**
>
> **½ teaspoon salt**
>
> **1 teaspoon ground cinnamon**
>
> **2 cups old-fashioned or quick-cooking rolled oats**
>
> **1 cup light or dark raisins**

Preheat the oven to 400°F. Cover two large cookie sheets with parchment paper or grease lightly.

In a large mixing bowl, mix the butter and sugar together until creamy. Add the egg, egg white, apple juice, and molasses and blend well.

Stir the flour, baking soda, salt, and cinnamon together in another bowl and slowly stir into the creamed mixture. Stir in the rolled oats and raisins until well mixed.

Drop rounded teaspoonfuls of the cookie dough onto the cookie sheets, about 1 inch apart. Bake for 8 to 10 minutes, until golden. Cool on a wire rack.

MAKES 48 COOKIES

PER COOKIE: *81.3 calories, 26% calories from fat, 2.4 g fat, 14 mg cholesterol, 3.9 mg sodium, 0.69 g dietary fiber*

Oat Flour–Chocolate Chip Cookies

The *oat flour and whole wheat pastry flour combined give a toasted, nutty flavor to these crispy cookies. Corn syrup adds sweetness and moisture. Be sure not to overbake these cookies—check for doneness when 8 minutes are up and remove them from the oven while they are still a little soft.*

- **1 cup old-fashioned or quick-cooking rolled oats**
- **1 cup whole wheat pastry flour**
- **1 teaspoon baking powder**
- **⅛ teaspoon salt**
- **¾ cup packed brown sugar**
- **4 tablespoons (½ stick) unsalted butter, at room temperature**
- **⅓ cup dark corn syrup**
- **1 tablespoon vanilla**
- **1 large egg, beaten**
- **¼ cup semisweet miniature chocolate chips**

Preheat the oven to 375°F. Cover two cookie sheets with parchment paper or lightly coat them with nonstick spray.

Put the oats into a food processor with the steel blade in place (see Note). Process until the oats are ground to a flour. Add the whole wheat pastry flour, baking powder, salt, brown sugar, and butter. Process until the mixture is blended. Add the corn syrup, vanilla, and egg and process until well blended. Transfer to a bowl and stir in the chocolate chips.

Drop the dough by teaspoonfuls 2 inches apart on the prepared cookie sheets.

Bake for 8 to 10 minutes, until lightly browned. Do not overbake. Slide the cookies on the parchment paper onto the countertop to cool, or if not using parchment paper, remove the cookies and place on a wire rack to cool.

MAKES 36 COOKIES

PER COOKIE: *59.3 calories, 30% calories from fat, 2.04 g fat, 9.37 mg cholesterol, 20.6 mg sodium, 0.7 g dietary fiber*

NOTE: If you do not use a food processor, grind the rolled oats into a flour in the blender. Turn into a mixing bowl and add all of the remaining ingredients in the same order, mixing until a cookie dough is formed.

Whole Wheat Chocolate Chip Cookies

Whole wheat pastry flour has a lower gluten content than regular whole wheat flour. It gives these cookies a nutty taste and a tender crumb, and because this flour absorbs less fat, it is necessary to cut the butter down so that the cookies will not be too rich. Nonfat sour cream softens the texture of the cookies, too, while adding some nutritional value.

- 1½ cups whole wheat pastry flour
- ¾ teaspoon baking soda
- ½ teaspoon salt
- ½ cup packed brown sugar
- ¼ cup sugar
- 2 tablespoons unsalted butter, at room temperature
- ½ teaspoon vanilla
- 1 large egg white
- ¼ cup nonfat sour cream
- ½ cup miniature semisweet chocolate chips
- ½ cup raisins (optional)

Preheat the oven to 350°F. Cover two cookie sheets with parchment paper or lightly grease or coat with nonstick spray.

Combine the flour, baking soda, and salt in a small bowl. In a mixing bowl, cream the sugars and butter until smooth. Stir in the vanilla, egg white, and sour cream. Add the dry ingredients, chocolate chips, and raisins, if using, and stir until well blended.

Drop the dough by rounded teaspoonfuls 2 inches apart onto the prepared cookie sheets. Bake for 10 to 12 minutes until just set. Slide the cookies on the parchment paper onto a countertop to cool, or remove the cookies from the sheets and cool on a wire rack.

MAKES 36 COOKIES

PER COOKIE: *66 calories, 20% calories from fat, 1.59 g fat, 1.73 mg cholesterol, 51.2 mg sodium, 0.84 g dietary fiber*

Crispy Applesauce Oatmeal Cookies

Crispy and delicious, with only 16 percent of calories from fat, these are cookies you'll want to remember. I replaced part of the oil with applesauce, which adds moistness and flavor. You can substitute 2 tablespoons water for the egg to make these cookies both dairy-free and egg-free.

- ½ cup whole wheat flour
- ½ cup all-purpose flour
- 1 teaspoon baking powder
- ½ teaspoon baking soda
- ½ teaspoon salt
- ½ teaspoon ground cinnamon
- ¼ cup unsweetened applesauce
- 2 tablespoons canola or corn oil
- ½ cup packed brown sugar
- ½ cup sugar
- 1 large egg
- 1 teaspoon vanilla
- 1⅓ cups uncooked old-fashioned or quick-cooking rolled oats
- ½ cup raisins

Preheat the oven to 350°F. Cover a cookie sheet with parchment paper or lightly coat it with nonstick spray.

Mix the flours, baking powder, baking soda, salt, and cinnamon together in a small bowl.

In a large mixing bowl, stir the applesauce, oil, sugars, egg, and vanilla together until well blended. Add the flour mixture and stir well. Stir in the oats and raisins.

Drop the mixture by rounded teaspoonfuls, 2 inches apart, on the prepared cookie sheet. Bake for 10 to 12 minutes, until very lightly browned. Do not overbake. Slide the cookies on the parchment paper onto the countertop to cool, or, if not using parchment paper, remove the cookies and place on a wire rack to cool.

MAKES 40 COOKIES

PER COOKIE: *56.8 calories, 16% calories from fat, 1.03 g fat, 5.32 mg cholesterol, 49.6 mg sodium, 0.7 g dietary fiber*

Peanut Butter—Chocolate Chip—Raisin Cookies

Nonfat sour cream replaces part of the butter to bring the percentage of calories from fat down to 30 percent, considerably reduced from the original 49 percent calories from fat. With a few chocolate chips mixed with raisins to add chewiness and flavor to these delicious "nuggetlike" cookies, you don't feel deprived at all. In fact, my testers said they preferred these cookies to the old high-fat ones. They don't spread much in the oven during baking.

4 tablespoons (½ stick) unsalted butter, at room temperature

¼ cup nonfat sour cream

¼ cup creamy or chunky peanut butter

¾ cup packed brown sugar

1 large egg, lightly beaten

1 cup whole wheat flour

1 cup all-purpose flour

¼ cup toasted wheat germ

1 teaspoon baking soda

½ teaspoon salt

½ cup semisweet chocolate chips

1 cup dark raisins

Preheat the oven to 350°F. Cover two cookie sheets with parchment paper.

In a large mixing bowl, cream the butter with the sour cream, peanut butter, and brown sugar until smooth. Stir in the egg. In a medium bowl, stir the flours, wheat germ, baking soda, and salt together. Stir the dry ingredients into the creamed ingredients until a smooth dough is formed. Mix in the chocolate chips and raisins.

Drop the dough by rounded teaspoonfuls evenly spaced, about 1½ inches apart, on the two cookie sheets. Bake for 10 minutes, or until the cookies are lightly browned and feel firm to the touch. Do not overbake. Serve warm, or cool on a wire rack.

MAKES 60 COOKIES

PER COOKIE: *56.6 calories, 30% calories from fat, 2.02 g fat, 5.62 mg cholesterol, 39.6 mg sodium, 0.64 g dietary fiber*

ROLLED AND SHAPED COOKIES

Pepparkaker

The secret to delectable and crispy Pepparkaker is to roll the chilled dough out very, very thin.

6 tablespoons (¾ stick) unsalted butter, softened

1 tablespoon canola or corn oil

¾ cup packed brown sugar

1 tablespoon cinnamon

2 teaspoons ground ginger

1½ teaspoons ground cloves

1 teaspoon baking soda

2½ cups all-purpose flour

3 tablespoons dark molasses

¼ to ⅓ cup water

Royal Icing (optional; see Note)

Preheat the oven to 375°F. Cover 2 cookie sheets with parchment paper or coat with nonstick spray.

In a large bowl, cream the butter and oil with the brown sugar. Combine the cinnamon, ginger, cloves, baking soda, and flour and blend in.

Stir the molasses into 2 tablespoons of the water and mix in until a stiff cookie dough forms. Add more water as necessary to form a stiff but smooth cookie dough. Wrap and chill for 10 to 30 minutes. Divide the dough into quarters. Roll out to about ¹⁄₁₆-inch thickness. Cut out cookies and place 1 inch apart on the cookie sheets.

Bake for 7 to 10 minutes or until lightly browned. Decorate the cookies with Royal Icing, if desired.

MAKES 60 COOKIES

PER COOKIE: *42 calories, 30% of calories from fat, 1.42 g fat, 3.1 mg cholesterol, 15.3 mg sodium, 0.13 g dietary fiber*

NOTE: To make Royal Icing, beat 1 egg white and gradually add 3 cups confectioners' sugar and 1 teaspoon vanilla. Add water if necessary to make a smooth icing that can be drizzled or piped over the cookies.

Crystallized Ginger Cookies

The burst of sweet-pungent crystallized ginger makes these sugar-topped ginger cookies very distinctive.

2¼ cups all-purpose flour

1 teaspoon baking soda

½ teaspoon salt

½ teaspoon ground ginger

½ teaspoon ground cinnamon

6 tablespoons (¾ stick) unsalted butter, at room temperature

⅓ cup packed brown sugar

1 large egg, lightly beaten

½ cup dark molasses

2 tablespoons orange juice

½ cup currants

2 tablespoons finely chopped crystallized ginger

⅓ cup sugar for rolling the cookies before baking

Preheat the oven to 350°F. Cover two cookie sheets with parchment paper or coat with nonstick spray.

Sift the flour, baking soda, salt, ginger, and cinnamon into a medium bowl.

In a large bowl, cream the butter and brown sugar until blended. Add the egg and beat until light. Beat in the molasses and orange juice. Stir in the flour mixture until well mixed, then stir in the currants and crystallized ginger.

Shape the dough into balls about 1 inch in diameter and roll them in the sugar. Place them onto the prepared cookie sheets, 3 inches apart. Bake for 10 to 12 minutes, or until firm. Cool on a wire rack.

MAKES 50 COOKIES

PER COOKIE: *54.7 calories, 25% calories from fat, 1.54 g fat, 7.99 mg cholesterol, 40.5 mg sodium, 0.24 g dietary fiber*

Cocoa-Nutmeg Snickerdoodles

S*nickerdoodles are old-fashioned sugar cookies that are rolled in cinnamon sugar before baking. In this version, the nutmeg-flavored butter cookie dough is rolled in cocoa and sugar before baking.*

1 cup plus 1 tablespoon sugar

6 tablespoons (¾ stick) unsalted butter, at room temperature

½ cup nonfat sour cream

1 large egg, lightly beaten

2 cups all-purpose flour

½ teaspoon ground nutmeg

1 teaspoon baking powder

½ teaspoon baking soda

¼ teaspoon salt

1 teaspoon vanilla

1 tablespoon unsweetened cocoa powder

In a large mixing bowl, cream 1 cup of the sugar and the butter until smooth. Add the sour cream and egg and beat until light. Place a wire sieve over the top of the mixing bowl. Measure the flour, nutmeg, baking powder, baking soda, and salt into the sieve. Stir with a spoon until the dry ingredients are sifted into the bowl. Add the vanilla and stir until a stiff dough is formed. Refrigerate the dough for 30 minutes to 1 hour, until firm enough to handle.

Preheat the oven to 375°F. Cover two cookie sheets with parchment paper or coat lightly with nonstick spray.

In a small bowl, combine the cocoa powder and the remaining tablespoon of sugar.

Shape the dough into 1-inch balls and roll each ball in the cocoa-sugar mixture. Place the balls, about 2 inches apart, on the prepared cookie sheets. Bake for 8 to 10 minutes, or until lightly browned. Slide the cookies on the parchment paper onto the countertop or remove and cool them on a wire rack.

MAKES 30 COOKIES

PER COOKIE: *80.2 calories, 27% calories from fat, 2.4 g fat, 6.21 mg cholesterol, 43 mg sodium, 0.26 g dietary fiber*

Ginger Crinkles

These spicy cookies with sugar-crinkle tops have always been a favorite of mine. My original recipe called for more butter and makes chewier cookies, but my husband thought they stuck to his teeth (though I liked them!). With less butter, the cookies are chewy but softer, still just as tasty, and keep remarkably well in an airtight container. If I plan to keep them longer than a couple of days, I put them into the freezer.

> 1 cup sugar
>
> ⅓ cup (5⅓ tablespoons) unsalted butter, at room temperature, or corn oil
>
> ¼ cup dark molasses
>
> 1 large egg, lightly beaten
>
> 2 cups all-purpose flour
>
> 1 teaspoon baking soda
>
> 1 teaspoon ground cinnamon
>
> 1 teaspoon ground ginger
>
> ½ teaspoon ground cloves
>
> 3 tablespoons sugar for the top

Preheat the oven to 375°F. Cover a cookie sheet with parchment paper or lightly coat it with nonstick spray.

In mixing bowl, mix the sugar, butter or oil, and molasses. Add the egg and beat until light. Add the flour, baking soda, cinnamon, ginger, and cloves. Mix well.

Shape the mixture into balls 1 inch in diameter. Dip the top of each into the sugar and place with sugar side up, 2 inches apart, on the prepared cookie sheet. Drop 2 to 3 drops of water onto the top of each cookie.

Bake for 8 to 9 minutes, until lightly browned. Do not overbake. Slide the cookies on the parchment paper onto the countertop to cool, or, if not using parchment paper, remove the cookies and place on a wire rack to cool.

MAKES 48 COOKIES

PER COOKIE: 53.2 calories, 24% calories from fat, 1.42 g fat, 7.85 mg cholesterol, 19 mg sodium, 0.15 g dietary fiber

White Ginger Cookies

These thin, spicy, and crisp cookie cutouts are pale in color but not in flavor!

> 6 tablespoons (¾ stick) unsalted butter, at room temperature
>
> ½ cup sugar
>
> ½ cup light corn syrup
>
> 1½ teaspoons cider vinegar
>
> 1¾ cups all-purpose flour
>
> ½ teaspoon baking soda
>
> ¾ teaspoon ground cinnamon
>
> ¾ teaspoon ground ginger
>
> ¼ teaspoon ground cloves
>
> 1 large egg white, lightly beaten
>
> Colored sugar for decoration

In a small saucepan, melt the butter over medium heat and add the sugar, corn syrup, and vinegar. Stir until the sugar is dissolved. Pour into a medium bowl and cool.

In a small bowl, combine the flour, baking soda, cinnamon, ginger, and cloves. Mix the dry ingredients and the egg white into the butter mixture until the batter is very smooth. Chill the dough until stiff, 1 to 2 hours.

Preheat the oven to 350°F Cover two cookie sheets with parchment paper. Divide the dough into two parts. Working with one part at a time, roll the dough on a lightly floured surface to ⅛-inch thickness. With your favorite shaped cookie cutter, cut into shapes and place on the prepared cookie sheets. Sprinkle with colored sugar. Bake for 7 to 8 minutes, or until lightly browned. Slide the cookies on the parchment paper onto a countertop to cool.

MAKES 36 COOKIES, ABOUT 2 INCHES IN DIAMETER

PER COOKIE: *61.4 calories, 28% calories from fat, 1.98 g fat, 5.18 mg cholesterol, 15.5 mg sodium, 0.16 g dietary fiber*

Mocha-Glazed Brown Sugar Butter Cookies

These are tender, simple little cookies that don't spread much while they bake. The chilling step is necessary only in hot weather when doughs, especially cookie dough, might become too warm to handle.

½ cup sugar

1 cup packed brown sugar

½ cup (1 stick) unsalted butter, at room temperature

1 large egg, lightly beaten

3 tablespoons skim milk

1 tablespoon vanilla

2½ cups all-purpose flour

½ teaspoon baking soda

¼ teaspoon salt

MOCHA ICING

1 cup confectioners' sugar

2 to 3 teaspoons strong, hot coffee

In a large mixing bowl, with an electric mixer, cream the sugars with the butter and blend in the egg, milk, and vanilla.

Stir the flour, baking soda, and salt together in another bowl and then stir the mixture into the butter mixture until smooth. Cover and chill for 30 minutes to 1 hour, until the dough is firm enough to handle.

Preheat the oven to 375°F Cover two cookie sheets with parchment paper or lightly grease them with nonstick spray.

Shape the dough into 1½-inch balls and place onto the prepared cookie sheets, about 2 inches apart. Bake for 10 to 12 minutes, or just until browned on the edges.

While the cookies bake, stir together the confectioners' sugar and enough coffee to make a thin glaze.

When the cookies are baked, remove from the oven and slide the cookies with the parchment paper onto the countertop or remove and cool them on a wire rack. Brush the tops of the warm cookies with the icing.

MAKES 48 COOKIES

PER COOKIE: *73.8 calories, 25% calories from fat, 2.08 g fat, 9.63 mg cholesterol, 23.9 mg sodium, 0.16 g dietary fiber*

Italian Anise Sticks

These are delicious crispy, crunchy, anise-flavored cookie sticks, perfect for any occasion.

> 2 cups all-purpose flour
>
> 1 teaspoon baking powder
>
> 1 teaspoon crushed anise seed
>
> 1/4 teaspoon salt
>
> 3/4 cup sugar
>
> 1/4 cup vegetable shortening
>
> 2 large eggs, beaten
>
> 1/8 teaspoon anise extract

Preheat the oven to 375°F. Cover two or three cookie sheets with parchment paper or lightly grease them with nonstick spray.

In a mixing bowl, combine the flour, baking powder, anise seed, salt, and sugar. With an electric mixer, blend in the shortening until the shortening is incorporated into the flour mixture. Stir in the eggs and anise extract and mix until cookie dough is stiff.

Working with half of the dough at a time, roll out on a lightly floured board to a 4 × 20-inch strip. Cut the strip crosswise into 1/2-inch strips. Place on the prepared cookie sheets about 1/2 inch apart. Bake for 10 to 12 minutes, until lightly browned. Slide the cookies on the parchment onto the countertop to cool, or lift with a spatula onto a wire rack.

MAKES 80 COOKIES

PER COOKIE: *25.3 calories, 28% calories from fat, 0.79 g fat, 5.32 mg cholesterol, 12.4 mg sodium, 0.08 g dietary fiber*

Peanut Butter and Jelly—Center Cookies

A dot of peanut butter and jelly in the center of these cookies gives them color and kid appeal.

> 1/2 cup sugar
>
> 4 tablespoons (1/2 stick) unsalted butter, at room temperature
>
> 1 large egg, lightly beaten
>
> 1 tablespoon lemon juice
>
> 1 1/2 cups all-purpose flour
>
> 1/2 teaspoon baking powder
>
> 1/2 teaspoon baking soda
>
> 1/4 teaspoon salt
>
> 2 tablespoons creamy or chunky peanut butter
>
> 1/2 cup fruit jelly (grape, raspberry, or strawberry)

In a large mixing bowl, with an electric mixer, cream the sugar and butter until smooth. Add the egg and lemon juice and beat until smooth. In a small bowl, combine the flour, baking powder, baking soda, and salt. Stir the dry ingredients into the creamed ingredients to make a stiff cookie dough. Cover and chill 1 hour.

Preheat the oven to 350°F. Cover cookie sheets with parchment paper or lightly coat with nonstick spray.

Shape rounded teaspoonfuls of the dough into balls and place about 2 inches apart onto the prepared cookie sheets. With your thumb, make a depression in the center of each one. Bake for 12 to 15 minutes, or until the cookies feel firm to the touch. Transfer to a wire rack and spoon a small dot of peanut butter along with a dot of jelly in the center of each baked cookie.

MAKES 30 COOKIES

PER COOKIE: *69.3 calories, 29% calories from fat, 2.3 g fat, 11.2 mg cholesterol, 58.4 mg sodium, 0.25 g dietary fiber*

Lemon-Frosted Sugar Cookies

Light *corn syrup adds moistness as well as tenderness to these cutout cookies. Lemon juice not only adds flavor but also tenderizes the protein in the flour. For Easter, I use bunny and flower cookie cutters and decorate the cookies with pastel icing.*

1 cup sugar

½ cup (1 stick) unsalted butter, at room temperature

1 large egg, lightly beaten

¼ cup light corn syrup

2 tablespoons fresh lemon juice

1 tablespoon vanilla

2¾ cups all-purpose flour

¾ teaspoon baking powder

½ teaspoon baking soda

½ teaspoon salt

ICING

1 cup confectioners' sugar

2 tablespoons lemon juice

2 to 3 tablespoons water

Food coloring

In a large mixing bowl, cream the sugar and butter together until crumbly. Add the egg, corn syrup, lemon juice, and vanilla and beat until light. In a small bowl, stir together the flour, baking powder, baking soda, and salt. Stir the flour mixture into the creamed mixture until it is well blended and the dough holds together when pressed into a ball.

Divide the dough into four parts. Flatten each part to make a disk about 5 inches in diameter. Wrap each disk in plastic and refrigerate 30 minutes or overnight, if desired.

Preheat the oven to 375°F Line three or four cookie sheets with parchment paper or coat with nonstick spray.

Place a chilled disk of cookie dough onto a lightly floured board. Roll out to ¼- to ⅛-inch thickness. Cut out cookies and transfer to the prepared cookie sheets, placing them 2 inches apart. Roll and cut out the remaining dough.

Bake for 5 to 9 minutes, depending on the size of the cookies. Do not overbake. Remove from the oven and slide the cookies on the parchment paper onto a countertop or a wire rack. Cool completely.

For the icing, combine the confectioners' sugar and lemon juice. Mix to blend well. Add water a little at a time to achieve the desired consistency. Divide the icing into parts, depending on how many colors you want to use. Add food coloring, a few drops at a time, to achieve desired tint. Spread the icing in a thin layer on the cooled cookies. Place the remainder of the icing in pastry bags fitted with a small writing tip. Or place in a small resealable plastic bag, snipping a small hole off one corner. Pipe designs onto the iced cookies.

MAKES ABOUT 48 COOKIES

ANALYSIS IS BASED ON 48 COOKIES. PER COOKIE: *71.4 calories, 26% of calories from fat, 2.09 g fat, 9.61 mg cholesterol, 38.5 mg sodium, 0.18 g dietary fiber*

Bar Cookies

Chocolate-Cherry Brownies

I used nonfat vanilla-flavored yogurt to add moistness and boost the flavor in these rich-tasting brownies.

1 cup cake flour

½ cup unsweetened cocoa powder

½ teaspoon salt

1½ cups packed brown sugar

½ cup dried tart cherries

4 tablespoons (½ stick) unsalted butter, melted

½ cup vanilla-flavored nonfat yogurt

1 large egg

2 teaspoons vanilla

DRIZZLE

1 cup confectioners' sugar

2 tablespoons unsweetened cocoa powder

2 to 3 teaspoons skim milk

Preheat the oven to 350°F. Coat a 9-inch square pan lightly with nonstick cooking spray and dust lightly with flour.

Place a wire sieve over a mixing bowl and measure the cake flour, cocoa powder, salt, and brown sugar into it. With a spoon, stir the mixture until it is sifted into the bowl. Add the dried cherries. In another bowl, stir the butter, yogurt, egg, and vanilla together. Pour the liquids over the dry ingredients and stir just until blended.

Pour the batter into the baking pan and bake for 25 to 30 minutes, or until a toothpick inserted into the center comes out clean.

Place the baking dish on a wire rack to cool. Combine the confectioners' sugar, cocoa powder, and milk to make a frosting that can be drizzled. Drizzle over the cooled brownies. Cut into squares.

MAKES 16 SQUARES

PER SQUARE: *166 calories, 20% calories from fat, 3.76 g fat, 21 mg cholesterol, 106 mg sodium, 1.18 g dietary fiber*

Orange and Fig Bars

Sometimes I make these bars with dates or dried apricots in place of the figs in the filling. I replaced some of the fat in the crumbly oat pastry with applesauce with great success.

2 cups chopped dried figs

1 tablespoon grated orange zest

4 tablespoons fresh orange juice

1 cup water

½ cup applesauce

6 tablespoons (¾ stick) unsalted butter, at room temperature, or canola oil

¾ cup packed brown sugar

1¾ cups all-purpose flour

1 teaspoon salt

½ teaspoon baking soda

1 cup quick-cooking rolled oats

Preheat the oven to 350°F. Coat a 9-inch square pan with nonstick spray.

In a saucepan, combine the figs, orange zest and juice, and water. Place over low heat and cook for 10 minutes, stirring occasionally, until the figs are soft and have absorbed most of the liquid. Purée the mixture in a food processor and add ¼ cup of the applesauce.

In a mixing bowl, cream the butter and brown sugar. Stir in the flour, salt, baking soda, and rolled oats. The mixture will be crumbly; stir in the remaining ¼ cup applesauce until the crumbs feel slightly moist. Press two thirds of the mixture into the bottom of the prepared pan. Top with the fig mixture. Crumble the remaining oat mixture over the top. Press down the top layer to pack firmly. Bake for 25 to 30 minutes, or until lightly browned. Cool in the pan on a wire rack. Cut into bars.

MAKES 32 BARS

PER BAR: *91.5 calories, 24% calories from fat, 2.47 g fat, 5.82 mg cholesterol, 49.8 mg sodium, 1.3 g dietary fiber*

Cinnamon-Pumpkin Bars

The original recipe for these pumpkin bars has been a family favorite for years. That recipe had twice the amount of oil and egg, bringing the calories from fat up to about 40 percent, so I removed one egg and replaced some of the oil with nonfat sour cream. The new low-fat bars are every bit as moist, cakelike, and tasty as the original.

1 cup canned pumpkin
1 large egg
1 cup sugar
¼ cup canola oil
½ cup nonfat sour cream
1 cup all-purpose flour
1 teaspoon baking powder
½ teaspoon baking soda
¼ teaspoon salt
1 teaspoon ground cinnamon

CREAM CHEESE FROSTING
4 ounces fat-free cream cheese, at room temperature
1¾ cups confectioners' sugar
1 teaspoon vanilla

Preheat the oven to 350°F. Lightly coat a 13 × 9-inch pan with nonstick spray. Line the bottom with wax paper or parchment paper and spray again.

In a large bowl, stir together the pumpkin, egg, sugar, oil, and sour cream. Add the flour, baking powder, baking soda, salt, and cinnamon and mix until well blended. Pour the mixture into the prepared pan. Bake for 25 to 30 minutes, or until the top springs back when lightly touched. Place the pan on a wire rack to cool.

In a small bowl, beat the cream cheese and add the confectioners' sugar and vanilla. Beat until smooth. When the bars are cooled, spread with the frosting. Cut into bars to serve.

MAKES 24 BARS

PER BAR: *114 calories, 20% calories from fat, 2.56 g fat, 9.7 mg cholesterol, 84.9 mg sodium, 0.32 g dietary fiber*

Whole Wheat and Pumpkin Bars

Brown sugar and sweet spices gives these bars holiday appeal. The original bar had twice the amount of shortening, and cream cheese in the frosting. These new, low-fat bars are every bit as irresistible as the original.

1 cup all-purpose flour

1 cup whole wheat flour

2 teaspoons baking powder

2 teaspoons ground cinnamon

$\frac{1}{2}$ teaspoon ground nutmeg

$\frac{1}{2}$ teaspoon ground ginger

$\frac{1}{4}$ teaspoon salt

1 cup packed brown sugar

1 cup canned pumpkin

$\frac{1}{2}$ cup (1 stick) unsalted butter, melted

1 large egg

2 teaspoons vanilla

$\frac{1}{2}$ cup raisins

FROSTING

1$\frac{1}{2}$ cups confectioners' sugar

3 tablespoons vanilla-flavored nonfat yogurt

1 teaspoon vanilla

Preheat the oven to 350°F. Coat a 15 × 11-inch rimmed baking pan with nonstick spray.

In a large bowl, combine the flours, baking powder, cinnamon, nutmeg, ginger, salt, brown sugar, pumpkin, butter, egg, and vanilla. Beat with an electric mixer for 2 minutes, until the mixture is smooth. Stir in the raisins. Pour the mixture into the prepared baking pan and bake for 25 to 30 minutes, or until a toothpick inserted into the center comes out clean and dry. Remove from the oven and cool completely on a wire rack.

Stir together the confectioners' sugar, vanilla yogurt, and vanilla and spread over the top of the bars. Cut into bars.

MAKES 48 BARS

PER BAR: *72.7 calories, 25% calories from fat, 2.13 g fat, 9.61 mg cholesterol, 29 mg sodium, 0.6 g dietary fiber*

Cocoa Mocha Brownies

These cakelike brownies had a fat quotient of 40 percent of calories from fat to start out. By reducing the butter by 25 percent and eliminating one egg, the total dropped to 27 percent calories from fat. This makes a large pan of brownies, just perfect for a large group of people.

2 cups all-purpose flour

2 cups sugar

1 teaspoon baking soda

$\frac{3}{4}$ cup (1$\frac{1}{2}$ sticks) unsalted butter, at room temperature

1 cup hot, strong coffee

$\frac{1}{4}$ cup unsweetened cocoa powder

$\frac{1}{2}$ cup low-fat buttermilk

1 large egg, lightly beaten

1 teaspoon vanilla

FROSTING

2 tablespoons unsweetened cocoa powder

3 cups confectioners' sugar

3 to 4 tablespoons skim milk

1 tablespoon vanilla

Preheat the oven to 400°F. Coat a 17½ × 11-inch jelly roll or sheet pan with nonstick spray.

In a large bowl, mix the flour, sugar, and baking soda. In a saucepan, combine the butter, coffee, and cocoa powder. Stir over medium heat until the cocoa is dissolved and the butter is melted. In another bowl, stir the buttermilk, egg, and vanilla together.

Pour the cocoa mixture and the buttermilk mixture over the flour mixture and stir until well blended. Pour the mixture into the prepared pan. Bake for 20 minutes, or until the center springs back when touched.

While the brownies bake, stir together the cocoa powder, confectioners' sugar, skim milk, and vanilla until smooth and spreadable. Spread over the hot baked brownies. Place the pan on a rack to cool. Cut into bars.

MAKES 36 BROWNIES

PER BROWNIE: *138 calories, 27% calories from fat, 4.24 g fat, 16.4 mg cholesterol, 30.3 mg sodium, 0.44 g dietary fiber*

Frosted Rich Brownies

Just when I was about to give up on the whole brownie idea, I was struck with this inspiration. What if I used nonfat dry milk plus nonfat evaporated milk to make a saucepan brownie? After three attempts, I came up with this nice, moist brownie that I will make again and again! The only fat in this brownie comes from semisweet chocolate morsels which, in combination with unsweetened cocoa, give the brownies richness.

½ cup nonfat evaporated milk
1 cup instant nonfat dry milk

¾ cup sugar
¾ cup semisweet chocolate chips
⅓ cup unsweetened cocoa powder
4 large egg whites
1 cup all-purpose flour
1 teaspoon baking powder
1 teaspoon vanilla

COCOA FROSTING
1 cup confectioners' sugar
⅓ cup unsweetened cocoa powder
1 teaspoon vanilla
1 to 2 tablespoons hot, strong coffee

Preheat the oven to 350°F. Lightly grease a 9 × 13-inch baking pan or coat it with nonstick spray. Line the bottom with wax or parchment paper and lightly grease the paper.

In a medium saucepan, combine the milks and sugar. Place over medium heat and stir until the sugar is dissolved and the mixture comes to a boil. Remove from the heat and stir in the chocolate chips and cocoa powder until the mixture is smooth and slightly thickened. Stir in the egg whites, flour, baking powder, and vanilla until well blended. Pour the mixture into the prepared baking pan. Bake for 20 minutes, or until the center feels firm and is set. Do not overbake. Cool on a wire rack.

In a small bowl, stir together the confectioners' sugar, cocoa powder, vanilla, and enough coffee to make the frosting smooth and spreadable. Spread over the top of the warm brownies. Cool until the frosting is set.

MAKES 18 BROWNIES

PER BROWNIE: *144 calories, 19% calories from fat, 3.24 g fat, 0.94 mg cholesterol, 61.5 mg sodium, 1.34 g dietary fiber*

Crunchy Rosemary and Dried Cherry Squares

Rosemary, an herb that we usually associate with savory dishes, makes a surprising addition to these chewy, fruit-stuffed cookie squares. There is no added shortening in the recipe.

2 large eggs

1 cup packed brown sugar

1 tablespoon vanilla

1 cup all-purpose flour

1 teaspoon baking powder

½ teaspoon salt

½ teaspoon chopped rosemary leaves, dried or fresh

1 cup dried tart cherries or golden raisins

⅔ cup dry-roasted sunflower seeds or chopped pecans

Preheat the oven to 350°F. Lightly grease or coat with nonstick spray a 9-inch square baking pan and dust lightly with flour.

In a large bowl, beat the eggs and brown sugar together until thick and fluffy. Add the vanilla. Stir the flour, baking powder, salt, and rosemary together in another bowl and add to the egg mixture. Beat until light.

Blend in the cherries and sunflower seeds. Pour the mixture into the prepared pan and smooth the top. Bake for 30 minutes, or until lightly browned and the top feels dry when touched. Cool in the pan on a wire rack. Cut into squares.

MAKES 36 SQUARES

PER SQUARE: *66.2 calories, 20% calories from fat, 1.5 g fat, 11.8 mg cholesterol, 45.5 mg sodium, 0.53 g dietary fiber*

TWICE-BAKED COOKIES

Anise-Almond Biscotti

One of the things I love most about these twice-baked Italian cookies is how easy they are to shape and bake. They certainly deliver the most "bang for the buck" in terms of effort! Biscotti are better two or three days after baking, when they have mellowed and softened a bit and the flavors have had a chance to blend.

2 tablespoons unsalted butter, at room temperature

⅔ cup sugar

1 tablespoon anise-flavored liqueur

3 large egg whites

2 cups all-purpose flour

2 teaspoons baking powder

1 teaspoon anise seed

¼ teaspoon salt

¼ cup toasted blanched almonds, finely chopped

Preheat the oven to 325°F. Cover a cookie sheet with parchment paper or coat it with nonstick spray and dust it lightly with flour.

In a large bowl, cream the butter, sugar, and anise-flavored liqueur together until smooth. Beat in the egg whites until light and fluffy. Add the flour, baking powder, anise seed, salt, and almonds and mix until the dough is smooth. Chill, covered, for 30 minutes or until firm.

Divide the dough into four parts. Shape each part into a log about ½ inch thick and 12 inches long. Place the logs onto the cookie sheet spaced about 2 inches apart.

Bake for about 30 minutes, until golden brown. Reduce the oven temperature to 250°F. Remove the cookies and cool on the cookie sheet for about 15 minutes.

With a thin, sharp knife, cut the logs diagonally into ½-inch slices. Arrange the slices, with one cut side down, on the cookie sheet and bake until dried, 15 to 20 minutes. Let cool completely on the cookie sheet. Store in an airtight container.

MAKES 48 BISCOTTI

PER COOKIE: *37.5 calories, 21% calories from fat, 0.88 g fat, 1.29 mg cholesterol, 28.6 mg sodium, 0.21 g dietary fiber*

Filbert Biscotti

Italians eat biscotti any time of day—breakfast, lunch, or dinner. It is typical to serve them with red wine or coffee for dunking.

2 tablespoons unsalted butter, at room temperature

⅔ cup sugar

1 teaspoon vanilla

3 large egg whites

2 cups all-purpose flour

2 teaspoons baking powder

¼ teaspoon salt

¼ cup toasted filberts or hazelnuts, skinned and finely chopped (see page xiii)

Preheat the oven to 325°F. Cover a cookie sheet with parchment paper or coat it with nonstick spray and dust it lightly with flour.

In a large bowl, cream the butter, sugar, and vanilla together until smooth. Beat in the egg whites until light and fluffy. Add the flour, baking powder, salt, and filberts and mix until the dough is smooth. Chill, covered, for 30 minutes or until firm.

Divide the dough into four parts. Shape each part into a log about ½ inch thick and 12 inches long. Place the logs onto the cookie sheet spaced about 2 inches apart.

Bake for about 30 minutes, until golden brown. Reduce the oven temperature to 250°F. Remove the cookies and cool on the cookie sheet for about 15 minutes.

With a thin, sharp knife, cut the logs diagonally into ½-inch slices. Arrange the slices, with one cut side down, on the cookie sheet and bake until dried, 15 to 20 minutes.

Let cool completely on the cookie sheet. Store in an airtight container.

MAKES 48 BISCOTTI

PER COOKIE: *35 calories, 14% calories from fat, 0.5 g fat, 1.29 mg cholesterol, 28.5 mg sodium, 0.13 g dietary fiber*

Cardamom Toast

This is a twice-baked cookie like a rusk or biscotti. I've reduced the fat grams by replacing ½ cup of the butter with nonfat sour cream.

½ cup (1 stick) unsalted butter, at room temperature

2 cups sugar

1½ cups nonfat sour cream

2 large eggs

2 teaspoons freshly ground cardamom

3½ cups all-purpose flour

3 teaspoons baking powder

½ teaspoon salt

Preheat the oven to 350°F. Lightly grease or coat a 13 × 9-inch baking pan with nonstick spray.

In a large bowl, cream together the butter and sugar until smooth. Add the sour cream, eggs, and cardamom and beat until light. In another bowl, stir the flour, baking powder, and salt together, then add to the creamed mixture. Mix until smooth and spread the dough into the prepared pan.

Bake for 40 to 50 minutes, or until light brown. Lower the oven temperature to 275°F. Remove the pan from the oven and cool on a wire rack for 10 minutes. Invert the pan and remove the cake. Cut into ½-inch slices crosswise. Lay the slices close together in a single layer with the cut side up on a cookie sheet. Cut each slice into 3-inch pieces and leave them in place. Bake until crisp and dry, 1 to 2 hours. Cool the cookies on the cookie sheet.

MAKES 78 COOKIES

PER COOKIE: *55 calories, 22% calories from fat, 1.36 g fat, 8.65 mg cholesterol, 24 mg sodium, 0.14 g dietary fiber*

Swedish Almond Rusks

Sweet twice-baked cookies are a summertime staple in Scandinavia. They keep well in an airtight tin or jar held in a cool pantry.

4 tablespoons (½ stick) unsalted butter, at room temperature

¾ cup sugar

3 large egg whites

1 teaspoon baking powder

1 teaspoon almond extract

¼ cup coarsely chopped unblanched almonds

2 cups all-purpose flour

Preheat the oven to 375°F. Lightly grease a large cookie sheet or coat it with nonstick spray, or cover with parchment paper.

In a large bowl, cream together the butter and sugar. Add the egg whites and beat until light. Stir in the baking powder, almond extract, and almonds. Mix in the flour just until incorporated. Turn the dough out onto a lightly floured surface, divide into three parts, and dust each part lightly with flour. Shape each piece into a log 12 inches long. Place on the cookie sheet, evenly spaced, about 3 inches apart.

Bake for 15 to 20 minutes, until light brown. Leave the oven on and cool for 5 minutes on the cookie sheet. Cut each log into 1-inch-wide slices on the diagonal. Turn the pieces so that one of the cut sides faces down and return to the oven. Turn the oven off and allow the rusks to dry about 2 hours.

MAKES 36 COOKIES

PER COOKIE: *57.5 calories, 28% calories from fat, 1.81 g fat, 3.45 mg cholesterol, 14.2 mg sodium, 0.28 g dietary fiber*

Cinnamon-Walnut Cookie Rusks

I've always loved twice-baked cookies and rusks. We used to make rusks from all kinds of coffee breads and cakes, to refresh and preserve baked goods. We used this method especially in the summertime when things could go stale quickly. Rusks are great for dunking in hot cocoa or coffee. The Italians, of course, use them as wine-dunkers.

2 tablespoons unsalted butter, at room temperature

$2/3$ cup brown sugar

1 tablespoon vanilla

3 large egg whites

$1\frac{1}{2}$ cups all-purpose flour

$1/2$ cup whole wheat flour

2 teaspoons baking powder

1 teaspoon ground cinnamon

$1/4$ teaspoon salt

$1/4$ cup toasted walnuts, finely chopped

Preheat the oven to 325°F. Cover a cookie sheet with parchment paper or coat it with nonstick spray and dust it lightly with flour.

In a large bowl, cream the butter, sugar, and vanilla together until smooth. Beat in the egg whites until light and fluffy. Add the flours, baking powder, cinnamon, salt, and walnuts and mix until the dough is smooth. Chill, covered, for 30 minutes or until firm.

Divide the dough into four parts. Shape each part into a log about $1/2$ inch thick and 12 inches long. Place the logs onto the cookie sheet spaced about 2 inches apart.

Bake for about 30 minutes, until golden brown. Reduce the oven temperature to 250°F. Remove the cookies and cool on the cookie sheet for about 15 minutes.

With a thin, sharp knife, cut the logs diagonally into $1/2$-inch slices. Arrange the slices, with one cut side down, on the cookie sheet and bake until dried, 15 to 20 minutes. Let cool completely on the cookie sheet. Store in an airtight container.

MAKES 48 COOKIES

PER COOKIE: *37.4 calories, 22% calories from fat, 0.92 g fat, 1.29 mg cholesterol, 28.6 mg sodium, 0.92 g dietary fiber*

CAKES

Ingredients, temperature, and techniques affect the ultimate success of a cake. But what is success? First of all, the cake must be delicious. It needs to have flavor. A cake also needs to be moist, with a tender texture. The simpler the cake, the fewer the ingredients, and consequently the more success depends on each of the ingredients that make up the cake.

It is no secret that fat carries flavor. The type of fat used in a cake makes a great difference in flavor, texture, moistness, and tenderness. Some cakes require little or no fat at all, such as angel food cakes, which are made light and delicate by beaten egg whites; sponge cakes, leavened by beating both the egg whites and the yolks; and chiffon cakes, with beaten egg and leavening. Butter cakes, such as layer cakes, pound cakes, and most coffee cakes also are made lighter when air is beaten into fat to make a light and tender texture. Rich flourless nut or chocolate cakes depend on a large amount of high-fat ingredients to create their individual characters.

In selecting cakes for this book, I chose angel food, sponge, chiffon, coffee, fresh fruit, and butter cakes. I didn't even consider torturing pound cakes or rich nut or chocolate cake recipes to make them fit into the guideline of less than 30 percent of calories from fat. They are best left as they are, in all their buttery, nutty, chocolatey glory.

It was such fun revisiting some of my favorite old cake recipes. One of the interesting things I discovered is that cakes have become richer and richer, fattier and fattier in the last three or four decades. There was a time when we ascribed to the theory that "too much of a good thing is never enough."

I selected beloved recipes from my own files of recipes I've developed and worked with over the years. First, I calculated the nutritional profile for each cake, then I calculated the amount of fat that theoretically needed to be removed from the recipe to bring it in line with the 30-percent guideline. The next step was to go to the kitchen and start baking.

I reduced the fat by using less butter, egg yolks, and nuts. Obviously, when you eliminate fat ingredients, you eliminate volume from the product. So I needed to replace the fat with another ingredient, preferably one that added its own attributes to the final product. Reduced-fat and nonfat dairy sour cream and yogurt as well as cooked or puréed fruits help to retain the cake's tender crumb, even texture, and moisture without altering the color or the flavor. But when I tried to replace all of the fat, the cake looked fine, but the flavor suffered. I could not enjoy an empty-tasting cake and I thought, Why bother, if it doesn't really taste good? Now, I prefer the flavor of my lower-fat cakes, and they still contain butter because butter makes them taste wonderful.

TIPS FOR FROSTING AND DECORATING CAKES

Not only should the cake taste moist and wonderful, it needs to *look* special. Presentation is almost as important as making a good cake in the first place. A white cake baked in a square or rectangular pan can be served just plain, cut into squares. But layer cakes need to be filled with something, and they call for some sort of topping. A filling of fresh fruit jam and a dusting of confectioners' sugar is simple and elegant. Or you can lay a doily on top of a cake and dust generously with powdered sugar, then carefully lift it to reveal a pretty design.

Gumdrops, jelly beans, and candied, fresh, or dried fruit make colorful nonfat adornments for a cake with a minimum of frosting. Fresh, nontoxic, chemical-free flowers, such as nasturtiums, violets, roses, pansies, and apple blossoms, make very attractive garnishes.

To make a simple decorating bag, mix frosting in a small, heavy-duty plastic bag. Snip off one corner and press the frosting out onto the cake to decorate.

TIPS FOR STORING LOW-FAT CAKES

1. To bake and keep cakes for serving a day or two later, let them cool completely and wrap them, unfrosted, in an airtight container, then freeze.

2. Frosted cakes or baked cheesecakes that will be eaten soon should be kept under a cake bell or an inverted large bowl.

3. Leftover cake or cheesecake pieces can be stored in rigid containers in the refrigerator or freezer.

A Basic Low-Fat Butter Cake

I am including this simple recipe because it illustrates the way I approached reducing the fat in all of the shortening-based recipes in this chapter. First, I used cake flour instead of all-purpose flour so that the cake would have a more tender texture. I used skim milk in place of whole milk. I did not change the eggs, although you may use 4 egg whites in place of the 2 whole eggs. (This will result in a white cake.) I replaced 2 tablespoons of the butter with 2 tablespoons nonfat sour cream. All of this reduced the calories from fat from 34 percent to 27 percent, and the fat grams per serving from 9 to 6. If you bake this cake in layers, you can fill the layers with a berry jam and simply dust it with powdered sugar. Cut into wedges, it is wonderful with a fresh fruit purée and perhaps softened nonfat ice cream. If you choose to bake cupcakes, frost them with the One-Minute Boiled Fudge Frosting (page 84) or Boiled Caramel Icing (page 84).

- 2-1/4 cups cake flour, sifted
- 3 teaspoons baking powder
- 1 1/4 cups sugar
- 1/2 teaspoon salt
- 6 tablespoons (3/4 stick) unsalted butter, at room temperature
- 2 tablespoons nonfat sour cream
- 1 cup skim milk
- 2 large eggs, lightly beaten
- 1 teaspoon vanilla

Preheat the oven to 375°F. Lightly grease or coat with nonstick spray two 9-inch round cake pans, one 7 × 11-inch rectangular pan, or 24 muffin cups and dust with flour.

Stir the flour, baking powder, sugar, and salt together in a large mixing bowl. Add the butter and mix with an electric mixer until the butter is thoroughly incorporated into the dry ingredients. In a small bowl, mix the sour cream, milk, eggs, and vanilla. Add the liquids to the dry ingredients and beat at low speed, scraping the bowl with a rubber spatula. Beat at high speed for 2 minutes, until the batter is light and fluffy.

Pour the batter into the prepared pans. Bake the layers for 20 to 25 minutes, the rectangular pan for 30 to 35 minutes, or the cupcakes for 18 to 20 minutes, until the cake springs back when touched in the center and begins to pull away from the sides of the pans. Cool the cakes in the pans on a rack for 5 minutes, then turn out onto a wire rack to finish cooling. Cool completely before filling or frosting.

MAKES 12 SERVINGS

PER SERVING: *228 calories, 27% calories from fat, 6.8 g fat, 51.4 mg cholesterol, 193 mg sodium, 0.57 g dietary fiber*

LAYER CAKES AND CUPCAKES

Banana-Filled Chocolate Cake

When we discovered that our grandson was allergic to both dairy products and eggs, I set out to make a birthday cake that he could eat. Not only is this dairy-free and egg-free, but everybody found it delicate and delicious! The recipe originally came from a collection of "wartime" cakes designed to conserve rationed ingredients.

3 cups all-purpose flour

½ cup unsweetened dark cocoa powder

2 teaspoons baking soda

½ teaspoon salt

1½ cups packed brown sugar

½ cup canola oil

2 cups water

1 teaspoon vanilla

¼ cup very strong coffee

BANANA FILLING AND FROSTING

2 ripe bananas, sliced

1 ripe banana, mashed, about ½ cup

3 cups confectioners' sugar

1 to 2 tablespoons fresh lemon juice

⅛ teaspoon salt

1 teaspoon canola oil

1 teaspoon vanilla

Banana slices and mint leaves for garnish (optional)

Preheat the oven to 350°F. Lightly grease or coat two 9-inch round cake pans with nonstick spray. Dust with flour.

Sift the flour, cocoa, baking soda, and salt into a large mixing bowl. Add the brown sugar and mix until blended into the dry ingredients. Pour the oil, water, vanilla, and coffee over the dry ingredients and mix with a whisk until the batter is smooth. Divide the batter between the two cake pans and smooth out evenly.

Bake for 25 to 30 minutes, or until a toothpick inserted into the center of the cake comes out clean and dry. Cool in the pans on a wire rack.

Remove the layers from the cake pans. Place one layer on a cake plate and cover with the sliced bananas.

To make the frosting, combine the mashed banana, confectioners' sugar, lemon juice, salt, oil, and vanilla in a bowl. With an electric mixer, beat until the frosting is smooth. Add a little more confectioners' sugar if the frosting seems too soft. Add water if it seems too stiff. (The variation depends on the moisture of the bananas.) Spread about ½ cup of the frosting over the banana slices on the cake layer. Top with the second layer. Spread the remaining frosting over the top and sides of the cake. Decorate with the extra slices of banana and fresh mint leaves, if desired.

MAKES 16 SERVINGS

PER SERVING: 308 calories, 22% calories from fat, 7.6 g fat, 0 mg cholesterol, 180 mg sodium, 1.67 g dietary fiber

Berry-Filled Sponge Cake Layers

This is one of our favorite cakes when berries are in season. We split it into layers and fill it with fresh berries to make a delicious birthday or celebration cake, covered with whipped cream, of course. But, to cut the amount of whipped cream and yet have a reasonable amount of frosting, I've begun using what I seldom used in the past: marshmallow creme. Just a half cup of whipping cream, whipped and folded into the fluffy creme, makes enough volume to fill the cake. I dust the top with confectioners' sugar and decorate it with more berries.

4 large eggs, at room temperature

1 cup sugar

⅛ teaspoon salt

1 teaspoon vanilla

1 cup all-purpose flour

BERRY FILLING

½ cup whipping (heavy) cream

½ cup marshmallow creme

2 cups fresh strawberries, sliced, or raspberries

DECORATION

Confectioners' sugar

Additional berries

Preheat the oven to 375°F. Cover the bottom of two 9-inch round cake pans with wax paper or parchment paper rounds, then lightly grease or spray with nonstick spray and dust lightly with flour.

In a clean, dry mixing bowl, beat the eggs with the sugar and salt at high speed with an electric mixer for 5 minutes, scraping the bowl often at first. Gently stir in the vanilla. Sift the flour into the bowl. With a rubber spatula, gently fold the flour into the egg foam until it is thoroughly mixed, being careful not to smash the foam down.

Pour the batter into the prepared pans. Bake the layers for 30 to 35 minutes, or until the cake feels firm to the touch in the center or a toothpick inserted in the center comes out clean and dry.

Remove from the oven. Cool the layers in the pans on a wire rack. Carefully loosen the layers from the pans by running a spatula around the edges of the pans, then turning out the cakes onto a rack. Peel off the papers.

Whip the cream until almost stiff, then whip in the marshmallow creme. Place one cake layer on a cake plate. Spread with the whipped cream mixture and top with the berries. Top with the second layer. Dust the top of the cake with confectioners' sugar and top with additional berries.

MAKES 8 SERVINGS

PER SERVING: *301 calories, 24% calories from fat, 8.28 g fat, 127 mg cholesterol, 79.1 mg sodium, 1.35 g dietary fiber*

Cocoa Layer Cake with Fast Fudge Frosting

This splendid cake is perfect for a birthday celebration. There's just enough frosting to fill between the layers and cover the top, leaving the sides of the cake exposed. But if you want to, you can double the frosting recipe to cover the sides as well.

2½ cups cake flour

⅓ cup dark unsweetened cocoa powder

1½ cups sugar

2 teaspoons baking powder

½ teaspoon baking soda

¼ teaspoon salt

½ cup (1 stick) unsalted butter, at room temperature

1 cup vanilla-flavored nonfat yogurt

3 large eggs

1 tablespoon vanilla

FAST FUDGE FROSTING

2 tablespoons unsalted butter

3 tablespoons unsweetened cocoa powder

3 tablespoons vanilla-flavored nonfat yogurt

1¾ to 2 cups confectioners' sugar

⅛ teaspoon salt

1 teaspoon vanilla

Preheat the oven to 375°F. Coat two 9-inch round cake pans with nonstick spray and dust lightly with flour.

Sift the flour, cocoa, sugar, baking powder, baking soda, and salt into a large bowl. Add the butter and, with an electric mixer, mix until the butter is completely blended into the dry ingredients.

In a small bowl, combine the yogurt, eggs, and vanilla. Pour the liquid ingredients into the dry ingredients. With the electric mixer, blend at high speed for 2 minutes, scraping the bowl often, until the batter is light and fluffy.

Pour the batter into the prepared pans, dividing it equally. Smooth the tops so that they are even. Bake for 30 to 35 minutes, or until a toothpick inserted into the center of the cake comes out clean and dry. Remove from the oven and cool on a wire rack for 10 minutes. Loosen the edges of the cakes using a knife or spatula and invert the cakes onto a wire rack to cool completely.

Prepare the frosting: In a small bowl, combine the butter and cocoa; mix until smooth. Add the yogurt and beat until smooth. Slowly beat in the confectioners' sugar until the frosting is light and fluffy. Beat in the salt and vanilla.

Place one of the cake layers on a cake plate. Spread about ½ cup of the frosting onto the layer. Place the second layer on top. Spread the remaining frosting over the top of the cake.

MAKES 16 SERVINGS

PER SERVING: *264 calories, 24% calories from fat, 8.12 g fat, 20.9 mg cholesterol, 103 mg sodium, 1.3 g dietary fiber*

Glazed Almond–Plum–Rum Torte

The light and airy base for this layer cake is a sponge cake made with cake flour and ice water, a revised version of a recipe I received many years ago from my friend Shirley Sarvis. I like to have the layers on hand in my freezer all ready for a quick shortcake when the raspberries in the garden are abundant, or when the meadow strawberries are in season. This makes a festive, low-fat dessert.

1¼ cups all-purpose flour

1 teaspoon baking powder

⅛ teaspoon salt

4 large eggs, separated, at room temperature

⅓ cup ice water

1⅓ cups sugar

½ teaspoon almond extract

1 teaspoon cream of tartar

FILLING

3 tablespoons slivered almonds

2 tablespoons sugar

4 tablespoons white rum

⅓ cup plum jelly

Preheat the oven to 375°F. Lightly grease or coat with nonstick spray two 8- or 9-inch round cake pans. Line the pans with parchment paper or wax paper and grease or spray again; dust with flour.

Sift the flour, baking powder, and salt in a small bowl.

In a large bowl, beat the egg yolks at high speed until light and fluffy. Gradually beat in the ice water until the mixture is pale and foamy. Gradually beat in the sugar until the sugar is completely dissolved. Beat in the almond extract. Fold in the flour mixture.

In a small bowl, beat the egg whites and cream of tartar until stiff. Gently fold the whites into the yolk mixture. Divide the batter between the prepared pans and spread evenly.

Bake for 15 to 20 minutes, or until the cake springs back when lightly touched. Loosen the edges and turn cakes out onto a wire rack to cool. Remove the papers.

While the cakes cool, spread the almonds on a cookie sheet. Sprinkle with 2 tablespoons sugar. Broil about 6 inches from the heat just until the nuts are toasted and the sugar is melted. Cool and crush the nuts with a mallet.

Place one cake layer on a plate. Sprinkle with 2 tablespoons rum. Spread with half of the jelly. Top with the second layer. Sprinkle with the remaining rum and spread with the remaining jelly. Sprinkle the top with the crushed almonds. Let stand several hours before slicing and serving.

MAKES 8 SERVINGS

PER SERVING: *293 calories, 12% calories from fat, 3.85 g fat, 106 mg cholesterol, 106 mg sodium, 0.87 g dietary fiber*

Gold Layer Cake

This moist and tender cake is wonderful filled with raspberry or apricot jam or preserves. Lightly drizzled with an orange glaze, it is pretty, too.

2¼ cups cake flour

2½ teaspoons baking powder

½ teaspoon salt

1¼ cups sugar

5 tablespoons vegetable shortening, at room temperature

1 cup skim milk

2 large eggs or ½ cup egg substitute

2 teaspoons grated orange zest

FILLING

1 cup raspberry or apricot jam

GLAZE

1½ cups confectioners' sugar

2 tablespoons fresh orange juice

Preheat the oven to 350°F. Coat two 8- or 9-inch round cake pans with nonstick spray and line the bottoms with rounds of parchment paper or wax paper. Spray again and dust with flour.

Place a wire sieve over a large mixing bowl and measure in the flour, baking powder, salt, and sugar. Stir the mixture until it is sifted into the bowl. Cut the shortening into ½-inch pieces and add to the bowl. With a hand-held electric mixer, mix until the shortening is blended completely into the dry ingredients. Pour the skim milk over and add the eggs or egg substitute and orange zest.

With the electric mixer, mix at low speed, scraping the sides of the bowl, until the mixture is blended. Turn mixer to high speed and beat until light and fluffy, about 3 minutes, scraping down the sides of the bowl several times.

Pour the batter into the prepared pans and bake for 30 to 35 minutes, or until a toothpick inserted in the center of the cake comes out clean and dry or the center of the cake feels firm to the touch.

Place the cakes in the pans onto a wire rack and cool for 30 minutes. Loosen the edges of the cakes and remove from the pans.

Place one layer on a cake plate. Spread evenly with the jam. Top with the second layer.

In a small bowl, mix the confectioners' sugar and orange juice until smooth. Place the frosting in a small, heavy-duty plastic bag with a zipper-top closure. With a pair of scissors, clip one corner to make a small hole. Grip the bag and drizzle the icing over the cake. Let stand until set.

MAKES 12 SERVINGS

PER SERVING: *368 calories, 23% calories from fat, 9.37 g fat, 74 mg cholesterol, 34.4 mg sodium, 1.8 g dietary fiber*

Lemon-Raspberry Cake

This is a wonderful, simple birthday or celebration cake. All the dry ingredients are blended together with the butter until the mixture is smooth and rather moist looking. The liquid ingredients are mixed together and then blended in. The secret to an even and delicate texture in the cake is to beat the batter until it is light and fluffy, about 2 minutes.

2½ cups cake flour

1¼ cups sugar

3 teaspoons baking powder

½ teaspoon salt

½ cup (1 stick) unsalted butter, at room temperature

3 large egg whites

¾ cup skim milk

1 tablespoon grated lemon zest

½ teaspoon lemon extract

SYRUP

⅔ cup sugar

1 cup water

Zest of 1 lemon, cut in strips

⅓ cup fresh lemon juice

2 tablespoons framboise (raspberry liqueur)

LEMON BUTTERCREAM

4 tablespoons (½ stick) unsalted butter, at room temperature

⅓ cup lemon-flavored nonfat yogurt

3¾ cups (1 pound) confectioners' sugar

2 teaspoons grated lemon zest

½ teaspoon lemon extract

GARNISH

1 pint raspberries

Preheat the oven to 350°F. Line two 8- or 9-inch round cake pans with wax paper or parchment paper. Coat with nonstick spray or lightly butter them and dust them with flour.

Sift the flour, sugar, baking powder, and salt into a bowl. Cut the butter into ¼-inch slices and add to the dry ingredients. With an electric mixer, mix at low speed, scraping the sides of the bowl with a rubber spatula, until the butter is evenly blended in and the mixture is smooth. Mix the egg whites, milk, lemon zest, and lemon extract in a small bowl. Pour the liquid ingredients over the dry ingredients and blend. Beat with the electric mixer at high speed until the batter is very light and champagne colored, about 2 minutes.

Divide the batter equally between the two prepared pans and smooth the tops. Bake for 35 to 40 minutes, or until a tester comes out clean. Cool the layers in the pans on a rack for 5 minutes, then invert the cakes onto the rack. Peel off the paper liners and cool completely.

In a small saucepan, combine the sugar, water, and lemon zest. Bring to a boil, stirring until the sugar is dissolved. Boil 1 minute. Remove the pan from the heat and let the syrup cool completely. Discard the lemon zest and stir in the lemon juice and framboise.

To make the buttercream, in a large bowl combine the butter, yogurt, and half the confectioners' sugar. Beat until the mixture is very smooth. Add the remaining sugar, the lemon zest, and the lemon extract. Beat at high speed about 2 minutes, scraping the bowl often, until the mixture is light and fluffy.

Halve each layer horizontally. Place the layers with the cut sides up on a long sheet of wax paper and brush each with the syrup, dividing the syrup equally. Place one of the halves on a cake plate with the cut side up. Spread with ⅓ cup of the buttercream. Top with a second layer, cut side down. Spread with another ⅓ cup buttercream. Repeat for the remaining layers. Finish the cake with the remaining buttercream and arrange the raspberries on top. Refrigerate until ready to serve.

MAKES 16 SERVINGS

PER SERVING: *364 calories, 22% calories from fat, 8.88 g fat, 23.5 mg cholesterol, 137 mg sodium, 1.43 g dietary fiber*

Luscious Lemon Layer Cake

Your guests will never believe that this cake is low in fat! The low-fat lemon cheese filling is made with low-fat or nonfat lemon-flavored yogurt, which, after it has been allowed to drain at least overnight, makes a smooth and spreadable cream. You do need to plan a day or two in advance of making the cake, but once made, it will keep for three or four days refrigerated. The easy lemon meringue frosting can be made a day ahead, too. And, if you're up to it, decorate the cake with homemade candied lemon peel. When strawberries are in season I decorate the cake with halved berries pressed in around the base of the cake.

LOW-FAT LEMON CHEESE FILLING

1½ cups lemon-flavored nonfat or low-fat yogurt

1 teaspoon grated lemon zest

LEMON CAKE

2¼ cups cake flour

3 teaspoons baking powder

1 cup sugar

2 teaspoons grated lemon zest

½ teaspoon salt

6 tablespoons (¾ stick) unsalted butter, at room temperature

¾ cup skim milk

1 large egg

1 teaspoon vanilla

1 teaspoon lemon extract

LEMON MERINGUE FROSTING

¾ cup sugar

1 large egg white

2 tablespoons water

1 tablespoon fresh lemon juice

1 teaspoon honey

Pinch of salt

Candied Lemon Peel (optional) (see Note)

A day or two before baking the cake, prepare the lemon cheese filling: Line a 4- to 5-inch wire sieve or strainer with a paper coffee filter. Place over a small bowl. Turn the yogurt into the coffee filter, cover with plastic wrap, and allow to drain, refrigerated, overnight, or until the texture is the consistency of soft butter. Stir in the lemon zest. Set aside.

Preheat the oven to 375°F. Coat two 9-inch round cake pans with nonstick spray. Dust with flour.

Sift the flour, baking powder, sugar, lemon zest, and salt into a large mixing bowl. Add the butter and half of the milk. With an electric mixer, beat at medium speed for 1 minute, scraping the bowl often with a rubber spatula. Add the egg, vanilla, lemon extract, and remaining milk and beat 2 minutes longer, until the batter is light.

Spread the batter into the pans, dividing equally. Bake for 20 minutes, or until the top springs back when lightly touched. Remove from pans and cool on a wire rack.

For the frosting, with an electric mixer, beat the sugar, egg white, water, lemon juice, honey, and salt in a large metal bowl for 1 minute. Place the bowl over, but not in, a saucepan of briskly simmering water. Beat the mixture until it forms fairly stiff peaks and is spreadable, about 4 minutes. Remove the bowl from over the water and beat the mixture until it is cool and the texture is light and fluffy, about 3 minutes. Cover and cool completely. (The frosting can be made a day ahead and refrigerated, if desired.)

To assemble the cake, stir ⅓ cup of the frosting into the lemon cheese filling. Place one layer on a cake plate and spread with the lemon filling. Top with the second layer. Spread the top and sides of the cake with the lemon meringue frosting. The cake can be assembled hours ahead. Cover with a cake dome and refrigerate. Before serving, decorate with curls of homemade candied lemon peel, if desired.

MAKES 12 SERVINGS

PER SERVING: 303 *calories, 19% calories from fat, 6.37 g fat, 33.5 mg cholesterol, 191 mg sodium, 0.57 g dietary fiber*

NOTE: It's easy to make your own candied lemon peel. Select thick-skinned lemons. Using the tip of a sharp knife, score through the yellow part of the peel to the white pith from one end to another into four lengthwise quarters. Pull the skin away from the flesh of the lemon (save the interior for another use). Place the lemon skin in a small saucepan with cold water to cover. Bring to a boil. Drain. Add more cold water and bring to a boil again. Repeat the boiling-and-draining process four times. After the final boiling and draining, add equal parts of sugar and water to the pan with the lemon skin (½ cup of each for the skins of two lemons). Simmer for a half hour or until the water and sugar are absorbed. (Be careful not to burn the bottom.) Cut the lemon peel into strips or dice. Toss in sugar. Store in an airtight container in a cool place.

Orange-Glazed Gold Cake

This is basically a good golden layer cake recipe that can be varied in many ways, depending on what fruits are in season. The layers are moistened with vanilla- or lemon-flavored nonfat yogurt and filled with sliced fresh fruit.

- 2½ cups cake flour
- 1½ cups sugar
- 3 teaspoons baking powder
- ½ teaspoon salt
- ½ cup (1 stick) unsalted butter, at room temperature
- 3 large eggs, lightly beaten, at room temperature
- 1 cup nonfat sour cream
- ¼ cup skim milk
- 2 teaspoons grated orange zest
- 1 teaspoon vanilla

FRUIT FILLING

- ½ cup lemon- or vanilla-flavored nonfat yogurt
- 2 cups sliced fresh peaches, strawberries, bananas, or fruit in season

ORANGE GLAZE

- 1 cup confectioners' sugar
- 1 teaspoon grated orange zest
- 1 to 2 tablespoons fresh orange juice
- Mint leaves or sliced fresh fruit for garnish (optional)

Preheat the oven to 350°F. Lightly grease two 9-inch round cake pans and dust the pans lightly with flour.

In a large mixing bowl, mix together the flour, sugar, baking powder, and salt until well blended. Cut the butter into ¼-inch slices and add to the flour mixture. With an electric mixer, mix at low speed until the butter is completely blended into the flour. In another bowl, stir the eggs, sour cream, milk, orange zest, and vanilla together. Pour the liquid ingredients over the dry ingredients and with the electric mixer beat at medium speed for 1 minute, scraping the bowl with a rubber spatula often, then increase the speed to high and beat for 2 minutes, scraping the bowl two or three times.

Pour the batter into the prepared cake pans, dividing it equally and smoothing the top of the batter.

Bake for 35 minutes, or until the cakes feel firm when gently touched in the center or a toothpick inserted in the center comes out clean and dry.

Remove the cakes from the oven and cool in the pans on a wire rack for about 15 minutes. Loosen the edges of the cakes with a metal spatula and invert onto the rack to finish cooling.

Place one layer on a serving plate. Spread with nonfat yogurt and top with the fresh fruit. Top the fruit with the second layer.

Mix the confectioners' sugar with the orange zest and orange juice to make a smooth, thin glaze. Drizzle the glaze over the cake. Garnish with fresh mint leaves, or additional fresh fruit, if desired.

MAKES 12 SERVINGS

PER SERVING: 343 calories, 24% calories from fat, 9.22 g fat, 74 mg cholesterol, 260 mg sodium, 1.29 g dietary fiber

Poppy Seed Layer Cake

Poppy seeds freckle this white cake and add a pleasant crunch to the texture. The lemon filling and white frosting are classic, and all of this can be yours without guilt! Dried lemon peel is a new product found in a cellophane bag in the produce section. It is not "hard" but chewy and full of flavor. It has the same texture as raisins and other dried fruit.

2½ cups cake flour

1½ cups sugar

3 tablespoons poppy seeds

3 teaspoons baking powder

½ teaspoon salt

½ cup (1 stick) unsalted butter, at room temperature

3 large egg whites, at room temperature

1 cup nonfat sour cream

¼ cup skim milk

1 teaspoon vanilla

LEMON FILLING AND FROSTING

⅓ cup lemon-flavored nonfat yogurt

2 tablespoons unsalted butter, at room temperature

3¾ cups (1 pound) confectioners' sugar

2 tablespoons finely chopped dried lemon peel

Preheat the oven to 350°F. Lightly grease two 9-inch round cake pans and dust the pans lightly with flour.

In a large mixing bowl, mix together the flour, sugar, poppy seeds, baking powder, and salt. Cut the butter into ¼-inch slices and add to the flour mixture. With an electric mixer, mix at low speed until the butter is completely blended into the flour. In another bowl, stir the egg whites, sour cream, milk, and vanilla together. Pour the liquid ingredients over the dry ingredients and with the electric mixer beat at medium speed for 1 minute, scraping the bowl with a rubber spatula often, then increase the speed to high and beat for 2 minutes, scraping the bowl two or three times.

Pour the batter into the prepared pans, dividing it equally and smoothing the tops of the batter.

Bake for 35 minutes, or until the cake feels firm when gently touched in the center or a toothpick inserted in the center comes out clean and dry.

Remove the cakes from the oven and allow to cool in the pans on a wire rack for about 15 minutes. Loosen the edges of the cakes with a metal spatula and invert onto the rack to finish cooling.

For the lemon filling and frosting, combine the lemon yogurt, butter, and confectioners' sugar in a large mixing bowl. With an electric mixer, beat at low speed until the sugar is moistened, scrape the sides of the bowl with a rubber scraper, then increase the speed to high and beat until the frosting is light and fluffy. Mix in the dried lemon peel.

Place one layer on a serving plate. Spread with ½ cup of the lemon filling and frosting. Top with the second layer. Spread the remaining frosting over the top and sides of the cake. Refrigerate until ready to serve.

MAKES 16 SERVINGS

PER SERVING: *349 calories, 21% calories from fat, 8.08 g fat, 19.5 mg cholesterol, 143 mg sodium, 1.08 g dietary fiber*

Raspberry—Chocolate Cake

Raspberries and chocolate are a classic flavor combination. By replacing half of the butter with applesauce and using egg whites, I was able to reduce the fat in this cake to 20 percent of calories from fat while retaining moistness and flavor. Fresh raspberries make a pretty garnish when they are available.

1 cup water

½ cup (1 stick) unsalted butter, at room temperature

2 cups sugar

2 cups all-purpose flour

1 teaspoon baking soda

½ teaspoon salt

¼ cup unsweetened cocoa powder

½ cup applesauce

2 large egg whites

1 teaspoon vanilla

RASPBERRY FILLING

¾ cup seedless raspberry jam

FROSTING AND DECORATION

1 cup confectioners' sugar

2 tablespoons unsweetened cocoa powder

2 tablespoons framboise (raspberry liqueur)

1 teaspoon vanilla

Fresh raspberries for garnish (optional)

Preheat the oven to 350°F. Coat two 8- or 9-inch round cake pans with nonstick spray and line the bottoms with rounds of parchment paper. Coat again with spray and dust with flour.

In a small pan, heat the water and butter to boiling; remove from heat and let cool slightly.

Place a wire sieve over a large mixing bowl and measure in the sugar, flour, baking soda, salt, and cocoa powder. Stir with a spoon until the dry ingredients are sifted into the bowl.

Pour the water-butter mixture over the dry ingredients and beat with an electric hand mixer. Beat in the applesauce, egg whites, and vanilla until the batter is smooth and light.

Pour into the prepared pans. Bake for 20 to 25 minutes, or until the cake springs back when lightly touched. Cool the cakes in the pans for 5 minutes; then turn onto a wire rack and let cool completely.

With a long, thin, serrated knife, split each layer into two thin layers. Place one layer on a cake plate, cut side up, and spread with ¼ cup of the raspberry jam. Top with a second layer, cut side down, and ¼ cup jam. Top with a third layer, cut side up, and spread with the remaining jam. Top with the remaining layer of cake, cut side down.

In a small bowl, combine the confectioners' sugar, cocoa powder, framboise, and vanilla and stir until smooth. Add warm water, if necessary, to make a smooth, spreadable glaze. Turn into a small heavy-duty plastic bag with a zipper-top closure. With scissors, cut one corner of the bag to make a small hole. Press the frosting through the hole zigzag fashion across the top of the cake, allowing some of it to dribble down the sides. Let stand until set. Decorate with fresh raspberries, if desired.

MAKES 12 SERVINGS

PER SERVING: 376 calories, 20% calories from fat, 8.39 g fat, 20.7 mg cholesterol, 172 mg sodium, 1.67 dietary fiber

Tropical Banana Cake

Bananas, *like applesauce or other puréed fruits, add moistness and flavor to cakes. This cake is not too sweet and is very moist and tender.*

6 tablespoons (¾ stick) unsalted butter, at room temperature

2 teaspoons grated lemon zest

1 cup sugar

½ teaspoon vanilla

2 large eggs, lightly beaten

2 cups all-purpose flour

1 tablespoon baking powder

¾ teaspoon salt

2 ripe bananas, mashed

4 tablespoons skim milk

BANANA FROSTING

4 tablespoons (½ stick) unsalted butter, at room temperature

½ cup ripe banana, mashed

3¾ cups (1 pound) confectioners' sugar

⅛ teaspoon salt

1 teaspoon vanilla

3 tablespoons coconut rum

Sliced bananas for garnish (optional)

Preheat the oven to 375°F. Lightly grease or coat two 9-inch round cake pans with nonstick spray and line them with rounds of parchment paper.

In a large mixing bowl, cream the butter, lemon zest, and sugar until smooth. Add the vanilla and eggs and beat until light and fluffy.

Mix the flour, baking powder, and salt together in another bowl and add to the creamed mixture along with the mashed bananas and milk. Beat until the batter is smooth. Pour the batter into the prepared pans, dividing it evenly. Smooth the batter to the edges. Bake for 25 minutes, or until a toothpick inserted in the center of the cake comes out clean and dry. Remove from the oven and cool the cakes in the pans for 5 minutes. Loosen the edges and invert onto a wire rack to finish cooling.

For the frosting, beat the butter, banana, and confectioners' sugar together until smooth and fluffy. Add the salt and vanilla and beat until well mixed.

To assemble the cake, place one layer on a cake plate. Drizzle with 1½ tablespoons coconut rum. Spread with about ½ cup of the frosting. Top with the second layer, drizzle with 1½ tablespoons coconut rum, and spread the top and sides with the remaining frosting. Garnish with sliced fresh bananas, if desired.

MAKES 12 SERVINGS

PER SERVING: *388 calories, 25% calories from fat, 10.8 g fat, 61.5 mg cholesterol, 98.2 mg sodium, 1.09 g dietary fiber*

Lemon Cupcakes

Perfect for kids' birthday parties, or bake them in miniature muffin cups and serve them at teatime. These tender, light-textured cupcakes are made using the old-fashioned, one-bowl method of mixing the dough. All the dry ingredients go into the bowl first, then the soft butter and liquid ingredients get mixed in. If you are making these for a child's birthday party, you will probably want to use lemon juice in the frosting. An interesting Italian liqueur, limone, is a more sophisticated choice, especially if you are planning to make tiny cupcakes for tea. Candied or fresh edible flowers would make a nice garnish, if you have them.

- 2 cups unbleached all-purpose flour
- 3 teaspoons baking powder
- 1 cup sugar
- 2 teaspoons grated lemon zest
- ½ teaspoon salt
- 6 tablespoons (¾ stick) unsalted butter, at room temperature
- ¾ cup skim milk
- 1 large egg
- 1 teaspoon vanilla

LEMON GLAZE

- 1 cup confectioners' sugar
- 1 tablespoon lemon liqueur or lemon juice
- 2 to 3 teaspoons water
- Candied or fresh edible flowers for garnish (optional)

Preheat the oven to 375°F. Line 18 regular-size muffin cups with paper baking cups, or lightly grease 36 miniature muffin cups.

Place a wire sieve over a large mixing bowl. Measure the flour, baking powder, sugar, lemon zest, and salt into it and stir with a spoon until the dry ingredients are sifted into the bowl. Add the butter and half of the milk. With an electric mixer, beat at medium speed for 2 minutes, scraping the bowl often with a rubber spatula. Add the egg, vanilla, and remaining milk and beat 2 minutes longer.

Scoop the batter into the muffin cups, dividing equally. Bake for 18 to 20 minutes for regular-size cupcakes, or 13 to 15 minutes for miniature cupcakes, until the top springs back when lightly touched. Remove from the pans and cool on a wire rack.

For the glaze, in a small bowl mix the confectioners' sugar with the lemon liqueur or lemon juice and enough water to make a smooth glaze. Spread the cooled cupcakes with the glaze and decorate with flowers, if desired.

MAKES 18 REGULAR-SIZE OR 36 MINIATURE CUPCAKES

PER REGULAR CUPCAKE: 153 calories, 25% calories from fat, 4.26 g fat, 22.4 mg cholesterol, 124 mg sodium, 0.34 g dietary fiber

PER MINIATURE CUPCAKE: 76.15 calories, 25% calories from fat, 2.13 g fat, 11.2 mg cholesterol, 62 mg sodium, 0.17 g dietary fiber

SHEET AND SPRINGFORM CAKES

Apple Date Cake

This is my favorite fresh apple cake. It is so moist, so loaded with apples, that it verges on being an apple pudding. I've left out the cupful of walnuts and reduced the butter that my original cake called for, thereby dropping the calories from fat from 40 percent down to 28 percent. It is still just as moist and wonderful as it ever was!

1 cup sugar

6 tablespoons (¾ stick) unsalted butter, at room temperature

2 large eggs, lightly beaten

1½ cups all-purpose flour

1 teaspoon baking soda

2 teaspoons unsweetened cocoa powder

1 teaspoon ground cinnamon

½ teaspoon ground cloves

4 cups peeled, cored, and chopped fresh tart apples

½ cup chopped pitted dates

½ cup cold strong coffee

Confectioners' sugar

Preheat the oven to 350°F. Lightly grease or coat with nonstick spray a 9 × 13-inch cake pan.

In a large mixing bowl, cream the sugar with the butter until blended, add the eggs, and beat until light. Combine the flour, baking soda, cocoa, cinnamon, and cloves in another bowl. Mix the apples and dates in a small bowl and sprinkle with 2 tablespoons of the flour mixture. Add the remaining flour mixture to the creamed mixture along with the coffee and beat until the batter is smooth. Stir in the apples and dates.

Turn the batter into the prepared pan and bake for 35 to 40 minutes, or until the cake springs back when touched in the center. Cool the cake in the pan on a wire rack. Dust with confectioners' sugar.

MAKES 12 GENEROUS SERVINGS

PER SERVING: *239 calories, 28% calories from fat, 7.65 g fat, 15.5 mg cholesterol, 80.2 mg sodium, 2.32 g dietary fiber*

Applesauce Gingerbread with Lemon Ginger Sauce

My original gingerbread cake weighed in at 45 percent calories from fat. But by replacing half of the oil with applesauce, the percentage of fat drops to a healthful 30 percent. To further reduce the fat, use ½ cup of commercial egg substitute in place of the eggs, or use 3 egg whites. Serve squares of the cake hot with lemon sauce that's textured with chunks of crystallized ginger. To produce the best texture, be careful not to overmix the batter.

- 1 cup sugar
- ¼ teaspoon salt
- 1 teaspoon ground ginger
- ½ teaspoon ground cinnamon
- ½ teaspoon ground cloves
- ½ cup canola oil
- ½ cup applesauce
- ½ cup light molasses
- 2 teaspoons baking soda
- 1 cup boiling water
- 2 cups all-purpose flour
- ½ cup whole wheat flour
- 2 large eggs, beaten
- Lemon Ginger Sauce (recipe follows)

Preheat the oven to 350°F. Coat a 9 × 13-inch cake pan with nonstick spray; set aside.

In a medium bowl, combine the sugar, salt, ginger, cinnamon, and cloves. Stir in the oil, applesauce, and molasses; blend well. Combine the baking soda and boiling water in another bowl and immediately stir into the molasses mixture. Add the flours gradually, stirring to prevent lumping. Add the eggs, then pour the mixture into the prepared pan. Do not overmix.

Bake for 40 to 45 minutes, or until a toothpick inserted in the center of the cake comes out clean and the cake starts to pull away from the sides of the pan. Place the pan on a wire rack to cool. Just before serving, make the Lemon Ginger Sauce.

MAKES 12 SERVINGS

PER SERVING: *307 calories, 30% calories from fat, 10.2 g fat, 35.5 mg cholesterol, 197 mg sodium, 0.85 g dietary fiber*

Lemon Ginger Sauce

- 1 cup sugar
- 2 tablespoons cornstarch
- 2 cups boiling water
- 2 tablespoons finely chopped crystallized ginger
- 1 tablespoon grated lemon zest
- 2 tablespoons lemon juice
- 1 tablespoon unsalted butter

Combine the sugar and cornstarch in a saucepan over low heat. Gradually whisk in the boiling water; boil 1 minute, stirring. Add the ginger, lemon zest, lemon juice, and butter. Serve hot, spooned over servings of the cake.

Applesauce Gold Cake

This is an easy mix-in-the pan cake that has no eggs and just a small amount of oil. For a nutty flavor, I like to substitute one tablespoon of good-quality, aromatic hazelnut or walnut oil for one tablespoon of the corn or canola oil.

> 1¼ cups all-purpose flour
>
> ⅔ cup sugar
>
> ¾ teaspoon baking soda
>
> ¼ teaspoon salt
>
> ¾ cup sweetened applesauce
>
> 4 tablespoons canola or corn oil, or part nut oil
>
> 1 teaspoon vanilla

Preheat the oven to 350°F.

Measure the flour, sugar, baking soda, and salt into a wire sieve or sifter placed over a 9-inch square cake pan. Stir to sift the mixture into the pan. Mix well with a fork or small whisk.

In a bowl, combine the applesauce, oil, and vanilla and pour them over the dry ingredients. With a fork, a small whisk, or a rubber spatula, stir the mixture until a smooth batter forms, being sure to get all the dry ingredients from the corners of the pan blended into the cake batter.

Bake for 25 to 30 minutes, or until golden and a wooden skewer inserted into the center of the cake comes out clean and dry. Cool slightly in the pan on a wire rack.

Cut into 3-inch squares and serve warm, or use the cake as a base for slightly crushed and sweetened fruit or berries.

MAKES 9 SERVINGS

PER SERVING: 184 calories, 30% calories from fat, 6.25 g fat, 0 mg cholesterol, 129 mg sodium, 0.73 g dietary fiber

Mocha Chocolate Cake

This cake is really quick to make and has minimal cleanup because it is mixed right in the baking pan.

> 1½ cups all-purpose flour
>
> ¼ cup unsweetened cocoa powder
>
> 1 teaspoon baking soda
>
> ¼ teaspoon salt
>
> ¾ cup packed brown sugar
>
> 4 tablespoons canola or corn oil
>
> 1 cup water
>
> ½ teaspoon vanilla
>
> 2 tablespoons strong coffee
>
> Confectioners' sugar

Preheat the oven to 350°F.

Measure the flour, cocoa, baking soda, and salt into a sieve or flour sifter placed over a 9-inch square cake pan. Stir to sift, then add the brown sugar and mix with a fork until completely blended and no lumps of the brown sugar remain.

Pour the oil over the dry ingredients. Mix the water with the vanilla and coffee in a small bowl and pour over. Blend with a fork or a small whisk until the cake batter is smooth. With a rubber spatula, check that all the dry ingredients from the corners of the pan are incorporated.

Bake for 25 to 30 minutes, or until a toothpick inserted into the center of the cake comes out clean and dry. Cool in the pan for 5 minutes, then turn onto a wire rack to cool. Dust with confectioners' sugar and cut into squares to serve.

MAKES 9 SERVINGS

PER SERVING: *198 calories, 30% calories from fat, 6.70 g fat, 0 mg cholesterol, 159 mg sodium, 1.23 g dietary fiber*

Quick Butter Cake

This cake has been my standby for years, whether I need a quick base for fresh berries or a hot square of cake for the carpenters, skiers, or my dad, who prefers something simple, good, and not too sweet. Using the food processor, it takes less than 5 minutes to mix up. Frost the cake with Boiled Caramel Icing (page 84) or One-Minute Boiled Fudge Frosting (page 84) if you wish.

1½ **cups all-purpose flour**

½ **cup nonfat dry milk**

1 **cup sugar**

2 **teaspoons baking powder**

¼ **teaspoon salt**

1 **tablespoon unsalted butter, sliced**

1 **large egg**

½ **cup water**

1 **teaspoon vanilla**

Preheat the oven to 350°F. Lightly grease or coat a 9-inch square pan with nonstick spray.

Measure the flour, dry milk, sugar, baking powder, and salt into the work bowl of a food processor with the steel blade in place, or into a mixing bowl. Process or blend with an electric hand mixer to combine the ingredients. Add the butter and process until it is completely mixed into the dry ingredients.

Mix the egg, water, and vanilla together in a small bowl. Add to the dry ingredients and process 1 minute, or mix with the electric mixer for 2 minutes, until the batter is very smooth. Pour the mixture into the prepared pan.

Bake for 25 to 30 minutes, or until the cake begins to pull away from the sides of the pan and the center springs back when touched. Cool in the pan on a wire rack. Cut into squares to serve.

MAKES 12 SERVINGS

PER SERVING: *176 calories, 27% calories from fat, 5.37 g fat, 31.2 mg cholesterol, 121 mg sodium, 0.39 g dietary fiber*

Carrot Kuchen

This classic Old World cake keeps well for several days.

4 large eggs, at room temperature

1 cup sugar

1½ cups very finely shredded carrots

1 cup all-purpose flour

1 cup finely ground rolled oats (see Note)

1½ teaspoons baking powder

½ teaspoon salt

1 cup orange marmalade

2 tablespoons rum

GARNISH

¼ cup sifted confectioners' sugar

2 tablespoons grated bittersweet chocolate

½ cup light whipped cream

Preheat the oven to 350°F. Coat a 10-inch springform pan with nonstick spray. Dust lightly with flour.

In a large bowl, with an electric mixer, beat the eggs and sugar until thick and light. Fold in the carrots. In another bowl, mix the flour, ground oats, baking powder, and salt together and carefully fold into the batter. Pour the batter into the prepared pan. Bake for 45 minutes, or until a toothpick inserted in the center of the cake comes out clean. Cool the cake in the pan on a wire rack.

Remove the cake from the pan and cut it horizontally into two layers using a long serrated knife. Set one cake layer on a serving plate, cut side up. Mix together the marmalade and rum in a small bowl. Spread the cake with half of the mixture. Top with the second layer, cut sit down. Spread the top with the remaining marmalade mixture.

To garnish, dust the edges of the cake with confectioners' sugar. Sprinkle the outside edge of the cake top with the grated chocolate. Serve each wedge with a dollop of whipped cream, about the size of a walnut.

MAKES 12 SERVINGS

PER SERVING: *265 calories, 16% calories from fat, 4.7 g fat, 77.8 mg cholesterol, 58.2 mg sodium, 2.09 g dietary fiber*

NOTE: To grind rolled oats, place quick-cooking or old-fashioned rolled oats in the food processor with the steel blade in place. Process until ground into flour. One cup rolled oats makes ⅔ cup oat flour.

Coconut Carrot Cake

Carrot cakes became popular in the 1970s, with most of the recipes so heavy with oil that you could actually squeeze it out of the cake with a fork. In my recipe I have simply cut back on the oil, and the cake is no less appealing. Light or nonfat cream cheese in the frosting and toasted coconut on the top make it appear and taste even better than the original. Be sure to use a fine shredder for the carrots for the very best texture.

1½ cups all-purpose flour

1 cup sugar

1 teaspoon baking powder

½ teaspoon baking soda

¼ teaspoon salt

1 teaspoon ground cinnamon

½ teaspoon ground allspice

1 cup finely shredded carrots (about 2 medium carrots)

½ cup raisins

1 cup canned crushed pineapple, packed in its own juices (1 8-ounce can)

¼ cup canola oil

1 teaspoon vanilla

1 large egg

FROSTING

2 ounces light or nonfat cream cheese

1½ cups confectioners' sugar

1 teaspoon vanilla

TOPPING

½ cup toasted flaked coconut

Preheat the oven to 350°F. Coat a 10-inch springform pan with nonstick spray and dust lightly with flour.

In a large mixing bowl, stir the flour, sugar, baking powder, baking soda, salt, cinnamon, and allspice together. With a fork, mix in the carrots and raisins until evenly blended in.

In a small bowl, mix the pineapple, oil, vanilla, and egg. Pour the liquids over the dry ingredients and mix gently, using a rubber spatula, just until the dry ingredients are moistened. Pour the batter into the prepared pan. Bake for 30 to 40 minutes, or until the cake springs back when lightly touched in the center and begins to pull away from the sides of the pan. Remove from the oven and place the pan on a wire rack to cool.

For the frosting, beat the cream cheese with the sugar and vanilla until smooth. Spread over the top of the cake. Sprinkle with the coconut. Cut into wedges to serve.

MAKES 12 SERVINGS

PER SERVING: 271 calories each, 20% calories from fat, 6.17 g fat, 19 mg cholesterol, 175 mg sodium, 1.74 g dietary fiber

Date-Frosted Date Cake

This is a dense, moist, and fruity cake that's perfect on an autumn dessert buffet served along with a bowl of fresh fruits. I bake it in a springform pan so that it is easy to unmold.

1 cup chopped pitted dates

1 cup water

½ teaspoon baking soda

1½ cups all-purpose flour

1 teaspoon baking powder

½ teaspoon ground cinnamon

¼ teaspoon salt

¼ cup unsweetened applesauce

4 tablespoons (½ stick) unsalted
    butter, at room temperature

1 cup sugar

1 large egg, lightly beaten

1 teaspoon vanilla

DATE FROSTING

1 cup water

1 cup packed light brown sugar

½ cup finely chopped pitted dates

1 tablespoon unsalted butter

Preheat the oven to 350°F. Coat a 9- or 10-inch round springform pan with nonstick spray and set aside.

Place the dates, water, and baking soda in a saucepan and bring to a boil. Stir and remove from the heat immediately. Set aside to cool.

Measure the flour, baking powder, cinnamon, and salt into a small bowl and mix well.

In a large mixing bowl, cream the applesauce, butter, and sugar until smooth; add the egg and vanilla and beat until fluffy. Add the flour mixture and date mixture and stir with a wooden spoon until the batter is well blended. Pour into the prepared pan. Bake for 40 to 45 minutes, or until a toothpick inserted in the center comes out clean. Cool in the pan on a wire rack before unmolding and frosting the cake.

For the frosting, combine the water, brown sugar, and dates in a 2-quart saucepan. Bring to a boil and cook for 10 minutes, stirring frequently, until the mixture is thickened slightly and drips slowly off a spoon. Add the butter and stir until it melts. Pour over the cake; the frosting will be slightly runny but will set upon cooling. Cool completely before cutting the cake.

MAKES 12 SERVINGS

PER SERVING: *338 calories, 16% calories from fat, 6.41 g fat, 33.3 mg cholesterol, 122 mg sodium, 2.3 g dietary fiber*

Simple White Cake

This is a cake that's quick to make, and a lovely snack just served plain. If you bake it in two 9-inch layers and use a fresh fruit jam as a filling, dust the cake with confectioners' sugar and decorate it with edible flowers for a gorgeous springtime dessert.

    2 cups all-purpose flour

    2 teaspoons baking powder

    ¼ teaspoon salt

    1½ cups sugar

    6 tablespoons (¾ stick) unsalted
        butter, at room temperature

    1 cup skim milk

    2 large eggs

    1 teaspoon vanilla

Preheat the oven to 375°F. Lightly coat a 13 × 9-inch pan or two 9-inch round cake pans with nonstick spray.

In a mixing bowl, combine the flour, baking powder, salt, and sugar. Add the butter and mix with an electric mixer until the butter is totally incorporated into the dry ingredients.

Add the milk, eggs, and vanilla and mix at high speed for 2 minutes, scraping the sides of the bowl often with a rubber spatula. Beat until the batter is light and fluffy. Pour the batter into the pan or pans. Smooth the batter to the edges.

Bake for 35 to 40 minutes for the 13 × 9-inch cake or 30 to 35 minutes for the round layers. Remove from the oven. Cool 5 minutes, then remove the cakes from the round pans. Finish cooling on a wire rack. Cool the 13 × 9-inch cake right in the pan on a wire rack.

MAKES 16 SERVINGS

PER SERVING: 178 calories, 26% calories from fat, 5.1 g fat, 38.5 mg cholesterol, 91.3 mg sodium, 0.39 g dietary fiber

Sour Cream—Apple—Cocoa Cake

This is one of my all-time favorite cakes, made with fresh apples, dates, and nuts. I've always iced it with a caramel frosting. It's perfect in the fall when the tart and juicy cooking apples are in season. The original recipe called for ¾ cup of butter and ½ cup of walnuts. The frosting had both butter and whipping cream in it. To lower the percentage of fat from calories, I reduced the butter and cut out the walnuts. Then, to replace the volume, I added nonfat sour cream. To replace the nuttiness, I substituted nut oil for part of the butter and flavored the caramelly frosting with Frangelico, a hazelnut-flavored liqueur.

1½ cups all-purpose flour

1 cup sugar

1 teaspoon baking soda

½ teaspoon salt

1 teaspoon ground cinnamon

¼ teaspoon ground nutmeg

⅛ teaspoon ground cloves

2 tablespoons unsweetened cocoa powder

4 tablespoons (½ stick) unsalted butter, at room temperature

2 tablespoons walnut or hazelnut oil

3 large egg whites or 2 large eggs, lightly beaten

½ cup nonfat sour cream

½ cup cold strong coffee

2 cups coarsely chopped and peeled tart apples (about 2 medium)

1 cup coarsely chopped pitted dates

FRANGELICO FROSTING

4 tablespoons nonfat half-and-half or evaporated skimmed milk

1 cup packed brown sugar

1 teaspoon dark corn syrup

⅛ teaspoon salt

1 tablespoon Frangelico or hazelnut-flavored liqueur

Preheat the oven to 350°F. Lightly grease or coat with nonstick spray a 9 × 13-inch pan.

In a large mixing bowl, combine the flour, sugar, baking soda, salt, cinnamon, nutmeg, cloves, cocoa, butter, oil, eggs, sour cream, and coffee. With an electric hand mixer, beat on low speed for 1 minute until the ingredients are well mixed. Increase the speed to high and beat until the mixture is light and fluffy, about 2 minutes, scraping the sides of the bowl two or three times. Stir in the apples and dates.

Pour the batter into the prepared pan and bake for 40 to 50 minutes, or until a toothpick inserted in the center of the cake comes out clean. Remove from the oven and place the cake in its baking pan on a rack to cool. Cool 10 minutes before covering with the frosting.

For the frosting, combine the half-and-half, brown sugar, corn syrup, and salt in a saucepan. Place over medium heat and bring to a boil, stirring. Cook, stirring, until the sugar is completely dissolved, 2 to 3 minutes. Remove from the heat and stir in the Frangelico. Pour the hot frosting over the warm cake.

MAKES 16 SERVINGS

PER SERVING: *255 calories, 21% calories from fat, 6.14 g fat, 7.92 mg cholesterol, 141 mg sodium, 2.2 g dietary fiber*

Whole Wheat Banana Cake

Applesauce and bananas together help to tenderize the crumb in this rather rustic cake. It's great served just plain, but sometimes I slice firm bananas and distribute them over the top of the cake, then spread it with Boiled Caramel Icing (page 84) for a company dessert.

2 cups sugar

2 cups unbleached all-purpose flour

1 cup whole wheat flour

3 teaspoons baking powder

1 teaspoon baking soda

½ teaspoon salt

1 teaspoon ground cinnamon

1 teaspoon ground ginger

½ teaspoon freshly ground nutmeg

½ cup (1 stick) unsalted butter or vegetable shortening, at room temperature

½ cup applesauce

2 very ripe bananas, mashed (about 1 cup)

2 large eggs, lightly beaten

¾ cup 1-percent-butterfat buttermilk

Preheat the oven to 350°F. Lightly grease or coat a 9 × 13-inch pan with nonstick spray.

In a large bowl, stir the sugar, flours, baking powder, baking soda, salt, cinnamon, ginger, and nutmeg together. Add the butter and mix with an electric mixer until it is completely blended into the dry ingredients.

In a small bowl, mix the applesauce, bananas, eggs, and buttermilk until well blended. Add the liquid ingredients to the dry ingredients and mix at high speed with an electric mixer for 2 minutes, scraping the bowl often. Pour the batter into the prepared baking pan.

Bake for 30 to 35 minutes, or until a toothpick inserted in the center comes out clean and dry. Remove from the oven and cool in the pan on a wire rack.

MAKES 20 SERVINGS

PER SERVING: *266 calories, 26% calories from fat, 8.06 g fat, 21.6 mg cholesterol, 162 mg sodium, 2.32 g dietary fiber*

Angel Food Cake

Angel food cake is the most obvious light cake to include in a light baking book. It has no fat at all and is a perfect base for berries or fresh fruit and a sauce made by allowing nonfat vanilla frozen yogurt to thaw slightly. There are, of course, angel food cake mixes, but you'll never use one again after you've compared the flavor of the freshly made cake with the mix cake.

> 1½ cups (about 12 large) egg whites, at room temperature
>
> 1¼ cups sifted cake flour
>
> 1¾ cups sugar
>
> ¼ teaspoon salt
>
> 1½ teaspoons cream of tartar
>
> 1 teaspoon vanilla
>
> Confectioners' sugar for dusting

Preheat the oven to 375°F.

Place the egg whites in a large mixing bowl.

Place a wire sieve over another bowl and measure the cake flour and ¾ cup of the sugar into it. Stir with a spoon until the cake flour and sugar are well mixed and sifted into the bowl.

Beat the egg whites and salt at high speed with an electric mixer until foamy. Add the cream of tartar and vanilla, beating until the whites form soft peaks. Gradually beat in the remaining 1 cup sugar until stiff peaks form. Put the flour-sugar mixture into the sieve again and dust over the whites, about one quarter at a time, gently mixing with a rubber spatula until the flour is incorporated.

Turn the batter into an ungreased 10-inch tube pan. Pull a clean butter knife through the batter once to remove any large air bubbles.

Bake for 35 to 45 minutes, or until a wooden skewer inserted in the center comes out clean and dry.

Invert the pan immediately, placing the tube over the top of a bottle to avoid smashing the cake. Cool 1 hour. Loosen the cake from the pan using a thin metal spatula. Remove the cake onto a serving plate.

To serve, dust with confectioners' sugar and tear straight pieces using two forks (cutting the cake into pieces with a knife will squash it).

MAKES 12 SERVINGS

PER SERVING: *166 calories, 0% calories from fat, 0 g fat, 0 mg cholesterol, 100 mg sodium, 0.28 g dietary fiber*

Apple Cake with Brown Sugar–Cinnamon Glaze

This comes from an old family favorite recipe that was always delicious but had a slightly too-tender quality. Here I've reduced the original 1 cup of walnuts to ¼ cup and sprinkled them in the bottom of the pan instead of mixing them into the cake. The original recipe called for a whole cup of butter, but I've substituted less than half the volume of canola oil. Sometimes I use part walnut oil to enhance the nutty flavor, so I have made it an optional ingredient. Some walnut oils on the market are mild, some have more flavor. If you have the kind with more flavor, substitute 2 tablespoons of the walnut oil for 2 tablespoons of the canola or corn oil. If you have the very mild walnut oil, use it at full strength.

- ¼ cup finely chopped walnuts
- 2 large eggs
- 2 cups sugar
- 6 tablespoons canola or corn oil, or a combination of canola and walnut oils
- 1 teaspoon vanilla
- 2 cups all-purpose flour
- 1 teaspoon baking powder
- 1 teaspoon baking soda
- ½ teaspoon salt
- 1 teaspoon ground cinnamon
- ½ teaspoon ground nutmeg
- ⅛ teaspoon ground cloves
- 4 cups peeled, diced, tart apples (about 4 medium)
- ½ cup cold strong coffee

BROWN SUGAR–CINNAMON GLAZE

- 1 cup packed dark brown sugar
- 2 teaspoons cornstarch
- 1 teaspoon ground cinnamon
- ¼ cup water
- 2 teaspoons unsalted butter
- 2 teaspoons vanilla

Preheat the oven to 350°F. Coat a 10-inch tube pan or Bundt pan with nonstick spray. Sprinkle the walnuts evenly around the bottom of the pan.

In a large bowl, with an electric mixer, beat the eggs until light and fluffy. Add the sugar, oil, and vanilla and beat until thick and frothy.

In a medium bowl, stir the flour, baking powder, baking soda, salt, cinnamon, nutmeg, and cloves together until well mixed. Stir the dry ingredients into the egg mixture until well blended.

Stir in the diced apples and coffee until well mixed. Turn the mixture into the prepared pan.

Bake for 60 to 65 minutes, or until the center of the cake feels firm when touched. Let stand 5 minutes in the pan. Then loosen the edges and turn the cake onto a plate.

Meanwhile, in a 2-quart saucepan, combine the brown sugar, cornstarch, cinnamon, and water. Stir and heat to boiling. Boil 30 seconds, stirring, then remove from the heat and stir in the butter and vanilla.

Pour the hot glaze over the cake.

MAKES 16 SERVINGS

PER SERVING: *288 calories, 23% calories from fat, 7.6 g fat, 27.9 mg cholesterol, 154 mg sodium, 1.09 g dietary fiber*

Banana—Poppy Seed Cake

Applesauce replaces the fat in this cake, and when it is whipped with the egg whites and sugar, it lightens up the mixture. The trick is to not overmix the batter when the dry ingredients are added. The cake has an even, light texture with a nice flavor, and it isn't too sweet.

1/2 **cup applesauce**

3/4 **cup sugar**

3 large egg whites

1 cup mashed ripe banana (about 2 medium)

1 teaspoon grated lemon zest

1 tablespoon vanilla

2 cups all-purpose flour or whole wheat pastry flour

1 teaspoon baking powder

1 teaspoon baking soda

1/4 **teaspoon ground cinnamon**

1/4 **teaspoon salt**

1 tablespoon poppy seeds

Preheat the oven to 350°F. Coat a 10-inch tube pan with nonstick spray.

Combine the applesauce, sugar, and egg whites in a large mixing bowl. Beat with an electric mixer at high speed until light and fluffy, about 5 minutes. The mixture will be meringuelike.

Process the banana, lemon zest, and vanilla in a food processor or blender until smooth.

In a medium bowl, stir the flour, baking powder, baking soda, cinnamon, salt, and poppy seeds together.

With a rubber spatula, fold the banana and flour mixtures alternately into the egg white mixture until well blended. Turn the batter into the prepared pan and bake until lightly browned and a toothpick inserted in the center comes out clean, 30 to 35 minutes. Cool in the pan for 5 minutes, then loosen the edges and turn the cake out onto a wire rack to cool completely.

MAKES 12 SERVINGS

PER SERVING: *148 calories, 4% calories from fat, 0.61 g fat, 0 mg cholesterol, 111 mg sodium, 1.11 g dietary fiber*

Banana Spice Cake

This spicy fruit-filled cake is quite moist and keeps well. You can use cholesterol-free egg substitute to further reduce the fat content, but expect the cake not to brown as well.

½ cup chopped pecans

1½ cups golden raisins

2 cups unbleached all-purpose flour

1 cup whole wheat flour

3 teaspoons baking powder

1 teaspoon baking soda

½ teaspoon salt

1 teaspoon ground cinnamon

1 teaspoon ground ginger

½ teaspoon ground nutmeg

½ cup (1 stick) unsalted butter, at
   room temperature

½ cup applesauce

2 cups sugar

2 very ripe bananas, mashed (about 1
   cup)

2 large eggs, lightly beaten

¾ cup 1-percent-butterfat buttermilk

Preheat the oven to 350°F. Coat a 10-inch tube pan with nonstick spray and dust lightly with flour.

In a small bowl, combine the pecans and raisins. In another bowl, stir the flours, baking powder, baking soda, salt, cinnamon, ginger, and nutmeg together. Mix a spoonful of the flour mixture into the pecans and raisins.

In a large mixing bowl, using an electric mixer, beat the butter with the applesauce, sugar, bananas, and eggs until light and fluffy. Add the buttermilk alternately with the flour mixture, beating until smooth. Add the pecan-raisin mixture, pour batter into the prepared pan, and smooth the top.

Bake for 60 to 65 minutes or until a toothpick inserted in the center comes out clean and dry. Remove from the oven and cool 5 minutes. Invert onto a wire rack and cool completely.

MAKES 16 SERVINGS

PER SERVING: 365 calories, 22% calories from fat, 9.43 g fat, 42.6 mg cholesterol, 153 mg sodium, 2.89 g dietary fiber

Chocolate Zucchini Cake

Shredded zucchini moistens and softens the texture of this cake. My original recipe incuded a cup of chopped walnuts and a cup of chocolate chips, plus 4 tablespoons more butter, adding up to a whopping 68 percent calories from fat. My new "skinny" version is every bit as moist and tasty, and far more "guilt-free."

> ½ cup (1 stick) unsalted butter, at room temperature
>
> 2 cups sugar
>
> 3 large eggs, lightly beaten
>
> 2 cups shredded zucchini
>
> ¾ cup nonfat vanilla yogurt
>
> 1 teaspoon vanilla
>
> 2½ cups all-purpose flour
>
> ½ cup unsweetened cocoa powder
>
> 1½ teaspoons baking soda
>
> 1 teaspoon salt
>
> ¾ teaspoon ground cinnamon
>
> Confectioners' sugar for dusting

Preheat the oven to 350°F. Lightly grease a 10-inch fancy tube pan or coat it with nonstick spray and dust with flour.

In a large mixing bowl, cream the butter and sugar. Add the eggs and beat until light. Mix in the zucchini, yogurt, and vanilla.

Sift the flour, cocoa, baking soda, salt, and cinnamon together in another bowl and add to the creamed mixture. Mix until the batter is very light and smooth. Pour into the cake pan.

Bake for 50 to 60 minutes, or until a wooden skewer inserted into the center of the cake comes out clean and dry. Remove from the oven, cool 5 minutes in the pan, then invert the cake onto a wire rack to cool completely. Dust with confectioners' sugar.

MAKES 16 SERVINGS

PER SERVING: *247 calories, 25% calories from fat, 7.57 g fat, 56.4 mg cholesterol, 224 mg sodium, 1.48 g dietary fiber*

Spiced Applesauce Cake

This is great to serve with tea or hot cocoa on a cold afternoon. Baked in a fancy tube pan, it doesn't need a frosting, just a dusting of confectioners' sugar. A sprinkling of edible flowers makes a nice finishing touch, though.

> ½ cup (1 stick) unsalted butter, at room temperature
>
> 1½ cups sugar
>
> 1 large egg, at room temperature
>
> 1½ cups applesauce
>
> 2 teaspoons baking soda
>
> 2 cups all-purpose flour
>
> 1 teaspoon ground cinnamon
>
> ¼ teaspoon ground cloves
>
> ¼ teaspoon salt
>
> 1½ cups chopped pitted dates
>
> Confectioners' sugar for dusting
>
> Edible flowers for garnish (optional)

Preheat the oven to 350°F. Lightly grease and flour a fancy 10-inch tube pan or coat with nonstick spray.

In a large bowl, cream the butter and sugar with an electric mixer until smooth. Add the egg and beat until light.

In a small bowl, mix the applesauce with the baking soda.

In another bowl, stir together the flour, cinnamon, cloves, and salt.

Add the dry ingredients to the creamed mixture alternately with the applesauce mixture and beat until smooth. Stir in the dates with a wooden spoon. Pour the batter into the prepared pan. Bake for 40 to 45 minutes, or until a wooden skewer or toothpick inserted into the center of the cake comes out clean. Cool for 5 minutes in the pan, then turn out onto a wire rack to finish cooling. Dust with confectioners' sugar and place edible flowers around the edge of the cake to garnish, if desired.

MAKES 16 SERVINGS

PER SERVING: *221 calories, 25% calories from fat, 6.27 g fat, 28.8 mg cholesterol, 175 mg sodium, 1.67 g dietary fiber*

Hot Milk Sponge Cake

I *think of this as a quick summertime cake. It's light, low-fat, and wonderful topped with lightly mashed wild strawberries. Of course, we added a bit of whipped cream to the top, but with such a low-fat cake, you can afford that!*

¼ **cup skim milk**

1¼ **cups all-purpose flour**

1½ **teaspoons baking powder**

¼ **teaspoon salt**

3 **large eggs**

1 **cup sugar**

2 **teaspoons lemon juice**

1 **teaspoon vanilla**

Preheat the oven to 350°F. Have an ungreased 8- or 9-inch sponge cake pan or tube pan ready.

Place the milk in a small saucepan over very low heat and bring to a boil very slowly.

Meanwhile, stir the flour, baking powder, and salt together in a small bowl and set aside. In a large mixing bowl, with an electric mixer (preferably one on a stand), beat the eggs until frothy. Gradually beat in the sugar and beat at high speed for 5 minutes, until very light and fluffy. Beat in the lemon juice and vanilla.

Turn the mixer to low speed and add the flour mixture and boiling milk. Mix about 15 seconds, until well blended, then pour the batter into the cake pan.

Bake for 30 to 35 minutes, until golden. Remove from the oven and invert the cake in the pan to cool. If the cake has risen over the top edge of the pan, place a small bottle into the tube so that the cake will be elevated enough that it will not get mashed down.

MAKES 8 SERVINGS

PER SERVING: *195 calories, 10% calories from fat, 2.08 g fat, 80 mg cholesterol, 158 mg sodium, 0.48 g dietary fiber*

Lemon Rum Cake

Lemon-flavored rum, patterned after an Italian lemon-flavored liqueur, gives this cake a distinctive flavor. Serve it with fresh fruit in season.

2 cups all-purpose flour

1 cup sugar

4 teaspoons baking powder

¼ teaspoon salt

½ cup skim milk

4 tablespoons (½ stick) unsalted
    butter, melted

1 teaspoon grated lemon zest

1 teaspoon vanilla

4 large eggs, lightly beaten

LEMON RUM SYRUP

1 cup sugar

1 cup water

¼ cup lemon-flavored rum

FOR SERVING

Raspberries, blackberries,
    blueberries, or cut-up fresh fruit

Fresh mint sprigs (optional)

Confectioners' sugar

Softened nonfat vanilla frozen yogurt
    or nonfat vanilla ice cream
    (optional)

Preheat the oven to 350°F. Lightly grease or coat an 8-cup ring mold with nonstick spray.

Measure the flour, sugar, baking powder, and salt into a mixing bowl. Stir until the dry ingredients are well mixed. Add the milk, butter, lemon zest, vanilla, and eggs and beat 2 minutes at medium speed with an electric mixer. Pour the batter into the prepared pan.

Bake for 30 to 40 minutes, or until a wooden skewer inserted in the center comes out clean.

While the cake is baking, make the lemon rum syrup. Combine the sugar and water in a saucepan. Heat to boiling, stirring, and boil 1 minute. Remove from the heat and add the rum.

When the cake is done, place it on a wire rack and pierce it in 1-inch intervals with a fork. Immediately pour the hot syrup over the cake. Cool the cake in the pan for 15 minutes, then invert it onto a serving plate and cool completely.

Fill the center of the cake with berries or fruit and garnish with fresh mint sprigs, if desired. Dust with confectioners' sugar. Cut into serving pieces and serve with the softened vanilla frozen yogurt, if desired.

MAKES 16 SERVINGS

PER SERVING: *225 calories, 17% calories from fat, 4.3 g fat, 61.1 mg cholesterol, 137 mg sodium, 0.5 g dietary fiber*

Light and Airy Sponge Cake

With its basic ingredients, this cake is amazingly simple to make, but you do need to have an electric mixer on a stand. The secret to its success is the ice water that is beaten into the egg yolks—and you need to beat at high speed with an electric mixer for at least 8 minutes.

4 large eggs, separated

½ cup ice water

¼ teaspoon vanilla

¼ teaspoon lemon extract

¼ teaspoon almond extract

1⅓ cups sugar

1¼ cups all-purpose flour

1 teaspoon baking powder

¼ teaspoon salt

1 teaspoon cream of tartar

FOR SERVING

Confectioners' sugar for dusting

Fresh strawberries or peaches, sliced, or raspberries or blueberries

Softened nonfat frozen yogurt or ice milk

Preheat the oven to 325°F. Have ready a 10-inch sponge cake or angel food cake pan, ungreased.

Put the egg yolks into a large mixing bowl, and with an electric mixer, beat at high speed until fluffy. Gradually beat in the ice water and vanilla, lemon, and almond extracts, beating until light and lemon colored. With the beater at high speed, gradually beat in the sugar; beat at high speed for 8 minutes. Meanwhile, mix the flour, baking powder, and salt in a small bowl.

In another bowl, beat the egg whites until frothy, add the cream of tartar, and continue beating until the whites are stiff but not dry.

Gently fold the flour mixture into the egg yolk mixture, then fold in the egg whites gently but thoroughly. Pour into the pan. Bake for 1 hour, or until the cake springs back when gently touched in the center. Invert the cake and allow it to cool in the pan on a wire rack.

Loosen the edges of the cooled cake and remove it from the pan. Dust with confectioners' sugar and serve with fresh fruit topped with softened frozen yogurt or ice milk.

MAKES 8 SERVINGS

PER SERVING: *232 calories, 10% calories from fat, 2.68 g fat, 106 mg cholesterol, 139 mg sodium, 0.48 g dietary fiber*

Mocha Sponge Cake with Mocha Buttercream

Your guests will not believe that this richly flavored sponge cake, iced with an "almost buttercream," falls into the "no guilt" category. Since this requires so much mixing, don't make this recipe unless you have a stand mixer.

6 large eggs, separated

¼ teaspoon salt

¾ teaspoon cream of tartar

½ cup cold strong coffee

1 teaspoon instant coffee powder

1⅓ cups sugar

1 teaspoon vanilla

1½ cups sifted cake flour

1 teaspoon baking powder

2 tablespoons unsweetened cocoa powder

MOCHA BUTTERCREAM

1 teaspoon instant coffee powder

1 teaspoon cold strong coffee

4 tablespoons (½ stick) unsalted butter, at room temperature

2 tablespoons unsweetened cocoa powder

1 teaspoon vanilla

¼ cup nonfat vanilla yogurt

2 cups confectioners' sugar

Preheat the oven to 350°F. Have an ungreased 10-inch tube pan ready.

In a mixing bowl, beat the egg whites with an electric mixer at high speed until foamy. Beat in the salt and cream of tartar. Beat until stiff but not dry.

In another bowl, beat the egg yolks at medium speed for 1 minute. Mix the coffee and the coffee powder together and add to the egg yolk mixture. Beat 1 minute longer. Gradually add the sugar, beating for 10 minutes at high speed until the sugar is completely dissolved into the mixture. Beat in the vanilla.

Sift the cake flour again with the baking powder and cocoa over the yolk mixture. Stir about one third of the beaten egg whites into the egg yolk mixture to lighten it; gently fold the whites and the flour mixture into the beaten yolks until blended, then fold in the remaining whites. Turn the batter into the tube pan. Bake for 50 to 55 minutes, or until a wooden skewer inserted into the cake comes out clean and dry. Invert the cake onto a wire rack to cool. When completely cool, remove from the pan.

To make the buttercream, mix the coffee powder with the cold coffee and combine with the butter, cocoa, and vanilla in a medium bowl. Mix in the yogurt. Gradually beat in the confectioners' sugar until the frosting is of spreading consistency. Spread the frosting over the cooled cake.

MAKES 12 SERVINGS

PER SERVING: *277 calories, 22% calories from fat, 6.8 g fat, 117 mg cholesterol, 77 mg sodium, 0.91 g dietary fiber*

Orange Chiffon Cake

This fabulous, light cake can be baked either in layers or in a tube pan, though I prefer the tube pan. It has been our family's favorite birthday cake since I was a little girl. In fact, when I was in my teens, I won a blue ribbon at the Minnesota State Fair as a 4-H member with my demonstration of this cake's preparation. Chiffon cakes are basically a sponge cake with oil added; the recipe was invented in the 1920s, then promoted by a flour company in the late '40s. Today, I'm still baking this cake but in a slimmed-down version. I've reduced the number of egg yolks to three and the oil from ½ cup to ⅓ cup, so that the cake has 27 percent calories from fat. With fresh berries and a dusting of sugar, it makes a perfect summertime dessert.

2 cups all-purpose flour

1½ cups sugar

3 teaspoons baking powder

½ teaspoon salt

⅓ cup vegetable oil

3 large eggs, separated

¾ cup cold water

1 tablespoon grated orange zest

1 teaspoon vanilla

5 large egg whites

½ teaspoon cream of tartar

Confectioners' sugar for dusting

Preheat the oven to 325°F. Have a 10-inch tube pan ready, ungreased.

In a large bowl, combine the flour, sugar, baking powder, and salt. Stir in the oil, egg yolks, water, orange zest, and vanilla.

In a large, dry bowl, whisk all 8 egg whites until frothy. Add the cream of tartar and continue beating until the whites hold soft but firm peaks. Fold the whites into the yolk mixture until blended. Turn the batter into the pan. Bake for 55 minutes, or until the cake springs back when touched in the center.

Remove from the oven and invert over a bottle so that the cake hangs free and cools completely.

Gently loosen the edges of the cake with a spatula or knife, then pull the cake free and place it onto a serving plate. Dust with confectioners' sugar.

MAKES 12 SERVINGS

PER SERVING: *251 calories, 27% calories from fat, 7.48 g fat, 53.2 mg cholesterol, 39.5 mg sodium, 0.56 g dietary fiber*

Sour Cream—Raspberry Jam Cake

Working from the old-fashioned Southern jam cake, which is loaded with fat, I reduced the butter and used nonfat sour cream to soften and tenderize the texture. My tasters couldn't believe it is low in fat!

2 cups all-purpose flour

1 cup sugar

2 teaspoons baking powder

1/2 teaspoon baking soda

1 teaspoon ground nutmeg

1/2 teaspoon ground cinnamon

1/4 teaspoon ground cloves

6 tablespoons (3/4 stick) unsalted butter, at room temperature

3 large eggs

1 cup seedless raspberry or black raspberry jam

1 cup nonfat sour cream

LEMON GLAZE

1 cup confectioners' sugar

1 to 2 tablespoons lemon juice

Preheat the oven to 375°F. Coat a 9-inch tube pan with nonstick spray and dust lightly with flour.

In a mixing bowl, combine the flour, sugar, baking powder, baking soda, nutmeg, cinnamon, and cloves. Cut the butter into pieces and, with an electric mixer at medium speed, mix until the butter is thoroughly blended into the dry ingredients. Add the eggs, jam, and sour cream all at once and beat at low speed, scraping the sides of the bowl, until all the dry ingredients are moistened. Beat at high speed for 2 minutes, until the batter is light and fluffy, scraping the bowl often.

Pour into the prepared pan and bake for 45 to 50 minutes, or until a wooden skewer inserted in the center comes out clean. Allow to cool in the pan for 5 minutes, then loosen around the edges with a thin spatula. Invert onto a wire rack to finish cooling.

While the cake cools, mix the confectioners' sugar and lemon juice to make a thin icing. Place the cake on a serving plate and drizzle with the icing.

MAKES 12 SERVINGS

PER SERVING: *333 calories, 19% calories from fat, 7.22 g fat, 68.8 mg cholesterol, 116 mg sodium, 0.77 g dietary fiber*

Rolled Cakes

Caramel Applesauce Cake Roll

This is such a simple way to make a delicious low-fat dessert. Simply spread the filling for the roll on the bottom of a jelly roll pan and pour the cake batter over the top. After baking, when you roll it up, the filling is automatically inside the cake.

FILLING
1 cup packed brown sugar
1 cup unsweetened applesauce
1 teaspoon ground cinnamon

CAKE
5 large eggs, separated
1 teaspoon baking powder
½ teaspoon salt
¾ cup sugar
1 teaspoon vanilla
2 tablespoons apple juice or water
1 cup all-purpose flour
¼ cup confectioners' sugar

Preheat the oven to 375°F. Line a 15 × 10-inch jelly roll pan with parchment paper or wax paper. Coat the paper with nonstick spray and dust lightly with flour.

In a small saucepan, combine the brown sugar, applesauce, and cinnamon and cook over medium heat about 5 minutes, or until the sugar is dissolved. Pour the mixture evenly into the prepared pan. Allow it to cool while preparing the cake.

In a large bowl, beat the egg whites, baking powder, and salt together at high speed until soft peaks form. Gradually add ¼ cup of the sugar and continue beating until stiff peaks form. In a small bowl, beat the egg yolks with the vanilla and apple juice until thick and lemon colored. Gradually add the remaining ½ cup sugar. Continue beating until light and fluffy. Fold the egg yolk mixture into the egg whites. Sift the flour over the mixture and gently but thoroughly fold the flour into the egg mixture. Pour the batter over the filling in the pan; spread carefully to cover the pan completely.

Bake for 15 to 18 minutes, or until light golden brown. While the cake bakes, cut a strip of paper toweling a little longer than the pan. Place the paper toweling on the countertop and dust generously with the confectioners' sugar. When the cake is done, remove it from the oven, loosen the edges of the cake with a knife, and turn it out immediately onto the paper toweling. Remove the parchment paper. Starting with a short side, roll up the cake, jelly-roll fashion. Place the cake with the seam side down on a serving platter and garnish with additional confectioners' sugar.

MAKES 12 SERVINGS

PER SERVING: *201 calories, 10% calories from fat, 2.19 g fat, 88.8 mg cholesterol, 151 mg sodium, 0.6 g dietary fiber*

Chocolate Jul Log

Perfect for a holiday buffet! I decorate this roll with a scattering of meringue mushrooms and soft candied fruits to make it festive.

  3 large eggs

  ½ cup packed light brown sugar

  ½ cup sugar

  ⅓ cup water

  1 teaspoon vanilla

  ¾ cup all-purpose flour

  ¼ cup unsweetened dark cocoa
      powder

  1 teaspoon baking powder

  ¼ teaspoon salt

  ½ teaspoon ground cinnamon

  Confectioners' sugar

CHOCOLATE CHIP–RICOTTA FILLING

  1 cup nonfat ricotta cheese

  3 tablespoons sugar

  ½ teaspoon ground cinnamon

  ¾ teaspoon instant coffee powder

  ¼ cup miniature chocolate chips

Preheat the oven to 375°F. Coat a 10 × 15-inch jelly roll pan with nonstick spray. Line with wax paper and spray again; lightly dust the pan with flour.

In a large bowl, with an electric mixer, beat the eggs at high speed until they are thick. Place a wire sieve over the bowl and press the brown sugar through it to sift it into the eggs. Continue beating at high speed until fluffy. Gradually beat in the sugar at high speed. Scrape the bowl often. Beat until the mixture forms a thick ribbon when beaters are lifted.

With a rubber spatula, mix in the water and vanilla. Place the sieve over the bowl again and add the flour, cocoa, baking powder, salt, and cinnamon. Stir the mixture until about one third of it has been sifted into the mixture. With a rubber spatula, fold the flour mixture carefully into the egg mixture. Add another third of the flour mixture; fold in. Add the remaining flour mixture and fold together until all the ingredients are well blended. Pour the batter into the prepared pan and spread to smooth the top and distribute the batter evenly.

Bake for 10 to 12 minutes, or until the top springs back when touched.

While the cake bakes, cut a strip of paper toweling a little longer than the pan. Place the paper toweling on the countertop and dust it generously with confectioners' sugar. Invert the baked cake immediately onto the toweling. Remove the wax paper and immediately roll the cake and paper toweling up, starting at a narrow end. Place on a wire rack and cool completely.

To prepare the filling, in a medium bowl, beat the ricotta with the sugar, cinnamon, and coffee powder. Fold in the chocolate chips.

Unroll the cake and discard the paper toweling. Spread with the filling. Reroll and place on a serving plate. Dust with additional confectioners' sugar.

If the cake is made ahead, wrap it in plastic wrap and refrigerate up to 24 hours. Allow the cake to come to room temperature before serving. Dust again with confectioners' sugar before serving.

MAKES 10 SERVINGS

PER SERVING: *192 calories, 16% calories from fat, 3.52 g fat, 66.3 mg cholesterol, 127 mg sodium, 1.03 g dietary fiber*

Fresh Strawberry Jam Roll

This is a light, tender sponge cake filled with a wonderful fresh homemade strawberry jam. You can wrap the filled roll and freeze it for up to two weeks. Decorate it with fresh strawberries before you serve it.

4 large eggs, separated

¾ cup sugar

1 teaspoon vanilla

¾ cup sifted cake flour

¾ teaspoon baking powder

¼ teaspoon salt

Confectioners' sugar

1 cup fresh strawberry jam (see Note)

Additional strawberries for serving

Preheat the oven to 375°F. Coat a 10 × 15-inch jelly roll pan with nonstick spray. Line with wax paper and spray again; dust the wax paper and pan lightly with flour.

In a large bowl, using clean, dry beaters, beat the egg whites until soft peaks form. Gradually beat in ¼ cup of the sugar. Continue beating until the whites form glossy peaks. Set aside.

In another bowl, without washing the beaters, beat the egg yolks until frothy. Gradually beat in the remaining ½ cup sugar until the mixture is light and fluffy and falls in a ribbon when the beaters are lifted. Stir in the vanilla. Place a wire sieve over the bowl and add the flour, baking powder, and salt. Stir the mixture until it is sifted into the yolks. Stir just until blended.

Mix about 1 cup of the beaten whites into the egg yolk mixture to lighten it, then fold in the remaining whites just until blended.

Pour the batter into the lined pan and spread it evenly. Bake the cake for 10 to 12 minutes, or until the top springs back when touched.

While the cake bakes, cut a strip of paper toweling about the length of the pan. Place on a countertop and dust generously with confectioners' sugar. Remove the cake from the oven and immediately invert it onto the toweling. Remove the wax paper and roll up the cake and the toweling, starting from a narrow end, into a cylinder. Place on a wire rack and cool completely.

Prepare the fresh strawberry jam. Unroll the cake and remove the toweling. Spread the cake with the jam and reroll. Dust with additional confectioners' sugar and serve with additional berries, or wrap the roll in plastic wrap and refrigerate until ready to serve.

MAKES 10 SERVINGS

PER SERVING: *204 calories, 9% calories from fat, 2.1 g fat, 85.2 mg cholesterol, 106 mg sodium, 0.53 g dietary fiber*

NOTE: To make fresh strawberry jam, crush enough fresh strawberries to measure 1 cup. Place in a large nonaluminum saucepan. Add 1 cup sugar and heat to boiling. Boil for 5 minutes, or until the jam reaches 218°F. on a candy thermometer. Remove from the heat and cool.

Mocha Sponge Roll

I *keep this quick and easy rolled cake in the freezer ready to slice to make a fast and delicious last-minute dessert.*

- ¾ cup cake flour
- 1½ teaspoons baking powder
- ⅛ teaspoon salt
- 3 large eggs, separated
- 1 teaspoon lemon juice or white vinegar
- ¾ cup sugar
- ¼ cup very strong hot coffee
- ½ cup confectioners' sugar

FILLING
- 1 pint mocha- or chocolate-flavored nonfat frozen yogurt, slightly softened

GARNISH
- 1 tablespoon confectioners' sugar

Preheat the oven to 375°F. Coat an 11 × 17-inch jelly roll pan with nonstick spray and line it with wax paper, leaving a 2-inch overhang beyond the edge of the short sides. Coat the paper with spray and dust lightly with flour.

Sift the cake flour, baking powder, and salt into a small bowl and set aside.

In a large bowl, with an electric mixer, beat the egg whites until frothy; add the lemon juice and beat until the whites are stiff and hold their shape, but are not overbeaten and dry.

In a medium bowl, beat the egg yolks, adding the sugar gradually until well blended. Beat in the coffee until well blended. Fold the egg yolk mixture and flour mixture into the egg whites until just combined.

Spread the batter into the prepared pan. Bake until light brown and set, about 10 minutes.

Dust a clean tea towel generously with confectioners' sugar and invert the baked cake onto the towel. Carefully remove the wax paper. Roll up carefully starting from a short end. Place the cake on a rack to cool completely.

To assemble, carefully unroll the cake and spread the softened frozen yogurt over the cake. Roll up. Wrap in plastic and keep the roll in the freezer until ready to serve. To serve, sprinkle with confectioners' sugar and cut into 1-inch slices.

MAKES 10 SERVINGS

PER SERVING: *167 calories, 8% calories from fat, 1.57 g fat, 63.9 mg cholesterol, 95 mg sodium, 0.23 g dietary fiber*

COFFEE CAKES

Blueberry Brunch Cake

Juicy with blueberries, this is most wonderful hot out of the oven! Can you tell I'm partial to blueberries?

1 cup all-purpose flour

1/3 cup sugar

1 1/2 teaspoons baking powder

1/4 teaspoon salt

1 large egg, lightly beaten

1/2 cup skim milk

2 tablespoons corn or canola oil

1 tablespoon lemon juice

1 cup fresh blueberries

TOPPING

1/3 cup sugar

1/4 cup all-purpose flour

1/4 cup quick-cooking or
old-fashioned rolled oats

1/4 teaspoon ground cinnamon

1 1/2 tablespoons unsalted butter,
melted

Preheat the oven to 400°F. Coat a 9-inch round cake pan with nonstick spray.

In a large mixing bowl, stir together the flour, sugar, baking powder, and salt. In a 1-cup liquid measure mix together the egg, skim milk, oil, and lemon juice. Pour the liquids over the dry ingredients. With a rubber spatula, gently fold the ingredients together just until the dry ingredients are moistened. Spread the batter into the prepared pan and spread the blueberries evenly over the top.

To make the topping: In a small bowl, stir together the sugar, flour, rolled oats, cinnamon, and melted butter until the mixture makes moist crumbs. Sprinkle over the blueberries in the pan. Bake for 20 to 25 minutes, or until a toothpick inserted into the center of the cake comes out dry and the crumbs are golden brown.

MAKES 8 SERVINGS

PER SERVING: *214 calories, 28% calories from fat, 6.62 g fat, 32.7 mg cholesterol, 146 mg sodium, 1.25 g dietary fiber*

Caramel Oatmeal Cake

This *old-fashioned oatmeal cake has a crunchy, caramelly broiled topping. Substituting rolled oats and rice cereal for some of the coconut in the topping reduces the fat count to 24 percent from fat with no sacrifice whatsoever.*

1¼ cups boiling water

1½ cups quick-cooking rolled oats

1½ cups unbleached all-purpose flour

1 teaspoon baking soda

1 teaspoon baking powder

1 teaspoon ground cinnamon

⅛ teaspoon salt

6 tablespoons (¾ stick) unsalted butter, at room temperature

1 cup packed brown sugar

½ cup sugar

2 large eggs, lightly beaten

½ cup dark raisins

CARAMEL TOPPING

2 tablespoons unsalted butter, at room temperature

¾ cup packed brown sugar

2 tablespoons skim milk

⅓ cup flaked coconut

⅓ cup quick-cooking rolled oats

⅓ cup crisp rice cereal

Preheat the oven to 350°F. Coat a 9 × 13-inch baking pan with nonstick spray and dust lightly with flour.

In a medium bowl, combine the boiling water and the rolled oats; let stand 20 minutes. In another bowl, mix together the flour, baking soda, baking powder, cinnamon, and salt. In a large bowl, beat the butter, sugars, and eggs until light and creamy. Add the oat mixture and flour mixture; mix well. Stir in the raisins. Spread into the prepared pan and bake for 30 to 35 minutes, or until a toothpick inserted into the center of the cake comes out clean and dry.

For the topping, in a small bowl, combine the butter, brown sugar, milk, coconut, oats, and rice cereal; blend well. Spoon evenly over the hot cake. Broil 6 to 8 inches from the heat for 1 to 2 minutes, or until the topping is bubbly. Remove from the oven. If necessary, spread the topping to cover the top of the cake evenly using a butter knife. Cool in the pan before cutting.

MAKES 16 SERVINGS

PER SERVING: *273 calories, 24% calories from fat, 7.59 g fat, 42.2 mg cholesterol, 96.2 mg sodium, 1.84 g dietary fiber*

...mon—Sour Cream Coffee Cake

...streak of nuts and cinnamon running
... this was my favorite coffee cake of all. But
... to go to get the fat grams out. The solu-
...e toasted whole-grain cereal, along with
... of hazelnut oil, provide the crunch, fla-
...ppearance of nuts. I reduced the butter by
...cing it with applesauce, and used nonfat
... in place of regular and egg whites instead
...ggs. The percentage of calories from fat
...y more than half, making this my new
favorite coffee cake!

- ½ cup (1 stick) unsalted butter, at room temperature
- 1¼ cups sugar
- 2 large egg whites
- ½ cup unsweetened applesauce
- 1 cup nonfat sour cream
- 1 teaspoon vanilla
- 2 cups all-purpose flour
- 1½ teaspoons baking powder
- ½ teaspoon baking soda
- ¼ teaspoon salt
- ½ cup Grape-Nuts cereal
- ¼ cup golden raisins
- 1 tablespoon hazelnut, walnut, or corn oil
- 2 teaspoons ground cinnamon

Preheat the oven to 350°F. Coat a 10-inch fancy tube pan with nonstick spray.

In a large mixing bowl, cream the butter with the sugar until blended. Add the egg whites and applesauce and beat until light. Stir in the sour cream and vanilla. In a small bowl, stir the flour, baking powder, baking soda, and salt together, then stir the dry ingredients into the creamed ingredients using a wooden spoon, until the mixture is well blended.

Spread half the mixture into the prepared pan. Combine the cereal, raisins, oil, and cinnamon. Sprinkle the mixture over the batter in the pan. Top with the remaining batter and smooth the top of the cake to the edges.

Bake for 50 to 55 minutes, or until a wooden skewer inserted in the center comes out clean and dry. Cool in the pan for 5 minutes, then invert onto a wire rack to finish cooling.

MAKES 16 SERVINGS

PER SERVING: 213 calories, 28% calories from fat, 6.77 g fat, 15.5 mg cholesterol, 86.6 mg sodium, 0.96 g dietary fiber

Cranberry Crumb Cake

I *always put a few bags of fresh cranberries into the freezer for use out of season. If you use frozen whole cranberries, add them to the cake batter while they are still frozen and add 5 to 10 minutes to the baking time.*

1¾ cups all-purpose flour

1 teaspoon baking powder

1 teaspoon baking soda

½ teaspoon salt

3 tablespoons unsalted butter, at room temperature

3 tablespoons vegetable shortening, at room temperature

1 cup sugar

2 large egg whites or 1 large egg, lightly beaten

1¼ cups nonfat sour cream

2 teaspoons grated orange zest

2 cups fresh, whole cranberries

TOPPING

1 cup packed light or dark brown sugar

¼ cup all-purpose flour

¼ cup quick-cooking or old-fashioned rolled oats

3 tablespoons unsalted butter, melted

Preheat the oven to 350°F. Coat a 13 × 9-inch cake pan with nonstick spray.

In a medium bowl, stir the flour, baking powder, baking soda, and salt together; set aside.

In a large mixing bowl, with an electric mixer, cream the butter, shortening, and sugar until smooth. Add the egg whites and beat until light at high speed. Blend in the sour cream and orange zest. Add the flour mixture and mix at low speed, scraping the bowl often, until the batter is smooth and light. Fold in the cranberries.

Spread the batter evenly into the prepared baking pan.

For the topping, combine the brown sugar, flour, oats, and melted butter and sprinkle over the top of the batter. Bake for 50 to 60 minutes, or until a toothpick inserted in the center of the cake comes out clean. Serve warm, or cool in the pan on a wire rack.

MAKES 16 SERVINGS

PER SERVING: *243 calories, 26% calories from fat, 6.96 g fat, 11.6 mg cholesterol, 153 mg sodium, 1.02 g dietary fiber*

Quick and Easy Apple Pie Cake

W*hen we were just too busy to make an apple pie, crust and all, we'd quickly stir up this cake, bake it in a pie pan, and call it apple pie.*

1 large egg

¾ cup sugar

1 teaspoon vanilla

1 teaspoon baking powder

¼ teaspoon salt

1 teaspoon ground cinnamon

½ cup all-purpose flour

3 medium-size tart apples, peeled, cored, and diced

Confectioners' sugar

Preheat the oven to 350ºF. Lightly coat a 9-inch pie pan with nonstick spray.

In a large mixing bowl, stir the egg, sugar, vanilla, baking powder, salt, cinnamon, flour, and apples together until blended. The mixture will be stiff. Spoon the mixture into the pan and smooth the top with a spatula. Bake for 30 minutes, or until browned.

Dust the cake with the confectioners' sugar. Cut into wedges to serve.

MAKES 6 SERVINGS

PER SERVING: *181 calories, 5% calories from fat, 1.14 g fat, 35.5 mg cholesterol, 155 mg sodium, 1.7 g dietary fiber*

Cinnamon Sugar Coffee Cake

This is so quick to stir up and bake, and so delicious hot out of the oven! It makes a great shortcake for dessert, too. When wild blueberries are in season, I throw a few handfuls onto the top of the batter before adding the cinnamon sugar. For the best texture and moistness, do not overmix the batter.

1 tablespoon unsalted butter, melted

1 large egg, beaten

½ cup skim milk

1 cup all-purpose flour

½ cup sugar

3 teaspoons baking powder

¼ teaspoon salt

TOPPING

¼ cup sugar

1 teaspoon ground cinnamon

Preheat the oven to 375ºF. Coat an 8-inch square cake pan with nonstick spray.

In a large mixing bowl, stir the butter, egg, and milk together. Place a wire sieve over the top of the bowl and add the flour, sugar, baking powder, and salt. Stir the dry ingredients until they are sifted onto the liquids. With a spatula, stir together until a lumpy dough forms, mixing just until the dry ingredients are moistened. Pour the dough into the prepared pan.

For the topping, mix the sugar and the cinnamon and sprinkle over the top of the cake. Bake for 15 minutes, or until a toothpick inserted in the center of the cake comes out clean and dry. Cool in the pan on a wire rack.

MAKES 9 SERVINGS

PER SERVING: *137 calories, 13% calories from fat, 1.99 g fat, 27.3 mg cholesterol, 184 mg sodium, 0.41 g dietary fiber*

Pineapple Coffee Cake

*A*lthough you can reduce the fat in this cake to almost nothing by using fat-free cream cheese and sour cream, it just isn't worth it. This coffee cake in its original incarnation is low enough in fat to easily come within our parameters of 30 percent calories from fat because there is no shortening added at all. It's irresistible served warm from the oven with its muffinlike texture. When there are houseguests around, we usually eat it all. But when there's just my husband and me, I put the remainder of the cake into a protective container and freeze it. If I remember to cut it into serving pieces ahead of time, we can just heat up a piece or two at a time in the microwave when we want "something to go with coffee."

1 can (8 ounces) crushed pineapple, packed in juice

4 ounces cream cheese

1 cup sugar

1 large egg

1 teaspoon vanilla

½ cup dairy sour cream

1 cup all-purpose flour

1 cup whole wheat pastry flour

1 teaspoon baking powder

1 teaspoon baking soda

¼ teaspoon salt

PINEAPPLE GLAZE

1 cup confectioners' sugar

1 to 2 tablespoons pineapple juice (from the crushed pineapple)

Preheat the oven to 375°F. Coat a 9- or 10-inch tube pan with nonstick spray and dust it with flour.

Place a wire strainer over a small bowl and turn the pineapple into the strainer to drain off most of the juices; reserve it.

In a large mixing bowl, with an electric mixer, cream the cream cheese and sugar together until smooth. Add the egg and vanilla; beat well. Stir in the sour cream and drained pineapple; mix until well blended.

In another bowl, mix the flours with the baking powder, baking soda, and salt. Add to the creamed mixture and stir just until blended. Turn into the prepared pan and bake for about 45 minutes, or until a toothpick inserted in the center comes out clean. Cool 10 minutes.

While the cake cools, mix the confectioners' sugar with enough pineapple juice to make a smooth glaze. Brush the glaze over the warm cake.

MAKES 10 SERVINGS

PER SERVING: *283 calories, 22% calories from fat, 7.22 g fat, 38.8 mg cholesterol, 183 mg sodium, 2.04 g dietary fiber*

Rhubarb-Strawberry Streusel Coffee Cake

I think of this as a coffee cake for springtime, when both rhubarb and strawberries are at their juiciest. Although my original recipe wasn't sinfully high in fat, reducing the butter and the number of whole eggs, replacing the nuts in the topping with the fat-free toasted wheat and barley cereal, and using just a tablespoon of hazelnut oil in place of a quarter cup of butter were the simple changes needed to bring the percentage of calories from fat down to a comfortable 23 percent.

2 cups diced fresh rhubarb

2 cups sliced fresh strawberries

1 tablespoon fresh lemon juice

½ cup sugar

2 tablespoons cornstarch

1½ cups all-purpose flour

⅓ cup sugar

½ teaspoon baking powder

½ teaspoon baking soda

¼ teaspoon salt

¼ teaspoon ground nutmeg

4 tablespoons (½ stick) unsalted butter, chilled and cut in pieces

½ cup lowfat (1 percent) buttermilk

1 large egg, lightly beaten

1 teaspoon vanilla

STREUSEL TOPPING

⅓ cup whole wheat pastry flour

⅓ cup packed brown sugar

¼ cup Grape-Nuts cereal

1 tablespoon hazelnut or walnut oil

Preheat the oven to 400°F. Coat a 9-inch round cake pan with nonstick spray and dust it lightly with flour.

In a 2-quart saucepan, combine the rhubarb, strawberries, and lemon juice. Place over medium heat for 5 minutes and cook until juicy, stirring often. In a small bowl, mix the sugar and cornstarch well. Stir the sugar mixture into the rhubarb mixture and bring to a boil; cook 2 minutes, until thickened and clear; remove from heat.

In a large mixing bowl, combine the flour, sugar, baking powder, baking soda, salt, and nutmeg; mix well. Cut in the butter with a fork or with a small hand mixer until the butter is in pea-size pieces. In a liquid 1-cup measure, beat the buttermilk, egg, and vanilla together. Pour the liquids over the dry ingredients and, with a rubber spatula, gently blend just until the dry ingredients are moistened. Spread the batter into the prepared pan, bringing it up the sides of the pan just a little so that it will encase the filling.

Pour the warm rhubarb-strawberry filling into the pan.

To make the topping, in a small bowl, combine the flour, sugar, cereal, and oil until crumbly. Sprinkle the mixture evenly over the fruit filling in the pan. Bake for 35 to 45 minutes, or until the topping is lightly browned.

MAKES 8 SERVINGS

PER SERVING: *322 calories, 23% calories from fat, 8.46 g fat, 46.6 mg cholesterol, 188 mg sodium, 3.28 g dietary fiber*

ICINGS AND FROSTINGS

Boiled Caramel Icing

Use this easy icing on a simple white cake, a cocoa cake, or an apple cake.

2 cups packed brown sugar

6 tablespoons (¾ stick) unsalted butter

½ cup whipping (heavy) cream

1 teaspoon vanilla

In a 2-quart saucepan, combine the brown sugar, butter, and cream. Boil for 1 minute, stirring, then beat the mixture until creamy and smooth. Add the vanilla and cool.

MAKES ABOUT 12 SERVINGS

PER SERVING: *191 calories, 28% calories from fat, 6.12 g fat, 16.9 mg cholesterol, 17.3 mg sodium, 0 g dietary fiber*

One-Minute Boiled Fudge Frosting

This is a delicious chocolatey frosting that is just perfect for any cocoa cake, plain white cake, or cupcakes.

1½ cups sugar

2 ounces (2 squares) unsweetened chocolate

1 tablespoon light corn syrup

¼ teaspoon salt

1 tablespoon vegetable shortening

2 tablespoons unsalted butter

7 tablespoons evaporated skimmed milk

1 teaspoon vanilla

In a large heavy saucepan, combine the sugar, chocolate, syrup, salt, shortening, butter, and milk. Place over medium heat and bring slowly to a boil, stirring. Boil for 1 minute. Remove from the heat and add the vanilla. Cool, then beat until the frosting has thickened.

MAKES 12 SERVINGS

PER SERVING: *159 calories, 29% calories from fat, 5.5 g fat, 5.54 mg cholesterol, 12.5 mg sodium, 0.73 g dietary fiber*

Simple Decorator Frosting

This makes enough frosting to cover a two-layer cake. This frosting is perfect for a fancy, special-occasion cake, such as a birthday cake. Multiply the recipe to decorate a wedding cake. The proportion of fat is surprisingly low!

2 large egg whites

1 teaspoon fresh lemon juice

¼ cup sugar

2 tablespoons water

6 tablespoons (¾ stick) unsalted butter, at room temperature

3¾ cups (1 pound) confectioners' sugar

1 teaspoon vanilla

In a metal mixing bowl, with a hand-held electric mixer, beat the egg whites until frothy, add the lemon juice, and beat until stiff.

In a saucepan, combine the sugar and water. Heat to boiling and boil for 1 minute. With the mixer at high speed, slowly beat the boiling syrup into the egg whites until smooth and frothy. Place the mixture over a pot of boiling water and beat at high speed for 2 minutes longer. Beat in the butter, sugar, and vanilla until light and fluffy.

MAKES 12 SERVINGS

PER SERVING: *215 calories, 23% calories from fat, 5.75 g fat, 15.5 mg cholesterol, 11 mg sodium, 0 g dietary fiber*

CHEESECAKES

Is it possible to make delicious cheesecakes that are low in fat and calories and taste good, too? Absolutely, with the help of low-fat and nonfat cream cheese, ricotta, yogurt, and other dairy products. When I first began making low-fat cheesecakes, there were few choices on the market. But today the dairy case has almost exploded with options. Nonfat and low-fat fruit and vanilla-flavored yogurts give a creamy cheesecake a subtle flavor boost. Nonfat cream cheese may not set up as well as the full-fat variety, so I sometimes add cornstarch to the mixture, or I'll use an additional egg white to boost the firmness.

All of the cheesecakes in this section received the critical approval of those who claim not to like or trust low-fat desserts! To make the cheesecakes healthier, I hard-heartedly slashed the thick fat-and-sugar-loaded crusts, which cheesecakes don't need anyway. A layer of spicy crumbs is sufficient to separate the cheesecake from the pan and give the illusion of a base to the cake. A fruit topping is one of my favorite ways to complement the creamy filling. Fresh fruits and berries, when available, are beautiful and irresistible counterpoints to the creamy flavor of the fillings.

Golden Delicious Apple-Topped Cheesecake

Made with regular cream cheese, this cheesecake figures out at 58 percent calories from fat! Fat-free cream cheese drops the percentage to 13 percent. For the topping, Golden Delicious apples are great because they hold their shape when they are cooked to tender succulence.

CRUST

1 cup graham cracker crumbs, made with low-fat graham crackers

2 tablespoons unsalted butter, melted

2 tablespoons brown sugar

CHEESECAKE

3 (8-ounce) packages fat-free cream cheese

1 cup sugar

1 teaspoon grated lemon zest

1 teaspoon vanilla

4 large eggs, lightly beaten

2 tablespoons all-purpose flour

APPLE TOPPING

1½ cups water

½ cup sugar

1 tablespoon fresh lemon juice

3 Golden Delicious apples, peeled, cored, and cut into 8 wedges each

1 tablespoon Calvados or apple brandy (optional)

Preheat the oven to 350°F. Lightly coat a 10-inch springform pan with nonstick spray.

In a small bowl, mix the graham cracker crumbs with the butter and brown sugar. Pat the mixture into the bottom of the springform pan.

In a large mixing bowl, with an electric mixer, cream the cream cheese and sugar together until evenly blended. Add the lemon zest, vanilla, eggs, and flour and mix well. Pour the mixture into the crust-lined pan. Place the filled pan onto a rimmed baking sheet. Bake for 60 to 65 minutes, just until set. Cool in the pan, then cover and chill overnight.

For the topping, in a 2-quart saucepan, bring the water, sugar, and lemon juice to a boil. Add the apples, reduce the heat, and simmer until the apples are just tender, 6 to 7 minutes. Remove the apple slices with a slotted spoon and cool them and arrange them over the cheesecake. Boil the remaining syrup until reduced to ¼ cup, about 20 minutes. Remove from the heat; stir in the Calvados, if using. Spoon the syrup over the apples.

MAKES 12 SERVINGS

PER SERVING: *265 calories, 13% calories from fat, 4.06 g fat, 86.3 mg cholesterol, 467 mg sodium, 1.52 g dietary fiber*

Ricotta Cheesecake with Glazed Apricots

Ricotta, *when blended in the food processor or blender, makes a silky, smooth, substantial base for this cheesecake that doesn't taste low in fat at all! Fat-free sour cream adds a creamy tang, too.*

CRUST

1½ cups graham cracker crumbs, made with low-fat crackers

4 tablespoons (½ stick) unsalted butter, melted

1 teaspoon ground cinnamon

CHEESECAKE FILLING

4 large egg whites, at room temperature

1 cup sugar

4 cups nonfat ricotta, blended until smooth in the food processor

1 cup fat-free sour cream

¼ cup all-purpose flour

¼ cup fresh lemon juice

1 tablespoon grated lemon zest

1 tablespoon vanilla

½ teaspoon ground nutmeg

½ teaspoon salt

APRICOT TOPPING

¼ cup apricot preserves

2 teaspoons Amaretto or almond-flavored liqueur

5 fresh apricots, halved and pitted

Preheat the oven to 350°F. Lightly coat a 9- or 10-inch springform pan with nonstick spray. Dust with flour.

In a small bowl, combine the graham cracker crumbs, butter, and cinnamon. Press the mixture into the bottom and about 1 inch up the sides of the prepared pan. Bake for 10 minutes, remove, and cool on a wire rack.

In a large mixing bowl, with an electric mixer, beat the egg whites with the sugar until the sugar is dissolved, scraping the sides of the bowl often. Add the ricotta, sour cream, flour, lemon juice, lemon zest, vanilla, nutmeg, and salt. Beat until the mixture is well combined. Pour into the crust-lined pan and place the pan on a baking sheet.

Bake for 1 hour and 15 minutes. Turn the heat off but do not open the oven door. Let the cake cool in the oven for 2 hours. Remove the cheesecake from the oven and chill, covered, overnight. Run a knife around the edge of the cake, remove the sides of the pan, and transfer to a cake stand or plate. Strain the apricot preserves into a glass bowl, or heat them in a small, heavy saucepan over low heat, stirring constantly until runny. Place in the microwave oven and heat for 1 minute, just until the preserves are runny. Stir in the Amaretto.

Arrange the apricot halves, cut side down, on top of the cake. Spoon the apricot preserves over.

MAKES 12 SERVINGS

PER SERVING: *292 calories, 22% calories from fat, 7.4 g fat, 23.5 mg cholesterol, 166 mg sodium, 0.8 g dietary fiber*

Cranberry-Raisin Streusel Cheesecake

This is a beautiful dessert for a festive holiday meal. When I made this cheesecake in its original version and served it with the low-fat version, my guests could hardly tell the difference. I reduced the butter in the crust, used nonfat cream cheese, and replaced the nuts in the topping with Grape-Nuts cereal. If you make the cheesecake ahead and refrigerate it, recrisp the top under the broiler for 2 to 3 minutes before serving.

CRUST

1 cup all-purpose flour

3 tablespoons sugar

2 tablespoons unsalted butter, at room temperature

FILLING

2 (8-ounce) packages nonfat cream cheese

2 tablespoons cornstarch

4 large egg whites, lightly beaten

½ cup sugar

1 tablespoon vanilla

CRANBERRY-RAISIN TOPPING

1 cup cranberries

½ cup dark or golden raisins

½ cup sugar

½ teaspoon ground cinnamon

STREUSEL TOPPING

½ cup brown sugar

½ cup all-purpose flour

4 tablespoons (½ stick) unsalted butter, at room temperature

½ cup Grape-Nuts cereal

Preheat the oven to 350°F. Lightly grease or coat a 9- or 10-inch springform pan with nonstick spray.

For the crust, in a small bowl, mix together the flour, sugar, and butter to make a crumbly mixture. Press evenly into the bottom and about ½ inch up the sides of the springform pan. Bake for 20 to 25 minutes, or until lightly browned and firm. Remove from the oven and cool on a wire rack. Increase the oven temperature to 450°F.

In a mixing bowl, with an electric mixer, beat the cream cheese, cornstarch, egg whites, sugar, and vanilla until the mixture is well blended. Pour the mixture over the baked crust. Return to the oven and bake for 20 to 25 minutes, or until the cake is set. Cool on a wire rack. Reduce the oven temperature to 400°F. (You may turn off the oven and preheat it to 400°F. when you are ready to finish baking the cheesecake.)

In a saucepan, combine the cranberries, raisins, and sugar with ½ cup water. Bring to a boil, stirring, and cook for 5 minutes. Add the cinnamon and cool slightly. Pour over the warm cheesecake evenly.

In a small bowl, stir together the brown sugar, flour, butter, and Grape-Nuts cereal to make a crumbly mixture. Sprinkle over the cranberry layer evenly. Bake for 15 minutes, until the top is browned. Remove from the oven and cool on a wire rack.

MAKES 16 SERVINGS

PER SERVING: *229 calories, 17% calories from fat, 4.47 g fat, 16.7 mg cholesterol, 242 mg sodium, 1.15 g dietary fiber*

Piña Colada Cheesecake

With the help of fat-free cream cheese and the flavors of pineapple, coconut, and rum, you'll never miss the missing fat in this cheesecake. In fact, it gives you more good nutrition than you'd ever expect in a dessert.

- ½ cup graham cracker crumbs, made with low-fat crackers
- 6 (8-ounce) packages fat-free cream cheese or 4 packages fat-free cream cheese plus 2 packages Neufchâtel cheese
- 1 cup sugar
- 1 tablespoon vanilla
- 1 cup well-drained crushed pineapple
- ½ cup canned cream of coconut
- 6 large egg whites, lightly beaten
- ¼ cup light rum
- Fresh seasonal fruit for garnish, such as fresh berries, sliced apricots, or sliced peaches

Preheat the oven to 325°F. Coat a 10- or 12-inch springform pan with nonstick spray and sprinkle the bottom and sides with the graham cracker crumbs.

Mix the cream cheese, sugar, and vanilla in a large bowl until light and fluffy. Add the pineapple, cream of coconut, egg whites, and rum and beat until light. Pour the mixture into the prepared pan.

Bake for 45 to 55 minutes, or until the center is almost set (it will jiggle a little when shaken). Cool in the pan on a wire rack, cover, and refrigerate for at least 3 hours or overnight. Serve with fruit on top.

MAKES 16 SERVINGS

PER SERVING WITH JUST FAT-FREE CREAM CHEESE: *163 calories, 5% calories from fat, 0.9 g fat, 15 mg cholesterol, 570 mg sodium, 0.25 g dietary fiber*
PER SERVING WITH FAT-FREE CREAM CHEESE AND NEUFCHÂTEL CHEESE: *212 calories, 30% calories from fat, 7.6 g fat, 32 mg cholesterol, 513 mg sodium, 0.25 g dietary fiber*

UPSIDE-DOWN CAKES, MERINGUES, AND SHORTCAKES

Gingered Pear Upside-Down Cake

A *sponge cake is the basis for this upside-down cake. Softened nonfat frozen yogurt or ice milk instead of ice cream further saves on fat grams.*

½ **cup packed brown sugar**

4 **tablespoons (½ stick) unsalted butter, melted**

1½ **pounds firm, ripe pears, peeled and cored**

1-**inch piece of fresh ginger, peeled and finely grated**

2 **large eggs, separated**

½ **cup sugar**

¾ **cup all-purpose flour**

½ **teaspoon baking powder**

¼ **teaspoon salt**

Nonfat vanilla frozen yogurt or ice milk, softened

Preheat the oven to 350°F. Lightly grease a 9-inch round cake or pie pan or coat with nonstick spray.

In a small bowl, mix the brown sugar and butter. Spread the mixture in the bottom of the prepared pan. Quarter the pears and toss them in a medium bowl with the grated ginger. Arrange the pears on top of the brown sugar and butter mixture in the pan.

In a medium bowl, beat the egg whites until stiff but not dry. In another bowl, using the same beaters without washing them, beat the egg yolks until thick and lemon colored. Gradually add the sugar; mix well. Combine the flour, baking powder, and salt and add to the egg yolk mixture. Fold in the whites until thoroughly incorporated. Pour the batter over the pears in the pan.

Bake for 30 to 35 minutes, or until a toothpick inserted in the center of the cake comes out clean. Cool in the pan for 2 minutes, then invert onto a serving plate. Serve warm, cut into wedges, topped with softened vanilla frozen yogurt or ice milk.

MAKES 8 SERVINGS

PER SERVING: *259 calories, 25% calories from fat, 7.45 g fat, 68.8 mg cholesterol, 110 mg sodium, 2.63 g dietary fiber*

Fresh Pineapple Upside-Down Cake

This is one of those old classics that, though rich and indulgent in flavor, actually is relatively low in fat. Fresh pineapple is easily available today and makes all the difference in flavor, too. I have a simple kitchen gadget that I use for cutting a fresh pineapple, making the process faster and easier.

- ½ **cup packed brown sugar**
- 4 **tablespoons (½ stick) unsalted butter, melted**
- 1 **ripe pineapple, about 1½ pounds**
- 2 **large eggs, separated**
- ½ **cup sugar**
- ¾ **cup all-purpose flour**
- ½ **teaspoon baking powder**
- ¼ **teaspoon salt**
- **Nonfat vanilla frozen yogurt or ice milk, softened**

Preheat the oven to 350°F. Lightly grease a 9-inch square cake pan or coat with nonstick spray.

In a small bowl, mix the brown sugar and butter. Spread the mixture in the bottom of the pan.

Cut the top and bottom off the pineapple and stand the pineapple on a plate. With a thin, sharp knife, cut straight down around the rind of the pineapple. With an apple corer, cut out the core of the pineapple. Cut the pineapple into ¾-inch-thick rings (save the juice that will collect on the plate), then cut the rings in half and arrange on top of the brown sugar and butter mixture in the pan.

In a medium bowl, beat the egg whites until stiff but not dry. In another bowl, using the same beaters without washing them, beat the egg yolks until thick and lemon colored. Gradually add the sugar; mix well. Add ¼ cup of the reserved pineapple juice. Mix the flour, baking powder, and salt and blend into the egg yolk mixture. Fold in the egg whites until thoroughly incorporated. Pour the mixture over the pineapple in the pan.

Bake for 30 to 35 minutes, or until a toothpick inserted in the center of the cake comes out clean. Cool in the pan for 2 minutes, then invert onto a serving plate. Serve warm, cut into wedges, and topped with softened vanilla frozen yogurt or ice milk.

MAKES 8 SERVINGS

PER SERVING: *243 calories, 27% calories from fat, 7.41 g fat, 68.8 mg cholesterol, 111 mg sodium, 1.33 g dietary fiber*

Cranberry Upside-Down Cake

When cranberries are not in season, I make this cake with fresh or frozen blueberries, adding a tablespoon of fresh lemon juice to the berries.

½ cup packed light brown sugar

¼ cup dark corn syrup

1 tablespoon unsalted butter

½ teaspoon ground cinnamon

⅛ teaspoon ground nutmeg

1 (12-ounce) package fresh cranberries

CAKE

1½ cups all-purpose flour

½ cup whole wheat pastry or cake flour

¼ cup packed light brown sugar

1 teaspoon baking powder

½ teaspoon ground cinnamon

¼ teaspoon salt

6 tablespoons (¾ stick) unsalted butter, at room temperature

1 cup vanilla-flavored nonfat yogurt

½ cup unsweetened applesauce

2 large eggs, lightly beaten

TO SERVE

Nonfat vanilla frozen yogurt, softened (optional)

Coat a 9-inch square cake pan with nonstick spray. In a saucepan, combine the brown sugar, corn syrup, butter, cinnamon, and nutmeg. Stir over low heat until the sugar is dissolved. Spread the mixture evenly over the bottom of the cake pan. Top with the cranberries.

Preheat the oven to 350°F.

Place a wire sieve over a medium bowl. Measure the flours, brown sugar, baking powder, cinnamon, and salt into the sieve. Stir the mixture until it is sifted into the bowl. Cut the butter into ¼-inch slices and, with an electric mixer on low speed, mix until the butter is blended into the dry ingredients. In another bowl, mix the yogurt, applesauce, and eggs until blended. Pour the liquids over the butter mixture and, with the mixer at medium speed, blend until the batter is smooth. Spoon the batter evenly over the cranberries in the baking dish. Bake for 45 to 50 minutes, or until the cake is firm to the touch and a toothpick inserted into the cake comes out clean and dry.

Cool the cake in the pan on a wire rack for 10 minutes. Loosen the edges of the cake with a knife and invert onto a serving plate. Serve warm or at room temperature. Top with the frozen yogurt, if desired.

MAKES 12 SERVINGS

PER SERVING: *264 calories, 26% calories from fat, 7.84 g fat, 53.6 mg cholesterol, 136 mg sodium, 2.38 g dietary fiber*

Pavlova

The base for this traditional Australian dessert is completely fat-free, as are the berries, but the whipped cream that is usually involved wrecks it all. So I started experimenting with blending a bit of whipped cream and various nonfat dairy products and was pleasantly surprised with the results. A mixture of ½ cup whipping cream, whipped, and nonfat sour cream tasted incredibly rich and delicious, made a great base for the summer fruits, and left the dessert at just 26 percent of calories from fat. I also tried blending the cream with vanilla-flavored yogurt, and the result again was quite delicious and made the percentage of calories from fat even lower at 22 percent, with only 5 grams of fat per serving. You can bake the Pavlova base and keep it in an airtight tin for several days, or frozen for several weeks. But once it is topped with cream and fruit it does not keep well, so plan to serve it the day that you assemble it.

4 large egg whites, at room temperature

¼ teaspoon salt

1 cup sugar

4 teaspoons cornstarch

½ teaspoon vanilla

2 teaspoons white vinegar

TO SERVE

½ cup whipping (heavy) cream

1 cup nonfat vanilla-flavored yogurt or ½ cup nonfat sour cream

Fresh raspberries, blackberries, strawberries, peeled and sliced kiwifruit, peeled and sliced fresh peaches, sliced bananas, or any other fresh soft fruit in season

Preheat the oven to 275°F. Line a baking sheet with parchment paper or foil. Butter the pan and sprinkle with flour.

In a large bowl, with an electric mixer, beat the egg whites and salt together until soft peaks form. In a small bowl, stir the sugar and cornstarch together. Turn the mixer to high speed and add the sugar mixture a heaping tablespoon at a time until the whites are stiff and glossy. Add the vanilla and vinegar, beating until very stiff but not dry.

Pile the egg white mixture onto the prepared pan to make an 8-inch circle. The meringue will be about 1½ inches deep. Smooth the sides and the top.

Bake for 1½ hours. Turn the oven off and leave the meringue in the oven with the door closed until cold, or overnight.

Before serving, place the Pavlova on a serving plate. Whip the cream until stiff; blend in the vanilla yogurt until well mixed. Spread the mixture over the top of the Pavlova and top with berries or fresh fruit. Cut into 8 wedges to serve.

MAKES 8 SERVINGS

PER SERVING: *225 calories, 22% calories from fat, 5.67 g fat, 20.4 mg cholesterol, 100 mg sodium, 1.93 g dietary fiber*

Raspberry-Chocolate Meringues

Meringues are made basically of two ingredients: egg whites and sugar. Cream of tartar, vinegar, or lemon juice are acid ingredients that stabilize the meringue, and other nonfat ingredients add flavor. Superfine sugar dissolves into the egg whites more quickly than granulated sugar, important for a light and airy texture. Meringues contain no fat at all. In fact, you need to be very careful not to allow any of the egg yolk into the egg whites, and you need to be sure that your bowl and your beaters are clean and free of any residual fat or grease, or the whites won't get stiff. Use a glass or metal bowl rather than plastic (which can have a greasy surface) for beating the egg whites. The filling makes all the difference: Whipped cream or fudge sauce are, of course, high in fat, but lightly sugared berries make a wonderful fat-free filling.

2 large egg whites, at room temperature

¼ teaspoon salt

¼ teaspoon lemon juice, vinegar, or cream of tartar

½ cup superfine sugar

½ teaspoon vanilla

1 tablespoon unsweetened cocoa powder

RASPBERRY SAUCE

1 (9-ounce) package frozen quick-thaw raspberries in a pouch

1 tablespoon white corn syrup

FILLING

2 cups fresh raspberries

Confectioners' sugar for dusting

Preheat the oven to 275°F. Line a baking sheet with parchment paper.

In a small, clean metal bowl, beat the egg whites, salt, and lemon juice until foamy. Gradually add the sugar and vanilla, beating until stiff peaks form. Sift the cocoa over the beaten egg whites and fold into the mixture.

Drop by heaping tablespoonfuls, making 6 individual mounds of the mixture on the parchment-lined baking sheet. Make a deep well in the center of each, spreading the mixture into a 3-inch circle.

Bake for 45 minutes, or until crisp. Turn off the oven and keep the door closed for 1½ hours. Remove the meringues from the oven. Slide the meringues and parchment paper onto a large wire rack.

To prepare the raspberry sauce, thaw the raspberries as directed on the package. Turn the contents of the pouch into a wire sieve placed over a small bowl. Drain and press the raspberries against the sieve. Add the corn syrup to the strained raspberry juice; mix well.

To serve, fill each meringue with fresh raspberries, dust with confectioners' sugar, and drizzle with the raspberry sauce.

MAKES 6 SERVINGS

PER SERVING: 145 calories, 3% calories from fat, 0.46 g fat, 0 mg cholesterol, 110 mg sodium, 4.78 g dietary fiber

Forgotten Torte

When I have a really busy day coming up, I whip up the base for this old-fashioned dessert in the evening and just put it into the oven, turn the oven off, and forget it until the next day. This meringue-based dessert is just perfect as a base for fresh berries and fruits. Instead of whipped cream, slightly thawed vanilla ice milk or nonfat frozen yogurt makes a perfect substitute.

- 5 large egg whites
- ¾ teaspoon cream of tartar
- ½ teaspoon salt
- 1½ cups sugar
- 1 teaspoon vanilla

FOR THE FILLING
- Fresh strawberries or peaches, sliced
- Sugar for sprinkling
- Vanilla or strawberry ice milk, softened

Preheat the oven to 500°F. Lightly coat a 10-inch springform pan or pie pan with non-stick spray and dust with flour.

In a large mixing bowl, with an electric mixer or a balloon whisk, beat the egg whites until foamy. Add the cream of tartar and salt. Beat until the whites are very stiff. On low speed, add the sugar, a tablespoon at a time. Add the vanilla. Turn into the prepared pan.

Place in the oven and turn the oven off immediately. Leave in the oven for 12 hours or overnight without opening the door.

To serve, remove the torte from the baking pan if using a springform pan. If you baked the torte in a pie pan, you can leave the torte right in the pan and fill with fruit. Sprinkle with sugar to taste. Pass the softened ice milk for each guest to spoon over servings of the torte.

MAKES 8 SERVINGS

PER SERVING: *231 calories, 6% calories from fat, 1.55 g fat, 4.5 mg cholesterol, 195 mg sodium, 0.97 g dietary fiber*

Pear and Apple Torte

This is such a delicious, quick, and easy dessert, you'll want to remember it when your time is short. If you leave out the nuts, the calorie count drops to 120 per serving, the fat grams to less than one, and the percentage of calories from fat to 6.

- 1 large egg, lightly beaten
- ¾ cup sugar
- 1 teaspoon vanilla
- ½ cup all-purpose flour
- 1 teaspoon baking powder
- ¼ teaspoon salt
- 1 teaspoon ground cinnamon
- ½ cup chopped walnuts or pecans (optional)
- 1 medium pear, peeled, cored, and chopped
- 1 medium-size tart apple, peeled, cored, and chopped
- Frozen nonfat vanilla yogurt, softened, for serving

Preheat the oven to 350°F. Lightly grease a 9-inch pie pan or coat with nonstick spray.

In a large mixing bowl, combine the egg, sugar, vanilla, flour, baking powder, salt, cinnamon, nuts, pear, and apple. With a wooden spoon, stir about 25 strokes, until blended. The mixture will be stiff. Scrape the mixture into the prepared pan and press down to level it into the pan.

Bake for 30 minutes, or until the torte is browned and slightly puffed. To serve, cut into wedges and top with softened vanilla frozen yogurt, if desired.

MAKES 8 SERVINGS

PER SERVING: *178 calories, 27% calories from fat, 5.47 g fat, 26.6 mg cholesterol, 117 mg sodium, 1.54 g dietary fiber*

Italian Plum Cake

Italian prune plums are perfect in this world-favorite dessert. The leftovers are wonderful for breakfast!

1 cup all-purpose flour

1 teaspoon baking powder

⅛ teaspoon salt

5 tablespoons unsalted butter, at room temperature

1 cup sugar

2 large eggs, at room temperature

1 pound Italian prune plums (about 12), halved and pitted

Preheat the oven to 375°F. Lightly grease or coat with nonstick spray a 10-inch springform pan or an 11-inch tart pan with a removable bottom and dust lightly with flour.

In a small bowl, mix the flour, baking powder, and salt. In a large bowl, cream the butter with ¾ cup of the sugar until well blended. Add the eggs and beat until light and fluffy. Stir in the flour mixture until well blended.

Spread the batter evenly into the prepared pan. Arrange the plums with their cut sides down on top of the dough in the pan. Sprinkle with the remaining ¼ cup sugar.

Bake for 50 to 55 minutes, or until a wooden skewer inserted into the center of the cake comes out clean. Cool on a wire rack.

MAKES 8 SERVINGS

PER SERVING: *262 calories, 30% calories from fat, 8.93 g fat, 72.7 mg cholesterol, 58.6 mg sodium, 1.49 g dietary fiber*

Rum Yeast-Cake Ring

A takeoff on the classic baba au rhum, this yeast-based batter cake is really simple to stir up and is the very best served warm. As with most yeast-based doughs, tenderness really doesn't depend on added fat. The small amount of butter that's added here is just for flavor. Soaked in a rum syrup and topped with a caramel-rum glaze, this cake goes well with fresh fruit and softened nonfat ice cream.

- **1 tablespoon (1 package) active dry yeast**
- **1/4 cup warm water (105°F. to 115°F.)**
- **3/4 cup nonfat sour cream**
- **1 large egg, lightly beaten**
- **2 tablespoons unsalted butter, melted**
- **2 cups all-purpose flour**
- **1/3 cup sugar**
- **1 teaspoon salt**

RUM SYRUP

- **1/2 cup water**
- **1/2 cup sugar**
- **4 tablespoons light or dark rum**

CARAMEL RUM GLAZE

- **2 tablespoons unsalted butter**
- **1/4 cup packed brown sugar**
- **1/4 cup evaporated skimmed milk or fat-free half-and-half**
- **1 cup confectioners' sugar**
- **1 to 2 tablespoons light or dark rum**

FOR SERVING

Fresh fruit or berries

Vanilla- or fruit-flavored nonfat ice milk, softened

In a large mixing bowl, dissolve the yeast in the warm water. Let stand 5 minutes, until the yeast is dissolved and begins to foam. Add the sour cream, egg, and butter; mix well. In another bowl, sift the flour, sugar, and salt together, and add half the mixture to the yeast mixture. With an electric mixer, beat at medium speed for 2 minutes. With a wooden spoon, stir in the remaining flour mixture until the batter is smooth and satiny.

Cover the bowl and let the dough rise for 1 hour, or until doubled in bulk.

Lightly grease a 6 1/2-cup ring mold or coat with nonstick spray. Beat the risen batter down and spoon evenly into the mold. Cover and let rise in a warm place until almost doubled, about 1 hour.

Preheat the oven to 350°F. Bake for 20 to 25 minutes, or until a wooden skewer inserted into the cake comes out clean.

While the cake bakes, make the rum syrup: Combine the water and sugar and bring to a boil. Boil 1 minute, or until the sugar is dissolved. Remove from the heat and add the rum.

To make the caramel rum glaze, in a saucepan, combine the butter, brown sugar, and milk. Heat to boiling, stirring, and cook for 1 minute. Remove from the heat and stir in the confectioners' sugar until a smooth, slightly thin icing is formed. Stir in the rum.

Pierce the hot cake, still in the pan, in 1-inch intervals with a skewer or a fork. Spoon the syrup over the cake, waiting for each spoonful to be absorbed before adding another. Let stand 10 minutes, then invert the cake onto a serving plate. Spoon the glaze over. Serve with fresh fruit and slightly softened nonfat ice milk.

MAKES 10 SERVINGS

PER SERVING: *293 calories, 17% calories from fat, 5.35 g fat, 34 mg cholesterol, 231 mg sodium, 0.86 g dietary fiber*

Strawberry Shortcake

Trimmed of 250 calories and 20 grams of fat, strawberry shortcake is on our menu again! Besides cutting the amount of butter in the shortcake itself, we now top it with softened nonfat frozen yogurt.

2 cups all-purpose flour

¾ cup sugar

3 teaspoons baking powder

¼ teaspoon salt

⅔ cup evaporated skimmed milk

5 tablespoons unsalted butter, melted

2 teaspoons vanilla

1 large egg, lightly beaten

6 cups sliced fresh strawberries

TOPPING

1 pint vanilla-flavored nonfat frozen yogurt

2 teaspoons vanilla

Preheat the oven to 375°F. Lightly grease a 9-inch round cake pan or coat with nonstick spray. Dust the pan with flour.

In a large bowl, combine the flour, ½ cup of the sugar, the baking powder, and the salt. Add the milk, butter, vanilla, and egg and lightly stir just until the dry ingredients are moistened. Spoon into the prepared pan.

Bake for 20 minutes, or until a toothpick inserted into the center of the cake comes out clean and dry. Turn the cake out of the pan and cool on a wire rack. Split the cake in half horizontally.

While the cake bakes, stir the strawberries with the remaining ¼ cup sugar in a bowl.

Place one half of the cake on a serving plate and top with half of the strawberries. Top the berries with the second half of the cake. Top with the remaining berries.

Before serving, soften the frozen yogurt and place it in a bowl. With an electric mixer, beat in the vanilla. Spoon the yogurt over individual servings of the shortcake.

MAKES 12 SERVINGS

PER SERVING: *232 calories, 22% calories from fat, 5.7 g fat, 31.2 mg cholesterol, 172 mg sodium, 2.45 g dietary fiber*

No-Fat Berries-and-Cream Shortcake

Corn syrup replaces the fat in this tender cake, which has a fine and even texture and forms a perfect base for berries. The simple, creamy topping is based on nonfat frozen ice cream or yogurt.

1½ cups cake flour

¾ cup sugar

2 teaspoons baking powder

½ teaspoon salt

2 large egg whites

¾ cup skim milk

½ cup light corn syrup

2 teaspoons vanilla

2 cups fresh berries, such as sliced strawberries, raspberries, or a combination

TO SERVE

1 pint vanilla nonfat ice cream or frozen yogurt, softened

2 tablespoons orange-flavored liqueur (optional)

Preheat the oven to 350°F. Coat a 9-inch square pan with nonstick spray.

Sift the cake flour, sugar, baking powder, and salt into a medium bowl. In another bowl, mix the egg whites, milk, corn syrup, and vanilla. Add the liquid ingredients to the dry ingredients and beat until smooth. Pour the batter into the prepared pan. Bake for 25 to 30 minutes, or until a toothpick inserted in the center comes out clean. Place the pan on a wire rack to cool.

Cut the cake into 9 equal squares. Split each square in half horizontally. Place the bottom halves on dessert plates and top with the berries, then with the top halves. Mix the softened nonfat ice cream with the orange-flavored liqueur, if desired, and spoon the sauce over the top of each serving.

MAKES 9 SERVINGS

PER SERVING: *244 calories, 1% calories from fat, 0.32 g fat, 0.33 mg cholesterol, 253 mg sodium, 1.37 mg dietary fiber*

COBBLERS,
CRISPS,
AND PUDDINGS

Cobblers, crisps, and baked puddings are down-home comfort desserts based on utilizing the abundance of fruits in season. You can combine fruits in season, or stick to just one variety. Some wonderful natural combinations are rhubarb and strawberry, blueberry and peach, or apples and pears. All of the combinations can be topped with a crunchy crumb mixture, a simple biscuit, or an easy-to-mix batter. The fruit beneath bakes into saucy deliciousness with minimal additional ingredients. Instead of whipped cream as a topping, I enjoy using the wide variety of high-quality nonfat ice milks and frozen yogurts that are available, slightly softened and spooned over a freshly baked crisp, cobbler, or pudding. I can't think of anything I enjoy more for dessert.

TIPS FOR STORING COBBLERS, CRISPS, AND PUDDINGS

1. To bake and keep cobblers, crisps, and puddings for serving a day or two later, let them cool completely and wrap them in an airtight container, then freeze.

2. I like to store extra freezable desserts in individually portioned dishes or cups, wrapped airtight in plastic or foil, in the freezer. Then I can remove as many servings as I wish and thaw them quickly in the microwave.

Berry Cobbler

Y*ou can use whatever berries are in season or frozen berries when the season is past. This dessert, which consists of fruit with a biscuit topping, used to be made on top of the stove. There were all kinds of funny names for cobblers in early American days, such as grunts and slumps, depending on where in the New World you lived.*

- **4 cups (1 quart) raspberries, blackberries, olallieberries, blueberries, or a combination of the four**
- **3 to 4 tablespoons cornstarch**
- **1 cup sugar**
- **1 tablespoon fresh lemon juice**
- **1¾ cups all-purpose flour**
- **1½ teaspoons baking powder**
- **½ teaspoon baking soda**
- **½ teaspoon salt**
- **6 tablespoons (¾ stick) unsalted butter, chilled and cut into pieces**
- **¼ cup hot water**
- **Nonfat vanilla frozen yogurt or light ice cream for serving**

Preheat the oven to 400°F.

In a large glass bowl, combine the berries with the cornstarch, ½ cup of the sugar, and lemon juice. Cover and cook in the microwave oven at high power for 10 minutes, or until the berries are cooked and the juices are thickened. Or place the mixture in a saucepan, add ¼ cup water, and place over medium heat. Cook, stirring, until the mixture comes to a boil and thickens. Turn the mixture into a 2½ to 3-quart shallow casserole.

In a mixing bowl, combine the flour, remaining ½ cup sugar, baking powder, baking soda, and salt. Mix in the butter until blended and the mixture resembles moist crumbs. Add the hot water and stir just until a soft dough forms. Drop spoonfuls of the dough onto the hot fruit mixture. Bake for 20 to 25 minutes, or until the topping is lightly browned. Serve warm with frozen vanilla yogurt or light ice cream.

MAKES 8 SERVINGS

P*ER SERVING: 314 calories, 26% calories from fat, 9.15 g fat, 23.3 mg cholesterol, 253 mg sodium, 2.66 g dietary fiber*

Apple-Raspberry Cobbler

The raspberries give the apples a pretty, rosy color, and since frozen berries are an option, you can make this dessert year round.

4 teaspoons cornstarch

¾ cup sugar

1 cup fresh raspberries or 1 (10-ounce) package frozen whole berries, thawed and drained

2 medium-size tart apples, such as Pippin or Granny Smith, peeled, cored, and diced

1 tablespoon fresh lemon juice

1¾ cups all-purpose flour

1½ teaspoons baking powder

½ teaspoon baking soda

½ teaspoon salt

6 tablespoons (¾ stick) unsalted butter, chilled and cut into pieces

¼ cup hot water

Nonfat vanilla frozen yogurt or light ice cream for serving

Preheat the oven to 400°F. In a medium saucepan, combine the cornstarch, ¼ cup of the sugar, raspberries, apples, and lemon juice. Cook for 3 to 5 minutes, stirring, until the apples are just tender and the juices are thickened. Pour the fruit mixture into an ungreased 2-quart shallow baking dish.

In a mixing bowl, combine the flour, the remaining ½ cup sugar, the baking powder, baking soda, and the salt. Mix in the butter until blended and the mixture resembles moist crumbs. Add the hot water and stir just until a soft dough forms. Drop spoonfuls of the dough onto the hot fruit mixture. Bake for 20 to 25

minutes, or until the topping is lightly browned and the juices are bubbling. Serve warm with vanilla frozen yogurt or light ice cream.

MAKES 8 SERVINGS

PER SERVING: 330 calories, 24% calories from fat, 9.15 g fat, 23.3 mg cholesterol, 216 mg sodium, 2.95 g dietary fiber

Summer Fruit Cobbler

The "soft" fruits of summer have a natural affinity to one another and are very appealing baked into this new old-fashioned dessert.

1¼ cups sugar

¼ cup cornstarch

2 cups peeled and sliced fresh nectarines or peaches

2 cups peeled, cored, and sliced fresh pears

2 cups pitted and sliced fresh plums

1¾ cups all-purpose flour

2 teaspoons baking powder

½ teaspoon salt

6 tablespoons (¾ stick) unsalted butter, chilled and cut into pieces

¼ cup hot water

TOPPING

½ cup nonfat sour cream

2 tablespoons brown sugar

Preheat the oven to 400°F. In a large saucepan, combine ¾ cup of the sugar, the cornstarch, and the fruit. Cook over medium heat until the mixture is hot and bubbly, stirring occasionally. Pour into an ungreased, shallow 2-quart baking dish.

In a mixing bowl, combine the flour, the remaining ½ cup sugar, the baking powder, and the salt. Mix in the butter until blended and the mixture resembles moist crumbs. Add the hot water and stir just until a soft dough forms. Drop spoonfuls of the dough onto the hot fruit mixture. Bake for 20 to 25 minutes, or until the topping is lightly browned and the juices are bubbling.

While the cobbler bakes, mix the sour cream and brown sugar. Serve the cobbler warm, topped with the sour cream mixture.

MAKES 8 SERVINGS

PER SERVING: *391 calories, 21% calories from fat, 9.45 g fat, 23.3 mg cholesterol, 154 mg sodium, 3.32 g dietary fiber*

Blueberry Peach Cobbler

Peaches and blueberries are in season at the same time in July and August. To make this cobbler, I lightened the biscuitlike dough by cutting down on the shortening and by using nonfat sour cream instead of cream.

3 pounds fresh peaches, peeled, pitted, and sliced (about 6 cups)

1 pint fresh blueberries, washed

¾ cup plus 1 tablespoon sugar

6 tablespoons (¾ stick) unsalted butter, chilled

2 cups all-purpose flour

1 tablespoon baking powder

½ teaspoon salt

1 cup nonfat sour cream

Nonfat vanilla ice cream (optional)

Preheat the oven to 400°F. Lightly grease a 2½-quart baking dish or coat with nonstick spray.

In a medium bowl, toss the peaches and blueberries with ¾ cup of the sugar. Turn the fruit into the baking dish. Dot with 1 tablespoon of the butter.

In another bowl, mix the flour, baking powder, salt, and the remaining 1 tablespoon sugar. Cut in the remaining 5 tablespoons butter until the mixture resembles coarse meal. With a fork, stir in the sour cream until the dough holds together like pie pastry. Shape the dough into a ball and place it on a sheet of well-floured wax paper or plastic wrap. Pat it into the shape that matches the top of the baking dish you are using, then dust the dough with flour and lightly roll it out to cover the fruit. Using the paper or plastic as a carrier, place the dough on the fruit, paper or plastic side up. Carefully remove the paper or plastic. Pat the dough into place and pierce several times with the tip of a knife.

Bake for 30 minutes, or until the pastry is golden brown and the juices are bubbling. Let cool for 15 minutes. Serve warm with nonfat vanilla ice cream, if desired.

MAKES 8 SERVINGS

PER SERVING: *378 calories, 21% calories from fat, 9.2 g fat, 23.3 mg cholesterol, 394 mg sodium, 4.68 g dietary fiber*

Maple Apple Crisp

Softened nonfat or low-fat vanilla or mocha frozen yogurt is wonderful over this dessert.

3 pounds tart, firm apples, such as Granny Smith or Golden Delicious, peeled, cored, and cut into ½-inch wedges

1 tablespoon fresh lemon juice

¼ cup pure maple syrup

½ cup all-purpose flour

½ cup whole wheat flour

¼ cup old-fashioned rolled oats

1 tablespoon ground cinnamon

¼ teaspoon ground ginger

¾ cup packed light brown sugar

6 tablespoons (¾ stick) unsalted butter, chilled and cut into small pieces

Nonfat vanilla or mocha frozen yogurt (optional)

Preheat the oven to 375°F. Coat an 8-inch square baking pan with nonstick spray.

Combine the apples in a large mixing bowl with the lemon juice and maple syrup.

In another large bowl, combine the flours, oats, cinnamon, ginger, and brown sugar. With an electric mixer, blend in the butter until the mixture is crumbly.

Place 1 cup of the crumb mixture in the bottom of the baking pan and press it into an even layer. Bake for 10 minutes. Remove from the oven.

Arrange the apple slices on top of the baked crust. Drizzle any juices over the apples. Sprinkle the remaining crumb mixture over the apples.

Bake for 35 to 45 minutes, until the top is browned and the apples are tender. Serve warm with softened vanilla or mocha frozen yogurt, if desired.

MAKES 8 SERVINGS

PER SERVING: *342 calories, 24% calories from fat, 9.55 g fat, 23.3 mg cholesterol, 13.4 mg sodium, 5.26 g dietary fiber*

Blueberry Buckle

The original recipe for my favorite buckle has twice the amount of butter in it. In order to retain the tenderness of the cakelike base to the buckle, I used fat-free sour cream here and added just a tablespoon of melted butter. The remaining butter gives the crumb topping crispness. This small change brought the percentage of fat down to 24 and the grams of fat per serving down to 6.72.

- ½ cup sugar
- 1 tablespoon unsalted butter, melted
- ½ cup fat-free sour cream
- 1 large egg, beaten
- 1 teaspoon vanilla
- 1 cup all-purpose flour
- 1 teaspoon baking powder
- ¼ teaspoon salt
- 2 cups fresh blueberries or frozen unsweetened blueberries

CRUMB TOPPING

- ½ cup sugar
- ⅓ cup all-purpose flour
- ½ teaspoon ground cinnamon
- ⅛ teaspoon ground nutmeg
- 3 tablespoons unsalted butter, melted

Preheat the oven to 375°F. Lightly grease a 9-inch square pan or coat it with nonstick spray.

In a mixing bowl, stir the sugar, butter, sour cream, egg, and vanilla together. Combine the flour, baking powder, and salt in another bowl and add to the egg mixture. Spread the mixture in the prepared pan. Top with the blueberries.

To make the topping, combine the sugar, flour, cinnamon, nutmeg, and butter together until the mixture is crumbly. Sprinkle the topping evenly over the blueberries. Bake for 40 minutes, or until the blueberries are bubbly and the topping is lightly browned.

MAKES 8 SERVINGS

PER SERVING: 251 calories, 24% calories from fat, 6.72 g fat, 42.3 mg cholesterol, 125 mg sodium, 1.49 g dietary fiber

Farm-Style Baked Peach Pudding

Some old-fashioned desserts like this pudding never depended on fat for flavor, especially when peaches were fresh and in season. You can use whole milk or low-fat milk, if you wish, without adding significantly to the percentage of fat in your dessert.

5 large peaches, peeled and quartered

1 tablespoon fresh lemon juice

⅔ cup skim milk

⅓ cup plus 2 tablespoons sugar

⅓ cup all-purpose flour

2 large eggs, lightly beaten

1 teaspoon vanilla

1 teaspoon ground cinnamon

1 tablespoon unsalted butter, chilled and cut into tiny pieces

Maple syrup for serving

Preheat the oven to 425°F. Lightly grease a 9-inch square pan or coat with nonstick spray.

In a large bowl, toss the peaches with the lemon juice. Arrange the peach quarters in the pan.

In a blender, combine the milk, ⅓ cup of the sugar, flour, eggs, and vanilla and process until combined. Pour the batter over the peaches. In a small bowl, combine the remaining 2 tablespoons sugar with the cinnamon and sprinkle the mixture on top of the batter. Dot with the butter. Bake for 40 to 45 minutes, or until the top is golden and the pudding is set. Serve warm with maple syrup.

MAKES 6 SERVINGS

PER SERVING: *196 calories, 19% calories from fat, 4.23 g fat, 76.7 mg cholesterol, 36.9 mg sodium, 2.4 g dietary fiber*

Blueberry Baked Indian Pudding

This simple, earthy pudding, a perfect ending to an autumn meal, is usually served with plain vanilla ice cream. Nonfat frozen yogurt or light ice cream keeps it within the boundaries of 30 percent of calories or less from fat. This is wonderful made with fresh wild blueberries, but when they're not available, you can use dried or frozen blueberries.

1 cup fresh or frozen blueberries or ½ cup dried blueberries

2 cups skim milk

¼ cup sugar

¼ cup stone-ground white cornmeal

1 large egg, lightly beaten

1 teaspoon grated orange zest

½ teaspoon ground ginger

¼ teaspoon ground cinnamon

½ teaspoon salt

¼ cup light molasses

¼ cup packed brown sugar

Preheat the oven to 300°F. Lightly grease a 1½-quart baking dish or coat with nonstick spray. Pour the blueberries into the pan and spread them out evenly.

In a heavy saucepan, mix the milk with the sugar. Place over medium-high heat and stir until the milk is simmering; gradually sprinkle in the cornmeal and whisk until smooth.

In a small bowl, whisk the egg, orange zest, ginger, cinnamon, salt, molasses, and brown sugar together. Whisk in a small amount of the cornmeal mixture. Return the whole mixture to the saucepan and stir to blend. Pour the mixture into the prepared baking dish over the berries. Bake for 45 to 55 minutes, or until a knife inserted into the center of the pudding comes out clean.

MAKES 4 SERVINGS

PER SERVING: *256 calories, 15% calories from fat, 1.75 g fat, 55.2 mg cholesterol, 90.1 mg sodium, 1.61 g dietary fiber*

Apricot-Apple-Raisin Crisp Squares

A *fruit filling made with a mixture of dried fruits, sandwiched between crispy oat layers, makes this a wholesome and delicious dessert.*

1½ **cups raisins**

1 **cup dried apples, chopped**

½ **cup dried apricots, finely chopped**

½ **cup sugar**

2 **tablespoons fresh lemon juice**

2 **tablespoons cornstarch**

1 **teaspoon ground cinnamon**

¼ **teaspoon ground nutmeg**

¼ **teaspoon ground ginger**

2 **cups water**

¾ **cup (1½ sticks) unsalted butter, at room temperature**

1 **cup packed brown sugar**

1½ **cups all-purpose flour**

½ **teaspoon baking powder**

½ **teaspoon salt**

1½ **cups quick-cooking rolled oats**

Combine the raisins, apples, apricots, sugar, lemon juice, cornstarch, cinnamon, nutmeg, ginger, and water in a 2-quart saucepan. Place over medium heat and heat to simmering; cook 5 minutes, stirring, until the mixture is thickened. Remove from the heat and cool.

Preheat the oven to 375°F. Coat a 13 × 9-inch baking pan with nonstick spray.

In a large mixing bowl, with an electric mixer, cream the butter and brown sugar. Place a wire sieve over the top of the bowl and measure in the flour, baking powder, and salt. Stir until the dry ingredients are sifted into the bowl. Stir in the rolled oats.

Pat half of the oat mixture into the prepared pan. Spoon the cooled fruit mixture over the top evenly. Top with the remaining oat mixture, spreading it evenly. Pat down with the back of a spoon. Bake for 22 to 25 minutes, until firm in the center and the topping is crisp. Cool completely. Cut into 2-inch squares.

MAKES 24 SQUARES

PER SQUARE: *194 calories, 28% calories from fat, 6.21 g fat, 15.5 mg cholesterol, 61.1 mg sodium, 2.0 g dietary fiber*

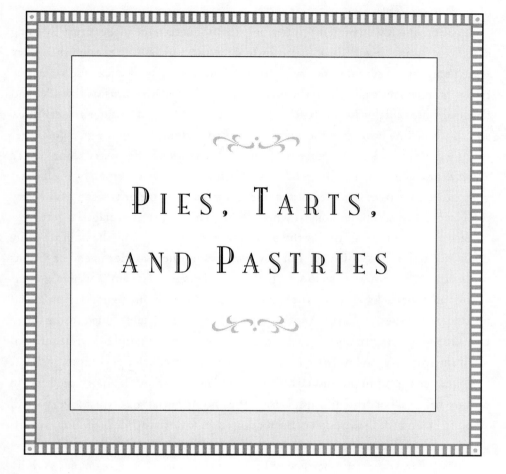

PIES, TARTS, AND PASTRIES

Pies, tarts, and pastries present a special challenge in low-fat baking. A basic pie pastry is made with one part of fat to three parts of flour by measure and just enough water is added to bind the ingredients. This standard pastry recipe offers 60 percent of its calories from fat.

A flour that is low in protein (gluten) helps to produce a more tender crust. By using cake flour, I was able to reduce the fat by more than half, but even though the pastry wasn't tough, the flavor was "floury." By adding a little low-fat cream cheese to the pastry, I was able to return flavor to the final product. The resulting crust was tender and flavorful, but not flaky. To remedy this, I used the old-fashioned "cheater's pastry" idea: add a little baking powder to the mixture. The final formula brings the grams of fat per serving down to 4.3, or 35 percent of the total calories for the pastry alone. That's about as low as you can go. The good news is that pastry is never served by itself if it is going to be a pie or a tart. The bottom line is that a slice of pie or tart can have a very respectable total of calories from fat when all the components are averaged together.

Pastry based on solid fat isn't the only choice we have. Phyllo, the delicate, thin, nonfat strudel pastry, which you can buy frozen, is another wonderful choice. Crusts made of crumb mixtures from low-fat graham crackers, low-fat vanilla wafers, gingersnaps, and zwiebacks are always delicious and easy to make and do not depend on fat for their tenderness or flavor. Another delicious choice is a meringue crust made of egg whites beaten with sugar into stiff peaks, spread into a pan, and baked either until totally crisp (as in a Pavlova) or to make a soft meringue cradle for pie fillings.

To reduce the fat in pie and tart fillings, I use nonfat or low-fat dairy products in creamy fillings. For fruit fillings, I use either no butter at all or just a very small amount. I found that a teaspoon of butter dotted on top of an apple pie filling is as satisfying as two tablespoons!

Unfortunately, we must sacrifice whipped cream toppings for cream pies. A fluffy meringue will appeal to the eye, but, alas, nothing can really replace the richness of whipped cream—although a dollop of low-fat frozen yogurt or ice milk is excellent consolation.

Most of the pies in this chapter can be made ahead and refrigerated before serving. Meringue-crusted pies can be made ahead and frozen, but I find the flavor and texture are best if they are still slightly frozen when they are served. Meringue shells will weep when totally thawed.

Lemon Berry Pie

This pie is best if eaten the same day you assemble it. To make the components ahead of time, bake the meringue shell, and when it is completely cooled, slip the shell, pan and all, into a large plastic bag, seal well, and freeze. The lemon filling can be made ahead, covered, and refrigerated for up to two days. The berries are best when absolutely fresh.

MERINGUE SHELL

3 large egg whites, at room temperature

1/4 teaspoon cream of tartar

Dash of salt

3/4 cup sugar

1/2 teaspoon vanilla

LEMON FILLING

3/4 cup sugar

3 tablespoons cornstarch

1/4 teaspoon salt

3/4 cup water

2 tablespoons grated lemon zest

6 tablespoons fresh lemon juice

2 teaspoons unsalted butter

BERRY FILLING

2 cups sliced strawberries, raspberries, or blackberries, or a combination

3/4 cup blueberries

3 tablespoons red currant jelly

1 teaspoon orange liqueur or orange juice

Fresh mint leaves (optional)

Preheat the oven to 275°F. Coat a 9-inch pie pan with nonstick spray and dust it lightly with flour.

To make the meringue shell, in a mixing bowl, beat the egg whites, cream of tartar, and salt until soft peaks form. Gradually add the sugar and beat until stiff peaks form. Add the vanilla; beat well. Spread the meringue over the bottom and sides of the prepared pan, building up the sides as high as possible. Bake for 1 hour. Turn the oven off. Let stand in the oven with the door closed for 1 hour or overnight.

For the lemon filling, combine the sugar, cornstarch, salt, and water in a 2-quart saucepan (see Note). Stir over medium heat until the mixture comes to a boil; boil 1 minute, stirring. Remove from the heat and add the lemon zest, lemon juice, and butter. Cover and refrigerate until cool.

Up to 2 hours before serving, pour the lemon filling into the meringue shell. Arrange the strawberries and blueberries over the lemon filling. In a small saucepan, heat the jelly and liqueur; cool slightly and drizzle over the fruit. Garnish with mint leaves, if desired. Store in the refrigerator.

MAKES 6 GENEROUS SERVINGS

PER SERVING: *272 calories, 5% calories from fat, 1.54 g fat, 3.54 mg cholesterol, 68.5 mg sodium, 1.87 g dietary fiber*

NOTE: To cook the filling in a microwave oven, combine the sugar, cornstarch, salt, and water in a microwave-safe bowl and stir well. Microwave at high power for 5 minutes, stirring once or twice, or until the mixture comes to a boil. Add the remaining ingredients and refrigerate, covered, until completely cool.

Strawberry Pie

Strawberry-glazed strawberry pie is a real spring-time treat.

PASTRY

1 cup all-purpose flour

1 tablespoon cornstarch

¼ teaspoon salt

4 tablespoons canola or corn oil

3 tablespoons cold water

FILLING

6 cups (3 pints) fresh strawberries, stemmed and cleaned

1 cup sugar

1 teaspoon fresh lemon juice

3 tablespoons cornstarch

½ cup water

1 pint vanilla nonfat frozen yogurt, softened

Preheat the oven to 425°F. Lightly grease a 9-inch pie pan or coat with nonstick spray. Dust with flour.

To make the pastry, in a small bowl, stir the flour, cornstarch, and salt together. In another bowl, combine the oil and water. With a fork, stir the liquid ingredients into the dry ingredients until the mixture resembles the texture of cottage cheese. Press the crumbs onto the bottom and sides of the pie pan. Bake for 10 to 12 minutes, or until lightly browned. Cool on a wire rack.

For the filling, in a small bowl, mash enough of the berries to make 1 cup. Cut the remaining berries in half. In a small saucepan, combine the crushed berries with the sugar, lemon juice, cornstarch, and water. Cook over medium heat, stirring constantly, until the mixture comes to a boil, about 4 minutes. Reduce the heat to low and cook until thickened and clear, about 2 minutes. Remove from the heat and let the mixture cool slightly.

Fill the baked crust with the halved berries, cut side down, and pour the cooked berry mixture over the top. Refrigerate until set, about 3 hours. Serve topped with frozen yogurt.

MAKES 8 SERVINGS

PER SERVING: *299 calories, 22% calories from fat, 7.37 g fat, 0 mg cholesterol, 36 mg sodium, 3.33 g dietary fiber*

Summertime Peach and Blueberry Pie

Here's another great single-crust pie made with my low-fat cream cheese pastry. I added a little sugar to the crust to further bring out the flavor of the fruit. Because of the sugar, the pastry can be slightly tacky to roll out, so I like to chill and roll out the dough between sheets of plastic wrap. The streusel topping replaces a rich top crust, and the filling, a combination of fresh peaches and blueberries, is one of my favorites.

PASTRY

1½ cups cake flour

½ teaspoon baking powder

¼ teaspoon salt

1 tablespoon sugar

2 tablespoons unsalted butter, chilled and cut into ¼-inch slices

3 tablespoons low-fat cream cheese, well chilled

2 teaspoons lemon juice

About 4 tablespoons ice water

FILLING

4 cups fresh peeled, sliced peaches

3 cups (1½ pints) fresh blueberries

1 cup sugar

3 tablespoons fresh lemon juice

3 tablespoons cornstarch

1 teaspoon grated lemon zest

½ teaspoon salt

STREUSEL TOPPING

½ cup all-purpose flour

⅓ cup packed brown sugar

¼ teaspoon salt

¼ teaspoon ground cinnamon

2 tablespoons unsalted butter, melted

Preheat the oven to 400°F. Coat a 9-inch pie pan with nonstick spray.

To make the pastry, measure the flour, baking powder, salt, and sugar into the work bowl of a food processor. Cut the butter and cream cheese into pieces and add to the flour. Pulse 10 to 15 times until the mixture resembles very coarse crumbs. Turn the mixture into a mixing bowl. Mix the lemon juice with 2 tablespoons of the water and sprinkle over the dry ingredients. With a fork, stir the mixture until the dry ingredients are moistened, adding water, if necessary, until the dough is no longer dry and crumbly. It should hold together when you pinch a small amount between your fingers. Gather the dough into a ball and press it into a disk 4 inches in diameter.

Place the dough between two sheets of plastic wrap and, with a rolling pin, roll out to a 13-inch diameter to fit the bottom and sides of the pie pan. Remove the top sheet of plastic wrap and center the pastry, dough side down, on the pie pan. Remove the top piece of plastic wrap. Fit the dough into the pie pan without stretching it. Fold the edges under and crimp. Chill 15 minutes.

To make the filling, in a bowl, combine the peaches, blueberries, sugar, lemon juice, cornstarch, lemon zest, and salt. Turn the mixture into the pastry shell.

For the streusel topping, in a small bowl, combine the flour, brown sugar, salt, cinnamon, and butter until crumbly. Sprinkle this mixture over the peach and blueberry filling.

Bake for 45 to 55 minutes, until the pastry is browned and the filling is bubbly. Remove from the oven and cool on a wire rack.

MAKES 8 SERVINGS

PER SERVING: *370 calories, 11% calories from fat, 4.68 g fat, 11.9 mg cholesterol, 120 mg sodium, 3.78 g dietary fiber*

Open-Faced Blueberry Pie

I have reduced the fat in the pastry for this single-crust pie, but to compensate I've added a bit of baking powder to lighten and leaven it. The filling is a combination of both cooked and fresh blueberries, so this pie is one to make in the late summer when the berries are in season. The pie is best when served the day it is assembled. To make ahead, bake the pie shell, cover, and keep in a cool place, and cook the filling, cover, and refrigerate. Up to 4 hours before serving, assemble and refrigerate the pie to keep the crust as tender as possible.

PASTRY

1⅓ cups all-purpose flour

½ teaspoon baking powder

1 tablespoon sugar

¼ teaspoon salt

6 tablespoons (¾ stick) unsalted butter, chilled and cut into ¼-inch slices

3 to 4 tablespoons ice water

FILLING

6 cups (3 pints) fresh blueberries

¼ cup water

⅔ cup sugar

3 tablespoons cornstarch

½ teaspoon ground cinnamon

Pinch of salt

Zest of 1 lemon (see Note), in strips

2 tablespoons fresh lemon juice

Preheat the oven to 400°F. Coat a 9-inch pie pan with nonstick spray.

To make the pastry, in a food processor, combine the flour, baking powder, sugar, and salt. Process 15 seconds to mix the ingredients. Add the butter and pulse 8 to 10 times, until the butter is cut into pieces no larger than ¼ inch. Turn the mixture into a mixing bowl and sprinkle with 3 tablespoons of the water. With a fork, stir the mixture until the dry ingredients are moistened, adding more water, if necessary, until the dough is no longer dry and crumbly. It should hold together when you pinch a small amount between your fingers. Gather the dough into a ball and press it into a disk 4 inches in diameter.

Place the dough between two sheets of plastic wrap and, with a rolling pin, roll out to a 13-inch diameter. Remove the top sheet of plastic wrap and center the pastry, dough side down, on the pie pan. Remove the top piece of plastic wrap. Fit the dough into the pie pan without stretching it. Fold the edges under and crimp. Chill 15 minutes.

Line the pastry with foil and fill with pie weights. Bake for 15 to 20 minutes, or until the pastry is lightly browned. Remove the foil and pie weights and cool on a wire rack.

For the filling, combine 2 cups of the blueberries and the water in a saucepan. Heat to boiling. In a small bowl, mix the sugar, cornstarch, cinnamon, and salt and stir into the boiling mixture. Stir and cook for 5 minutes, until the filling is very thick.

Meanwhile, chop half of the lemon zest and reserve the rest. Remove the filling from the heat and stir in the lemon juice and the chopped lemon zest. Cover and chill for 1 hour. Reserve 1 cup of the berries and stir the remaining berries into the cooked mixture. Pour the filling into the cooled pie shell. Top with the reserved berries and sprinkle with the reserved strips of lemon zest.

MAKES 8 SERVINGS

PER SERVING: *285 calories, 28% calories from fat, 9.23 g fat, 23.3 mg cholesterol, 96.1 mg sodium, 3.47 g dietary fiber*

NOTE: Remove the zest from the lemon using a zester, or use a vegetable peeler and cut the pieces into very thin strips.

Lemon Cake Pie

As this citrusy pie bakes, a cakelike topping forms over a sweet-tart lemon filling.

CRUST

1 cup all-purpose flour

¼ teaspoon salt

¼ cup canola oil

2 tablespoons ice water

FILLING

1 cup sugar

⅓ cup all-purpose flour

¼ teaspoon salt

½ teaspoon grated lemon zest

5 tablespoons fresh lemon juice

3 large eggs, separated

1 cup skim milk

Preheat the oven to 425°F

To make the crust, in a small bowl, stir the flour and salt together. In another bowl, combine the oil and water. With a fork, stir the liquid ingredients into the dry ingredients until the mixture resembles the texture of cottage cheese. Press the crumbs onto the bottom and sides of a 9-inch pie pan. Bake for 10 to 12 minutes, or until lightly browned. Cool on a wire rack. Reduce the oven temperature to 375°F

For the filling, in a large bowl, stir together the sugar, flour, salt, lemon zest, and lemon juice. In a small bowl, beat the egg yolks with the milk. Stir the egg mixture into the lemon mixture. In a medium bowl, beat the egg whites until they are stiff but not dry. Gently fold the egg whites into the lemon mixture.

Pour the filling into the pastry shell. Bake for 45 to 55 minutes, or until the top and center feel set when lightly touched. Cool on a wire rack. Serve at room temperature.

MAKES 8 SERVINGS

PER SERVING: *265 calories, 30% calories from fat, 8.93 g fat, 80.4 mg cholesterol, 106 mg sodium, 0.51 g dietary fiber*

Lemon Meringue Pie

"Mile-high" pies always fascinated me as a young cook. I would use double the amount of egg whites to make a huge mountain of meringue on top of my favorite lemony meringue pie. I've always added much more butter to the filling, but now I've cut that down to 2 teaspoons, which is just enough to smooth out the flavor and texture.

PASTRY

1 cup all-purpose flour

1 tablespoon cornstarch

¼ teaspoon salt

4 tablespoons canola or corn oil

3 tablespoons cold water

FILLING

1½ cups sugar

6 tablespoons cornstarch

¼ teaspoon salt

1¼ cups cold water

½ cup fresh lemon juice

3 large egg yolks, beaten

2 teaspoons unsalted butter

1 teaspoon grated lemon zest

MERINGUE

6 large egg whites

½ teaspoon cream of tartar

¾ cup sugar

Preheat the oven to 425°F. Lightly grease a 9-inch pie pan or coat with nonstick spray. Dust with flour.

To make the pastry, in a small bowl, stir the flour, cornstarch, and salt together. In another bowl, combine the oil and water. With a fork, stir the liquid ingredients into the dry ingredients until the mixture resembles the texture of cottage cheese. Press the crumbs onto the bottom and sides of the pie pan. Bake for 10 to 12 minutes, or until lightly browned. Cool on a wire rack. Reduce the oven temperature to 350°F.

For the filling, mix the sugar, cornstarch, salt, and water in a heavy saucepan. Place over medium-high heat and cook, stirring with a whisk, until the mixture comes to a boil. Boil for 1 minute. Beat the lemon juice and egg yolks in a small bowl. Add a small amount of the boiling mixture to the egg yolk mixture; mix quickly and well, then pour the mixture back into the saucepan and mix well. Cook 1 minute and add the butter and lemon zest. Pour the hot mixture into the baked pie shell. Let stand, allowing a thin film to form on the top, while preparing the meringue.

For the meringue, beat the egg whites until frothy. Add the cream of tartar and beat until stiff. Gradually beat the sugar into the egg whites until smooth and glossy. Spread the meringue over the pie. Use a narrow spatula to gently push the meringue against the inner edge of the pie crust, sealing it well. Cover the rest of the filling by swirling the meringue from the edge of the pie to the center, forming a large "mountainlike" peak in the center. Bake for 12 to 15 minutes, or until light golden brown. Cool completely on a wire rack. When cutting the pie, use a sharp knife and dip it into hot water after each cut, to make clean-cut servings.

MAKES 8 SERVINGS

PER SERVING: *394 calories, 22% calories from fat, 9.84 g fat, 82.5 mg cholesterol, 179 mg sodium, 0.51 g dietary fiber*

Pineapple Pie

Using new nonfat and low-fat dairy products, I've found it simple to revamp some of my favorite old-fashioned treats—like this creamy pie. Without the fat, the flavor of the pineapple is clearer, more pronounced. A touch of aniseed in the easy, press-in pastry further emphasizes the flavor of the filling.

ANISEED CRUST

1 cup all-purpose flour

1 tablespoon cornstarch

½ teaspoon salt

½ teaspoon aniseed

4 tablespoons canola or corn oil

3 tablespoons cold water

SPONGE FILLING

2 large eggs, separated

1 (14-ounce) can low-fat condensed (not evaporated) milk

1 (8-ounce) can crushed pineapple, packed in its own juice

2 tablespoons all-purpose flour

2 teaspoons grated lemon zest

1 large egg white

Preheat the oven to 425°F. Lightly grease a 9-inch pie pan or coat with nonstick spray. Dust with flour.

To make the crust, in a small bowl, stir the flour, cornstarch, salt, and aniseed together. In another bowl, combine the oil and water. With a fork, stir the liquid ingredients into the dry ingredients until the mixture resembles the texture of cottage cheese. Press the crumbs onto the bottom and sides of the pie pan. Bake for 10 to 12 minutes, or until lightly browned.

Cool on a wire rack. Reduce the oven temperature to 350°F.

For the filling, in a large mixing bowl, combine the egg yolks; condensed milk; pineapple, including the juices; flour; and lemon zest. In a small bowl, beat the 3 egg whites until stiff but not dry. Fold the whites into the pineapple mixture. Pour into the prepared pastry shell. Bake 25 to 30 minutes, or until just set. Cool. Serve warm or chilled.

MAKES 8 SERVINGS

PER SERVING: *312 calories, 30% calories from fat, 10.2 g fat, 59.6 mg cholesterol, 207 mg sodium, 0.73 g dietary fiber*

Sour Cream—Rhubarb Pie

The first cutting of rhubarb from our garden always goes into a pie at our house. I used my favorite press-in-the-pan oil pastry for the base of this mellow, custardy pie. Then, by simply using nonfat sour cream and reducing the butter in the crumbly topping, I lowered the calories from 453 to 382 a slice, and the percentage of calories from fat fell from 45 percent to an easy-to-swallow 28 percent.

LEMON OIL PASTRY

1 cup all-purpose flour

1 tablespoon cornstarch

1/4 teaspoon salt

4 tablespoons canola or corn oil

2 tablespoons lemon juice

1 tablespoon ice water

FILLING

3 tablespoons all-purpose flour

1 1/4 cups sugar

1/2 teaspoon salt

1 large egg, lightly beaten

1 cup nonfat sour cream

1 teaspoon vanilla

1/2 teaspoon lemon extract

3 cups finely diced rhubarb

CRUMB TOPPING

1/3 cup sugar

1/3 cup all-purpose flour

1 teaspoon ground cinnamon

1/4 teaspoon salt

3 tablespoons unsalted butter, at room temperature

Preheat the oven to 375°F. Lightly grease a 9-inch pie pan or coat with nonstick spray. Dust with flour.

To make the pastry, in a bowl, mix the flour, cornstarch, and salt together. In a cup, mix the oil, lemon juice, and water. Stir the liquids into the dry ingredients using a fork, until the mixture resembles the texture of cottage cheese. Press the mixture evenly into the bottom and sides of the pie pan.

To make the filling, in a large bowl, mix the flour, sugar, and salt. Stir in the egg, sour cream, vanilla, and lemon extract until well mixed. Add the rhubarb and mix well. Pour the mixture into the pie shell. Bake for 40 to 45 minutes, or until the filling is set.

While the pie bakes, make the topping. Mix the sugar, flour, cinnamon, salt, and butter until crumbly. Sprinkle the mixture over the top of the pie evenly. Return to the oven and bake for 15 minutes, or until the topping is lightly browned. Cool on a wire rack before serving.

MAKES 8 SERVINGS

PER SERVING: *382 calories, 28% calories from fat, 12 g fat, 38.3 mg cholesterol, 278 mg sodium, 1.78 g dietary fiber*

Maple Pumpkin Pie

*Pumpkin pie in its original form is not terribly high
in fat, but I reduced the fat content even more by using
evaporated skimmed milk in the filling and only two
eggs instead of four. The easy press-in pastry makes
this pie simple to make.*

PRESS-IN CRUST

1 cup all-purpose flour

1 tablespoon cornstarch

½ teaspoon salt

5 tablespoons canola or corn oil

3 tablespoons ice water

MAPLE PUMPKIN FILLING

2 cups (1 16-ounce can) pumpkin
   purée

1 cup evaporated skimmed milk

2 large eggs, beaten

2 tablespoons cornstarch

½ cup packed brown sugar

¾ cup pure maple syrup

1½ teaspoons vanilla

1½ teaspoons ground cinnamon

1½ teaspoons ground ginger

¼ teaspoon ground allspice

½ teaspoon salt

Preheat the oven to 425°F Lightly grease a
9-inch pie pan or coat with nonstick spray.
Dust with flour.

   To make the crust, in a medium bowl, mix
the flour, cornstarch, and salt. In a small bowl,
mix the oil and ice water together with a fork.
Stir the oil and water into the flour until the
mixture makes large, moist crumbs. Press the

crumbs into the pie pan, covering the sides and
bottom of the pan evenly.

   For the filling, in a large bowl, mix the
pumpkin purée, milk, eggs, cornstarch, brown
sugar, maple syrup, vanilla, cinnamon, ginger,
allspice, and salt. Pour the mixture into the
pastry-lined pan. Bake at 425°F for 15
minutes, then reduce the heat to 350°F and
bake for 40 to 50 minutes longer, or until the
pie is set. Cool and chill before serving.

MAKES 8 SERVINGS

PER SERVING: *303 calories, 29% calories from
fat, 10 g fat, 53.3 mg cholesterol, 163 mg
sodium, 1.54 g dietary fiber*

Phyllo-Crusted Apple Pie

Phyllo (or filo), the paper-thin sheets of nonfat pastry, come frozen in long, skinny packages. It is used by Greeks to make baklava and by Eastern Europeans to make strudel. Brushed with a mixture of egg white and butter, the pastry bakes up flaky and crispy, with very little fat, making it a perfect pastry for a low-fat apple pie.

PASTRY

6 sheets phyllo pastry, thawed

2 tablespoons unsalted butter, melted

1 large egg white, lightly beaten

APPLE FILLING

1 cup packed brown sugar

4 tablespoons cornstarch

2 tablespoons lemon juice

1 teaspoon ground cinnamon

6 cups tart apples, such as Granny Smith, peeled, cored, and thinly sliced

Preheat the oven to 400°F. Lightly grease a 9-inch pie pan or coat with nonstick spray.

For the pastry, cover the sheets of phyllo with a slightly damp towel so they will not dry out. (Wrap the remainder of the pastry so that it will not dry out and save it for another use.) In a small bowl, mix the butter and egg white.

Center one of the phyllo sheets on the greased pie pan and carefully fit the pastry into the bottom of the pan. Brush with the egg white mixture. Lay another sheet of the phyllo, in the opposite direction, and brush lightly with the egg white mixture. Repeat this method with another 4 sheets of phyllo placed in opposite directions; brush each sheet with the egg white mixture, to make a 6-phyllo layer crust.

For the filling, in a bowl, combine the brown sugar, cornstarch, lemon juice, and cinnamon. Add the apple slices and toss to coat.

Turn the apple mixture into the phyllo-lined pie pan. Gently bring the overlapping sides of phyllo up to cover the apples.

Bake for 15 minutes, then reduce the temperature to 350°F and continue baking for 20 to 30 minutes, until well browned. Remove from the oven and let stand 20 minutes before slicing.

MAKES 6 SERVINGS

PER SERVING: *256 calories, 14% calories from fat, 4.23 g fat, 10.4 mg cholesterol, 27.3 mg sodium, 2.7 g dietary fiber*

Apple Strudel

Although I often use frozen phyllo dough for apple strudel, I feel very creative when I make the pastry myself. Strudel pastry must be pulled until it is very thin. If you leave out the almonds in the filling, the calories from fat drop to only 13 percent and the calories drop to 208 per serving.

PASTRY

2 cups all-purpose flour

¼ teaspoon salt

1 large egg, beaten

½ cup water

2 teaspoons unsalted butter, melted

FILLING

6 teaspoons unsalted butter, melted

1 tablespoon ground cinnamon

¼ cup toasted fresh white bread crumbs

1 tablespoon grated lemon zest

1 cup packed brown sugar

¾ cup raisins

½ cup chopped blanched almonds (optional)

6 to 8 cups tart apples, such as Granny Smith, peeled, cored, and finely chopped

To make the pastry, put the flour and salt into a food processor with the steel blade in place. In a bowl, mix the egg, water, and butter. Turn the processor on and slowly add the egg mixture; process until the dough is smooth and elastic and comes away from the sides of the bowl, about 2 minutes. The dough will be quite soft to the touch, but because of the long processing time, the gluten is developed so well that the dough is not sticky. Coat a small bowl with nonstick spray and turn the dough out into the bowl. Coat the top of the dough with spray also and cover the bowl with plastic wrap. Let it rest for 1 hour so the dough will "tighten."

Place a pastry cloth or a large, square muslin dish towel on a countertop and tape down the edges, pulling the towel taut. Sprinkle with flour, rubbing it into the weave of the fabric. Turn the dough out onto the floured pastry cloth and roll the dough out with a floured rolling pin as thin as possible, dusting with flour as needed. When the dough is as thin as you can get it with a rolling pin, let it rest for 5 minutes. With your hands, stretch the dough out to 24 inches in each direction, keeping the surface under the dough lightly floured and dry.

Preheat the oven to 400°F.

To fill the dough, brush the dough with 4 teaspoons of the melted butter. Combine the cinnamon and bread crumbs and sprinkle the mixture over the dough to within 1 inch of the edges. Mix the lemon zest with the brown sugar and sprinkle over the crumbs. Sprinkle the raisins, almonds, if using, and apples.

Turn two opposite short sides over the filling by about 3 inches. Remove the tape from the edges of the towel. Lift the towel starting from one end of the pastry where the edges are not turned over the filling. With the aid of the towel, roll the pastry with the filling inside to make a rather tight roll.

Cover a baking sheet with parchment paper or coat with nonstick spray. Place the strudel with the seam side down on top of the prepared baking pan. Brush with the remaining 2 teaspoons butter. Bake for 20 minutes, then turn the heat down to 350°F and bake for 10 minutes longer, or until the roll is golden brown. Remove from the oven and cool on a wire rack.

MAKES 12 SERVINGS

PER SERVING: *240 calories, 21% calories from fat, 5.88 g fat, 23.8 mg cholesterol, 57.5 mg sodium, 2.83 g dietary fiber*

Apple Tarte Tatin

Tarte Tatin is one of my favorite apple pastries. This is an adaptation of the classic, which I first tasted in the South of France several years ago. To reduce the calories from fat as much as possible, I use phyllo dough and brush it with a mixture of egg white and a nutty flavored oil. The result is an irresistibly succulent apple tart.

½ pound (about 12 sheets) phyllo dough, thawed

1 large egg white, lightly beaten

2 tablespoons hazelnut, walnut, or canola oil

6 large (about 3½ pounds) Golden Delicious apples

¾ cup sugar

1 teaspoon ground cinnamon

½ teaspoon salt

2 tablespoons unsalted butter

¼ cup packed brown sugar

Confectioners' sugar

Preheat the oven to 375°F. Cover the phyllo with a slightly damp dish towel to prevent it from drying out.

Beat the egg white in a small bowl until no longer stringy; beat in the oil. Set aside.

Pare, core, and cut the apples into ½-inch-thick slices. In a large bowl, toss the apples with ¼ cup of the sugar, the cinnamon, and the salt.

Melt the butter in a heavy 10- to 12-inch ovenproof skillet over medium heat. Add the brown sugar and stir until the brown sugar is melted.

Arrange the apples concentrically in layers in the pan over the brown sugar. Sprinkle with the remaining ½ cup sugar and with a spatula or the palm of your hand press the apples down firmly. Cook over medium-low heat, covered, for 10 minutes, until the apples are tender.

On a clean, dry work surface, place one of the sheets of phyllo dough. Brush it lightly with the egg white mixture. Top with a second sheet of dough, placing it crosswise over the first layer, and brush it with the egg white mixture. Continue stacking and brushing the phyllo sheets in the same manner. When all of the sheets are stacked and brushed, pick up the whole stack and place it on top of the apples in the skillet. Tuck the edges inside the rim of the pan.

Bake for 45 to 55 minutes, until the filling is bubbly and the phyllo is evenly browned. Remove from the oven and cool in the pan. Loosen the edges with a flexible spatula.

Just before serving, invert the tarte onto a large heatproof serving platter. Preheat the broiler. Dust the top of the tarte with confectioners' sugar and place under the broiler for 3 to 4 minutes, until the top of the tarte is glazed. Cut into wedges to serve.

MAKES 8 SERVINGS

PER SERVING: *273 calories, 22% calories from fat, 6.89 g fat, 7.77 mg cholesterol, 145 mg sodium, 4.24 g dietary fiber*

Crumb-Topped Apple Tart

An apple tart tastes the very best in the fall, when the apples are fresh from the orchard. By reducing the fat in the streusel topping and using my cake flour pastry, I brought the total fat from calories down to 17 percent, with only 6 grams of fat per serving, without losing any of the delicious flavor of a classic fresh apple tart.

PASTRY

1½ cups cake flour

½ teaspoon baking powder

¼ teaspoon salt

2 tablespoons unsalted butter or vegetable shortening

3 tablespoons low-fat cream cheese

2 teaspoons lemon juice

About 4 tablespoons ice water

FILLING

¾ cup sugar

2 tablespoons all-purpose flour

1 teaspoon ground cinnamon

⅛ teaspoon nutmeg

¼ teaspoon salt

2½ pounds (7 cups) tart apples, such as Granny Smith, peeled and sliced

CRUMB TOPPING

½ cup packed brown sugar

¾ cup all-purpose flour

1 teaspoon ground cinnamon

2 tablespoons unsalted butter, melted

Preheat the oven to 425°F.

To make the pastry, measure the flour, baking powder, and the salt into the work bowl of the food processor. Cut the butter or shortening and cream cheese into pieces and add to the flour. Pulse 10 to 15 times until the mixture resembles very coarse crumbs. Turn the mixture into a mixing bowl. Mix the lemon juice with 2 tablespoons of the water and sprinkle over the dry ingredients. With a fork, stir the mixture until the dry ingredients are moistened, adding water, if necessary, until the dough is no longer dry and crumbly. It should hold together when you pinch a small amount between your fingers. Gather the dough into a ball and press it into a disk 4 inches in diameter.

On a lightly floured board, roll the pastry out to fit the bottom and sides of an 11-inch tart pan with a removable bottom. Fold the excess pastry over itself around the edge of the pan, pressing it firmly.

To make the filling, combine the sugar, flour, cinnamon, nutmeg, and salt and then toss with the apples. Heap the mixture into the pastry-lined pan.

For the crumb topping, mix the brown sugar, flour, cinnamon, and butter until crumbly. Sprinkle over the top of the apples.

Bake for 50 to 60 minutes or until the crust and topping are browned and the apples are tender.

MAKES 10 SERVINGS

PER SERVING: *310 calories, 17% calories from fat, 6.2 g fat, 15.7 mg cholesterol, 93 mg sodium, 3.12 g dietary fiber*

Blueberry Angel Tarts

These pretty tarts make a spectacular dessert for lunch or dinner. Because I feel strongly that the flavor of whipped cream, even in a small amount, totally enhances berries and fruit, I began experimenting with ways to "stretch" the cream without adversely affecting the flavor. I tried blending the whipped cream with nonfat sour cream: While the result was passable, the cream lost the light texture I was looking for. I had a jar of marshmallow creme on the shelf from some long-ago project, and thought I'd just try mixing it with the cream. I was amazed at the result. The whipped cream flavor and light texture were retained, sweetened subtly by the marshmallow creme. This combination holds up well while cutting the fat calories by half.

TART SHELLS

3 large egg whites, at room temperature

¼ teaspoon cream of tartar

Dash of salt

¾ cup sugar

1 tablespoon cornstarch

BLUEBERRY FILLING

1 pint fresh blueberries

1 tablespoon fresh lemon juice

2 tablespoons superfine sugar

TOPPING

½ cup whipping (heavy) cream

1 cup marshmallow creme

Preheat the oven to 275°F Lightly grease 6 individual-size tart or pie pans or coat with nonstick spray. Dust with flour.

To make the tart shells, in a metal mixing bowl, beat the egg whites with the cream of tartar and salt until soft peaks form. In a small bowl, mix the sugar and the cornstarch. Gradually add the sugar mixture to the egg whites, beating at high speed, until stiff peaks form. Divide the meringue among the tart pans and spread over the bottom and sides, making an indentation in the center so that the meringues form shells. Bake for 1 hour. Turn the oven off. Let the shells stand in the oven for 1 hour.

Meanwhile, to make the filling, mix the blueberries with the lemon juice and the sugar. Remove the tarts from the oven and fill with the berry mixture, dividing evenly.

For the topping, whip the cream until stiff. With a metal spoon, stir in the marshmallow creme until well blended. Divide the topping among the tarts.

MAKES 8 SERVINGS

PER SERVING: *270 calories, 18% calories from fat, 5.64 g fat, 20.4 mg cholesterol, 48.4 mg sodium, 0.99 g dietary fiber*

Chocolate-Banana Cream Pie

I *like this pie even better after reducing the fatty ingredients. I replaced a high-fat pastry shell with a light and easy-to-make meringue and used skim milk in place of whole milk in the rich-tasting chocolate filling. And I used my new trick of mixing whipped cream with marshmallow creme to make a light and creamy-tasting topping.*

MERINGUE SHELL

3 large egg whites, at room
    temperature

1/4 teaspoon cream of tartar

Dash of salt

3/4 cup sugar

1/2 teaspoon vanilla

CHOCOLATE-BANANA FILLING

1 cup sugar

1/4 teaspoon salt

2 squares unsweetened chocolate,
    chopped

2 1/2 tablespoons cornstarch

2 cups skim milk

1 teaspoon vanilla

3 large bananas, sliced

TOPPING

1/4 cup whipping (heavy) cream

1/4 cup marshmallow creme

Preheat the oven to 275°F. Coat a 9-inch pie pan with nonstick spray and dust it lightly with flour.

To make the meringue shell, in a small bowl, beat the egg whites, cream of tartar, and salt until soft peaks form. Gradually add the sugar and beat until stiff peaks form. Add the vanilla; beat well. Spread the meringue over the bottom and sides of the prepared pan, building up the sides as high as possible. Bake for 1 hour. Turn the oven off and let the meringue cool in the oven for 1 hour. Remove the meringue shell from the oven.

Meanwhile, for the chocolate-banana filling, in a 2-quart saucepan combine the sugar, salt, chocolate, cornstarch, and skim milk. Place over medium-low heat and stir until the chocolate is melted. Increase the heat to medium and cook, stirring constantly, until the mixture thickens and boils. Boil 1 minute. Remove from the heat. Blend in the vanilla. Cover and chill.

Pour half of the chocolate filling into the baked meringue shell. Top with the sliced bananas and the remaining chocolate filling. Refrigerate until cold.

To make the topping, whip the cream until stiff and beat in the marshmallow creme. Spread the mixture over the pie. Refrigerate until ready to serve.

MAKES 8 SERVINGS

PER SERVING: *335 calories, 19% calories from fat, 7.42 g fat, 12.5 mg cholesterol, 128 mg sodium, 2.17 g dietary fiber*

Mango Angel Pie

Mango, *the tropical fruit of an evergreen tree belonging to the cashew family, has a delicious, spicy flavor. You can tell a ripe mango not so much by a golden-blush color but by a slight give when you squeeze the fruit. Cradled by a soft meringue crust, this is a wonderful, elegant pie to serve to guests. It is best when assembled the day that you serve it. You can, if it is more convenient, leave the crust in the oven overnight with the oven turned off.*

ANGEL CRUST

4 large egg whites

1 teaspoon vinegar or lemon juice

1 teaspoon vanilla

1 cup superfine sugar

MANGO FILLING

2 large ripe mangoes

3 tablespoons lime juice

1 (14-ounce) can low-fat sweetened condensed milk

¼ teaspoon almond extract

½ cup whipping (heavy) cream

Preheat the oven to 275°F. Lightly grease a 9-inch pie pan or coat with nonstick spray. Dust lightly with flour.

To make the angel crust, in a metal or porcelain mixing bowl, beat the egg whites until thick but not stiff. Beat in the vinegar and the vanilla. Gradually beat in the sugar until the whites are stiff and glossy. Spread the mixture into the bottom and sides of the pie pan. Bake for 1 hour. Turn the oven off and without opening the oven door, allow the crust to cool as the oven cools for 2 to 3 hours or overnight.

For the filling, peel and pit the mangoes (see Note). Put the mango flesh into a blender or food processor and purée. Add the lime juice, sweetened condensed milk, and almond extract to the mangoes and mix well. In another bowl, whip the cream until stiff and blend into the mango mixture. Pour into the angel crust, cover, and chill for 2 to 3 hours.

MAKES 8 SERVINGS

PER SERVING: *314 calories, 21% calories from fat, 7.25 g fat, 25.8 mg cholesterol, 78 mg sodium, 1.45 g dietary fiber*

NOTE: To pit mangoes, cut alongside the seed through the skin and flesh on both flat sides of the fruit. Scoop the mango flesh out of the skin. Cut the remaining flesh from around the seed.

Old-Fashioned American Banana Cream Pie

The *typical American banana cream pie is loaded with fat and calories, but many low-fat versions lack satisfying flavor. I think graham cracker crusts often overpower the delicate flavor of a cream filling. So I combined gingersnaps and low-fat vanilla wafers to complement the creamy flavor of the filling. I used fat-free cream cheese in the filling to add to the flavor and smooth out the texture. To smooth the texture even more, I added a very small amount of unflavored gelatin. The pie is topped with a light meringue instead of whipped cream.*

GINGERSNAP-AND-VANILLA-WAFER CRUST

1/2 cup gingersnap crumbs (about 8 gingersnaps)

3/4 cup low-fat vanilla wafer crumbs (about 20 wafers)

2 tablespoons melted unsalted butter

1 teaspoon vanilla

1 tablespoon water

BANANA CREAM FILLING

3/4 cup sugar

1/3 cup all-purpose flour

1/4 teaspoon salt

1 3/4 cups skim milk

1 teaspoon unflavored gelatin

1 teaspoon vanilla extract

2 egg yolks

1 teaspoon unsalted butter

1 (8-ounce) package fat-free cream cheese, cut into 1-inch cubes

3 bananas, peeled and sliced

1 teaspoon fresh lemon juice

MERINGUE

3 egg whites

1/2 teaspoon cream of tartar

6 tablespoons sugar

Preheat the oven to 375°F. Coat a 9-inch pie pan lightly with nonstick spray.

To make the crust, in a large bowl, combine the gingersnap crumbs, vanilla wafer crumbs, butter, vanilla, and water. Mix until well blended. Press the mixture into the bottom and sides of the pie pan. Bake for 10 to 12 minutes or until lightly browned. Remove from the oven and cool on a rack. Increase the oven temperature to 400°F.

To make the filling, combine the sugar, flour, salt, milk, and gelatin in a heavy saucepan. Place over low heat and stir with a whisk constantly until the mixture comes to a boil. Boil 1 minute. Blend in the vanilla. Beat the egg yolks in a small bowl just until the yolks are broken. Add about 1/2 cup of the hot mixture to the yolks and mix quickly until blended. Return the mixture to the pan and cook 1 minute longer. Remove from the heat and stir in the butter and cream cheese until smooth. Cover and cool the filling over a bowl of ice.

To make the meringue, in a large bowl, beat the egg whites and cream of tartar until frothy. With the mixer at high speed, beat in the 6 tablespoons sugar, 1 tablespoon at a time, and continue beating until the mixture forms stiff peaks.

Toss the banana slices with the lemon juice and arrange them on the baked crust. Spoon the cooled custard over the bananas. Spread the meringue over the top, swirling it decoratively with the tip of a metal spatula and being sure to seal the meringue to the crust. Bake for 8 to 10 minutes, or until the meringue is lightly browned. Let the pie cool to room temperature, then refrigerate, uncovered, until the filling has set.

MAKES 8 SERVINGS

PER SERVING: *335 calories, 19% calories from fat, 7.09 g fat, 68.2 mg cholesterol, 332 mg sodium, 1.22 g dietary fiber*

Frozen Cranberry—Cream Cheese Pie

MAKES 8 SERVINGS

PER SERVING: *324 calories, 15% calories from fat, 5.59 g fat, 19.2 mg cholesterol, 302 mg sodium, 1.44 g dietary fiber*

This is a terrific pie to make ahead for holiday entertaining. And it clocks in at a mere 15 percent of calories from fat! Your guests will thank you.

CRUMB CRUST

1½ cups low-fat vanilla wafer crumbs (about 40 wafers)

2 tablespoons unsalted butter, melted

CRANBERRY FILLING

1 (8-ounce) package nonfat cream cheese

1 (14-ounce) can low-fat sweetened condensed milk

⅓ cup fresh lemon juice

1 teaspoon vanilla

1 (16-ounce) can whole berry cranberry sauce

Preheat the oven to 350°F.

In a mixing bowl, combine the vanilla wafer crumbs and butter. Press firmly into the bottom and up the sides of a 9-inch pie pan. Bake for 10 minutes until toasted, then cool completely.

In a large mixing bowl, beat the cream cheese until fluffy. Gradually beat in the condensed milk, lemon juice, and vanilla. Reserve ½ cup of the cranberry sauce and fold the remainder into the cheese mixture.

Pour the filling into the cooled crust. Cover and freeze for 6 hours, or until firm. Just before serving, spoon the reserved cranberry sauce over the pie.

MUFFINS

My sister-in-law Eileen relayed a story of "muffin deception" the other day. She had purchased muffins that were absolutely delicious, and best of all, the label indicated that they were only 250 calories per serving. A year later, after enjoying one of these muffins every day for breakfast, she read the fine print on the label: "one serving = ¼ muffin"!

All of the muffins in this chapter are "one muffin per serving"!

To make delicious low-fat muffins, there are a few tricks and rules. Moistness comes from "moist" ingredients. Fruits such as apples, applesauce, bananas, and berries are wonderful because they don't add fat. Low-fat and nonfat dairy products, such as sour cream and yogurt, add tenderness and flavor without significantly contributing to the fat content. Muffin batter can be loaded with moist and tender ingredients for delicious results, but too much of a liquid ingredient, such as juice or milk, can result in a tough muffin with large holes and little flavor.

When mixing muffin batter, it's better to undermix than overmix. Overmixed batter will produce a tough and tunneled baked muffin with a pointed top. Mix the dry ingredients and liquids just until the dry ingredients are moistened, or no more than twelve to fifteen strokes.

Overbaking will result in dry muffins. Begin checking the muffins a couple of minutes before the suggested baking time is up. Ovens vary. I have three ovens in my kitchen and all three bake slightly differently even though they are all calibrated to be the same.

If you bake the muffins in paper-lined muffin cups, coat the liners with nonstick spray before spooning the muffin batter into the cups to prevent sticking. Remove the muffins from the pan immediately after baking to prevent them from becoming soggy.

You can bake any of the muffins in this chapter in either jumbo- or mini-muffin pans. Be prepared to alter the baking times. Jumbo muffins may take almost twice the time to bake, while mini-muffins may bake in about half the time.

All of the muffins should be stored either in an airtight container or in airtight plastic bags in the freezer if they are made ahead. Package them for freezing after they have cooled thoroughly. Be sure to label the package and include the date. (I always think I'll remember what I've packed away, and I never do.) To thaw and serve, remove just the number of muffins you need from the freezer and thaw them in a warm oven (300°F) for ten minutes, or in the microwave for thirty seconds each on high power, or simply at room temperature for about 30 minutes.

Crumb-Topped Apple Spice Muffins

Just perfect for a morning coffee meeting, these are so moist and flavorful that they surprise even the most skeptical judges of low-fat baking.

2 cups all-purpose flour

2 teaspoons baking powder

½ teaspoon baking soda

¼ teaspoon salt

1 teaspoon ground cinnamon

¼ teaspoon ground nutmeg

1 large egg, lightly beaten

½ cup packed brown sugar

4 tablespoons (½ stick) unsalted butter, melted

1 cup plain nonfat yogurt, stirred

1 cup tart apples, such as Granny Smith, peeled and chopped

TOPPING

¼ cup packed brown sugar

¼ cup all-purpose flour

2 tablespoons unsalted butter, melted

Preheat the oven to 400°F. Lightly grease or coat with nonstick spray 12 standard muffin cups, or line with paper baking cups and spray lightly.

In a small bowl, dust the apples with 1 tablespoon of the flour. In a large bowl, combine the remaining flour, baking powder, baking soda, salt, cinnamon, and nutmeg until well mixed. In a small bowl, whisk the egg, sugar, butter, and yogurt together until well mixed. Stir the liquid ingredients into the dry ingredients just until blended, about 20 strokes. Gently fold in the apples.

Spoon the batter evenly into the muffin cups. To make the topping, in a small bowl, stir together the brown sugar, flour, and melted butter until the mixture resembles moist crumbs. Spoon the mixture over the muffins and pat down slightly. Bake for 15 to 20 minutes, or until the muffins are lightly browned and a wooden skewer inserted into the center of a muffin comes out clean. Cool 1 minute, then remove from the muffin tins and transfer to a wire rack to cool or to a basket to serve warm.

MAKES 12 MUFFINS

PER MUFFIN: *204 calories, 29% calories from fat, 6.42 g fat, 33.3 mg cholesterol, 102 mg sodium, 0.83 g dietary fiber*

Cranberry–Banana Chunk Muffins

Use ripe but not overripe bananas in these muffins. They will add a moist bite, while the apples add a chewiness and the cranberries a tart burst of flavor.

- 1 cup all-purpose flour
- 1 cup whole wheat pastry flour
- 4 teaspoons baking powder
- 1/2 cup sugar
- 1/4 teaspoon salt
- 2 medium bananas, sliced
- 1/2 cup chopped dried apples
- 1/4 cup dried cranberries
- 1 large egg
- 4 tablespoons (1/2 stick) unsalted butter, melted
- 1 cup skim milk
- 1 tablespoon vanilla

Preheat the oven to 425°F. Lightly grease or coat with nonstick spray 12 standard muffin cups, or line them with paper baking cups and coat with nonstick spray.

In a large bowl, stir together the flours, baking powder, sugar, and salt. Add the bananas, apples, and cranberries. Mix lightly to coat all the pieces of fruit. In a small bowl, mix the egg, butter, milk, and vanilla.

Pour the liquid ingredients over the dry ingredients and mix gently until the dry ingredients are moistened. Do not overmix. Spoon the batter evenly into the prepared muffin cups. Bake for 18 to 20 minutes, or until a wooden skewer inserted in the center of a muffin comes out clean.

MAKES 12 MUFFINS

PER MUFFIN: 190 calories, 22% calories from fat, 4.69 g fat, 28.4 mg cholesterol, 128 mg sodium, 2.49 g dietary fiber

Blueberry Oatmeal Muffins

When fresh blueberries are not in season, I prefer to use the dried berries. You can, however, use frozen berries, but they should be added in the frozen state or the muffins will discolor. If you use frozen berries, the entire mixture will be very cold and the muffins may take as much as 5 minutes longer to bake. These muffins taste wonderful and have a great texture, although they are somewhat flat on top rather than rounded.

- 1 cup fresh or 1/2 cup dried blueberries
- 1 1/2 cups all-purpose flour
- 1/2 cup quick-cooking rolled oats
- 1 tablespoon baking powder
- 1/2 teaspoon salt
- 1 large egg
- 1/3 cup sugar
- 3 tablespoons unsalted butter, melted
- 1 cup lemon- or vanilla-flavored nonfat yogurt

Preheat the oven to 400°F. Lightly grease or coat with nonstick spray 12 standard muffin cups, or line with paper baking cups and spray lightly.

In a small bowl, dust the berries with 1 tablespoon of the flour. In a large bowl, combine the remaining flour, rolled oats, baking powder, and salt until well mixed. In another small bowl, whisk the egg, sugar, butter, and yogurt together until well mixed. Stir the liquid ingredients into the dry ingredients just until blended, about 20 strokes. Gently fold in the blueberries.

Spoon the batter evenly into the muffin cups. Bake for 15 to 20 minutes, or until the muffins are lightly browned and a wooden skewer inserted into the center of a muffin comes out clean. Cool 1 minute, then remove from the muffin tins and transfer to a wire rack to cool or to a basket to serve warm.

MAKES 12 MUFFINS

PER MUFFIN: *160 calories, 21% calories from fat, 3.69 g fat, 25.5 mg cholesterol, 178 mg sodium, 1.08 g dietary fiber*

Bran and Applesauce Muffins

Here's a "branny" muffin that's moist, yet chewy, and not too sweet. Applesauce works well to replace part of the oil in the original recipe. Whole wheat flour was just too crumbly, but when I replaced some of the white flour with oat flour, that added a nuttiness and the tenderness that I was looking for.

2 cups bran breakfast cereal

1 cup milk

1 large egg, lightly beaten

½ cup unsweetened applesauce

1 tablespoon corn or canola oil

1 cup all-purpose flour

¼ cup oat flour (see Note)

1 tablespoon baking powder

¼ teaspoon salt

Preheat the oven to 400°F. Lightly grease or coat with nonstick spray 12 standard muffin cups, or line with paper baking cups and spray lightly.

In a large bowl, combine the cereal, milk, egg, applesauce, and oil. Stir well and set aside.

In another bowl, stir together the flours, baking powder, and salt. Stir the liquid ingredients into the dry ingredients just until the dry ingredients are moistened. Spoon the batter into the prepared muffin cups and bake for 18 to 20 minutes, or until a wooden skewer inserted into the center of a muffin comes out clean. Cool 1 minute, then remove from the muffin tins and transfer to a wire rack to cool or to a basket to serve warm.

MAKES 12 MUFFINS

PER MUFFIN: *134 calories, 15% calories from fat, 2.38 g fat, 18 mg cholesterol, 219 mg sodium, 3.92 g dietary fiber*

Variation

To make raisin-bran muffins, add 1 cup dark or golden raisins to the dry ingredients.

PER MUFFIN: *176 calories, 11% calories from fat, 2.44 g fat, 18 mg cholesterol, 221 mg sodium, 4.73 g dietary fiber*

NOTE: For oat flour, place quick-cooking or regular rolled oats into a food processor with the steel blade in place. Process until the oats are ground into flour.

Chili Corn Muffins

With the bite of green chilies and the crunch of cornmeal, these muffins are perfect with a steaming bowl of soup. And this was another case in which, once the fat was reduced, from $\frac{1}{2}$ cup oil to 3 tablespoons, the flavor and texture of the muffins were improved.

- 1 cup yellow cornmeal
- 1 cup all-purpose flour
- 4 teaspoons baking powder
- 3 tablespoons sugar
- $\frac{1}{2}$ teaspoon salt
- 1 cup skim milk
- 3 tablespoons canola oil
- 1 large egg
- $\frac{1}{4}$ cup seeded and chopped fresh hot green chili peppers or 1 (4-ounce) can chopped green chilies, drained

Preheat the oven to 425°F. Lightly grease or coat with nonstick spray 12 standard muffin cups.

In a large bowl, stir the cornmeal, flour, baking powder, sugar, and salt together. In another bowl, mix the milk, oil, egg, and peppers. Pour the liquid ingredients over the dry ingredients and stir just until moistened. Spoon the mixture into the prepared muffin cups. Bake for 15 minutes, or just until the muffins are lightly browned and a wooden skewer inserted in the center comes out clean and dry. Remove the muffins to a wire rack or a serving basket; serve hot.

MAKES 12 MUFFINS

PER MUFFIN: *133 calories, 29% calories from fat, 4.34 g fat, 18 mg cholesterol, 219 mg sodium, 1.5 g dietary fiber*

Ginger-Rhubarb Muffins with Cinnamon Sugar

The sophisticated flavor of these muffins makes an interesting change of pace. Serve them hot!

- $2\frac{1}{4}$ cups all-purpose flour
- 2 teaspoons baking powder
- 1 teaspoon baking soda
- $\frac{1}{2}$ teaspoon salt
- 2 tablespoons finely chopped crystallized ginger
- $\frac{3}{4}$ cup sugar
- $\frac{1}{2}$ cup skim milk
- $\frac{1}{2}$ cup vanilla nonfat yogurt
- 2 large egg whites
- 1 cup finely chopped fresh rhubarb stalks
- 1 tablespoon vegetable oil

CINNAMON SUGAR

- 2 tablespoons sugar
- 1 teaspoon ground cinnamon

Preheat the oven to 400°F. Lightly grease or coat with nonstick spray 12 standard muffin cups, or line with paper baking cups and spray lightly.

In a large bowl, stir the flour, baking powder, baking soda, salt, and ginger together.

In another bowl, whisk the sugar, milk, yogurt, egg whites, and rhubarb together. Pour the liquids over the dry ingredients and gently mix with a rubber spatula until almost all of the dry ingredients are moistened. Drizzle the oil over the top and very gently mix all of the ingredients. Fill each muffin cup about ¾ full with the batter. Bake for 15 to 17 minutes, or just until a wooden skewer inserted into the center of a muffin comes out clean.

Mix the sugar and cinnamon in a small bowl. Remove the hot muffins from the pan and immediately roll the top of each muffin in the cinnamon sugar mixture. Place in a basket and serve immediately.

MAKES 12 MUFFINS

PER MUFFIN: 174 *calories, 9% calories from fat, 1.8 g fat, 17.9 mg cholesterol, 155 mg sodium, 0.84 g dietary fiber*

Lemon-Thyme Muffins

These moist and tender muffins, topped with a lemon and thyme glaze, are great served with a chicken, seafood, or pasta salad.

2 cups all-purpose flour

½ cup sugar

3 teaspoons baking powder

½ teaspoon salt

1 tablespoon grated lemon zest

1 teaspoon dried thyme

¾ cup skim milk

¼ cup canola oil

1 large egg, lightly beaten

Preheat the oven to 400°F. Lightly grease or coat with nonstick spray 12 standard muffin cups, or line with paper baking cups and spray lightly.

In a mixing bowl, stir together the flour, sugar, baking powder, salt, lemon zest, and thyme. In a small bowl, mix the milk, oil, and egg. Add the liquid ingredients to the dry ingredients all at once. Stir just until the dry ingredients are moistened. Divide the batter between the muffin cups, filling them about ¾ full. Bake for 15 to 18 minutes, or until light golden brown and a wooden skewer inserted in the center of a muffin comes out clean and dry.

Cool 1 minute before removing from the pan. Cool the muffins on a wire rack or place them in a serving basket and serve right away.

MAKES 12 MUFFINS

PER MUFFIN: 166 *calories, 28% calories from fat, 5.17 g fat, 18 mg cholesterol, 185 mg sodium, 0.52 g dietary fiber*

Orange-Glazed Pineapple-Oatmeal Muffins

These are muffins that are almost indulgently full of flavor. They are great served with tea in the afternoon as well as for breakfast.

1 (8-ounce) can crushed pineapple, packed in natural juices

1 cup quick-cooking or old-fashioned rolled oats

1/3 cup nonfat sour cream

4 tablespoons (1/2 stick) unsalted butter, melted

1/3 cup packed brown sugar

1 teaspoon grated orange zest

1/2 teaspoon ground ginger

1 large egg, lightly beaten

1 1/4 cups all-purpose flour

1 teaspoon baking powder

1/2 teaspoon baking soda

1 teaspoon salt

ORANGE GLAZE

1 cup confectioners' sugar

1 to 2 tablespoons orange juice

Preheat the oven to 400°F. Lightly grease 12 standard muffin cups or coat with nonstick spray.

In a large mixing bowl, combine the pineapple, rolled oats, and sour cream and let stand 15 minutes. Stir in the butter, brown sugar, orange zest, ginger, and egg until blended. Sift the flour, baking powder, baking soda, and salt into the pineapple mixture. With a rubber spatula, mix just until the dry ingredients are moistened.

Spoon the batter into the muffin cups, dividing the batter equally. Bake for 15 to 17 minutes, or just until a wooden skewer inserted into the center of a muffin comes out clean.

While the muffins bake, mix the confectioners' sugar and orange juice to make a smooth, thin glaze. Drizzle the glaze over the hot muffins. Cool the muffins in the pan for 5 minutes, then remove and place in a basket and serve warm, or finish cooling on a wire rack.

MAKES 12 MUFFINS

PER MUFFIN: *151 calories, 28% calories from fat, 4.8 g fat, 28.1 mg cholesterol, 159 mg sodium, 1.25 g dietary fiber*

Upside-Down Cranberry Muffins

Spoon whole cranberry sauce into the bottom of the muffin cups before adding the muffin batter, bake, then invert the muffins and serve them hot! These muffins are perfect with any holiday meal.

6 tablespoons whole cranberry sauce

1 cup quick-cooking rolled oats

1 cup skim milk

3 tablespoons canola or corn oil

1 large egg, lightly beaten

1 cup all-purpose flour

1/2 cup packed brown sugar

2 teaspoons baking powder

1/4 teaspoon salt

1/4 teaspoon ground cinnamon

Preheat the oven to 400°F. Lightly grease or coat with nonstick spray 12 standard muffin cups, or line with paper baking cups and spray lightly. Spoon ½ tablespoon of the cranberry sauce into the bottom of each muffin cup.

In a large bowl, combine the oats, milk, oil, and egg and let the mixture stand for 5 minutes. In another bowl, stir the flour, brown sugar, baking powder, salt, and cinnamon together. Add the dry ingredients to the oat mixture and stir with a wooden spoon just until blended, about 20 strokes.

Spoon the batter into the muffin cups. Bake for 15 to 20 minutes, or until the muffins are lightly browned and a wooden skewer inserted into the center of a muffin comes out clean. Cool the muffins in the pan for 1 minute, then invert onto a serving tray and serve warm.

MAKES 12 MUFFINS

PER MUFFIN: *153 calories, 26% calories from fat, 4.38 g fat, 18 mg cholesterol, 122 mg sodium, 1.19 g dietary fiber*

Sour Cream Muffins

These muffins have the texture and nonsweet flavor of baking powder biscuits. I like them served hot out of the oven along with a bowl of vegetable chili. For teatime, serve them with Fat-Free Lemon and Cheese Spread (see page 152).

> **2 cups all-purpose flour**
> **1½ tablespoons sugar**
> **4 teaspoons baking powder**
> **1 teaspoon baking soda**
> **½ teaspoon salt**
> **1½ cups nonfat sour cream**
> **¼ cup skim milk**
> **1 large egg, beaten**

Preheat the oven to 425°F. Lightly grease 12 standard muffin cups or coat with nonstick spray.

Sift the flour, sugar, baking powder, baking soda, and salt into a large mixing bowl. In a small bowl, stir the sour cream, milk, and egg together. Stir the liquid ingredients into the dry ingredients just until the dry ingredients are moistened.

Spoon the batter into the muffin cups, dividing the batter equally. Bake for 15 to 17 minutes, or just until a wooden skewer inserted into the center of a muffin comes out clean and the muffins are lightly browned. Remove from the baking pan and serve immediately.

MAKES 12 MUFFINS

PER MUFFIN: *116 calories, 5% calories from fat, 0.62 g fat, 17.8 mg cholesterol, 275 mg sodium, 0.52 g dietary fiber*

Wild Rice Muffins

Wild rice, which is actually not a rice but a wild grass that grows in marshy northern lakes, has a nutty flavor and adds both moistness and texture to these muffins. The original recipe had twice the butter in it, and when I reduced the amount to 4 tablespoons, not only did the percentage of calories from fat drop considerably, the texture and the flavor improved as well!

- **1 cup cooked wild rice**
- **1 cup skim milk**
- **1 large egg, lightly beaten**
- **4 tablespoons (½ stick) unsalted butter, melted**
- **½ teaspoon salt**
- **3 teaspoons baking powder**
- **2 cups all-purpose flour**
- **⅓ cup sugar**

Preheat the oven to 400°F. Lightly grease or coat with nonstick spray 12 standard muffin cups, or line with paper baking cups and spray lightly.

In a small bowl, stir together the wild rice, milk, egg, and butter. In a large bowl, stir the salt, baking powder, flour, and sugar together. Add the liquid ingredients to the dry ingredients and stir just until the dry ingredients are moistened.

Spoon the batter evenly into the prepared muffin cups. Bake for 18 to 20 minutes, or until the muffins feel firm to the touch. Cool on a wire rack.

MAKES 12 MUFFINS

PER MUFFIN: *153 calories, 27% calories from fat, 4.52 g fat, 28.4 mg cholesterol, 188 mg sodium, 0.85 g dietary fiber*

QUICK BREADS
AND SPREADS

Easy-to-make quick breads, leavened with baking powder and baking soda, are mixed in minutes and baked without any time spent rising. They usually depend on shortening for their tenderness, flavor, and texture. Many of the breads I've enjoyed in the past contained much more shortening than necessary. Did you ever notice that a slice of quick bread placed on a paper napkin left a greasy spot? That's an indication that the bread contained more shortening than necessary.

When I started baking fruit and nut breads, scones, and corn sticks with less fat, their flavor actually improved. With reduced fat, the taste of spices, fruits, nuts, and whole grains is more pronounced and delicious. Today I automatically reduce the shortening in any quick bread that I make by at least 25 percent.

Soda bread and brown bread are two favorite savory quick breads that cooks around the world have baked for generations. They usually contain little or no sugar and rely on whole grains, spices, seeds, and herbs for flavoring. Best of all, they have always contained little or no fat.

Popovers also are low in fat, quick, and leavened with steam rather than baking powder or baking soda, making them low in sodium as well. When subjected to intense heat, the thin, liquid popover batter puffs quickly into a high and hollow shell.

I love to bake quick breads in small loaves so that I can freeze them individually. The rules are simple for successful freezing: Wrap the loaves airtight, then label and date them. Properly wrapped and frozen, they can be kept for up to four months.

Some quick breads are delicious with no spread at all. Low-fat and fat-free cream cheese are good options for on-hand spreads to pull out at a moment's notice. While there are a number of fat-free spreads in the dairy case at the supermarket, I like to make my own. The three included in this chapter are just suggestions. Dried fruits, such as prunes, raisins, cranberries, blueberries, and cherries, finely chopped and mixed with low-fat cream cheese, make delicious spreads. I make savory spreads using puréed beans, chickpeas, or split peas blended with herbs to go on savory breads. Cream cheese mixed with tomato salsa makes a great spread for corn sticks or corn-meal muffins. Fat-free pumpkin, apple, apricot, or prune "butters" are delicious on muffins, popovers, and quick breads, too.

High and Mighty Popovers

Popovers are puffy, steam-leavened breads that are baked in a hot oven. They're irresistible served hot from the oven with a bit of butter, jam, or a sandwich mixture.

2 large eggs, at room temperature

1 cup skim milk

$\frac{1}{2}$ teaspoon salt

1 cup all-purpose flour (see Note)

Preheat the oven to 450°F. Coat 6 (6-ounce) custard cups or popover pans with nonstick spray and preheat for 5 minutes in the oven.

Crack the eggs into the container of a blender; add the milk, salt, and flour and process for 10 seconds, scraping the sides of a container to blend in all of the flour, or mix for 30 seconds at high speed with an electric mixer until the batter is smooth.

Pour the batter into the preheated pans, dividing it equally. Bake for 15 minutes, then reduce the oven heat to 350°F. and bake for 25 to 35 minutes longer, or until the popovers are hollow and golden brown. Remove from the oven and tilt the popovers in the pan; pierce them with a knife to allow the steam to escape. Serve warm.

MAKES 6 POPOVERS

PER POPOVER: *109 calories, 16% calories from fat, 1.93 g fat, 71.7 mg cholesterol, 219 mg sodium, 0.52 g dietary fiber*

NOTE: Granulated flour (Wondra) makes wonderful popovers, although I've had good luck with all-purpose flour, too.

Scottish Buttermilk Scones

Unlike baking powder biscuits, these scones are relatively low in fat, yet light and fluffy. Serve them any time you would serve biscuits, with low-fat or fat-free cream cheese and fresh berry jam.

2 cups all-purpose flour

$\frac{1}{2}$ teaspoon baking soda

1 teaspoon cream of tartar

$\frac{1}{2}$ teaspoon salt

2 tablespoons unsalted butter, chilled, cut into small pieces

1 large egg, lightly beaten

$\frac{1}{2}$ to $\frac{3}{4}$ cup low-fat buttermilk

Preheat the oven to 425°F. Cover a baking sheet with parchment paper or coat with nonstick spray.

Sift the flour with the baking soda, cream of tartar, and salt into a large mixing bowl. Blend in the butter until completely incorporated into the dry ingredients.

Stir in the egg and then just enough buttermilk to make the dough hold together in a ball. Turn the dough out onto a lightly floured board and knead just a few seconds until smooth. Divide the dough into 12 equal pieces. Place them on the baking sheet and flatten with your knuckles or the tips of your fingers to form a roughly round shape. Pierce all over with a fork. Bake for 8 to 10 minutes, or until very lightly browned.

MAKES 12 SCONES

PER SCONE: *93.2 calories, 22% calories from fat, 2.24 g fat, 5.74 mg cholesterol, 140 mg sodium, 0.52 g dietary fiber*

Peppered Blue Corn Sticks

Blue cornmeal is actually blue in color and tastes a bit milder than yellow cornmeal. I buy it in the local whole-foods cooperative, but it is available in most health food stores and some supermarkets, as well as in Hispanic markets. You can, however, substitute yellow or white cornmeal if you cannot obtain blue cornmeal. Cayenne pepper gives the corn sticks a lot less heat than you'd think—$\frac{1}{2}$ teaspoon is just enough to create a mild burn.

- 1 cup blue cornmeal
- 1 cup all-purpose flour
- 2 tablespoons sugar
- 4 teaspoons baking powder
- $\frac{1}{2}$ teaspoon salt
- $\frac{1}{2}$ teaspoon cayenne pepper
- 1 large egg, lightly beaten
- 1 cup skim milk
- 3 tablespoons canola oil, olive oil, or melted butter

Preheat the oven to 425°F. Coat 14 corn stick molds with nonstick spray and place the pans in the oven as it preheats.

In a large mixing bowl, combine the cornmeal, flour, sugar, baking powder, salt, and cayenne; mix well. In a small bowl, beat the egg with the milk and oil. Make a well in the center of the dry ingredients and add the egg mixture; stir just to combine.

Remove the hot corn stick molds from the oven and fill each with 2 heaping tablespoons of the batter, spreading the batter out evenly so that it fills each corn shape completely.

Return the molds to the hot oven and bake for 9 to 10 minutes, or until the corn sticks are cooked through and lightly browned on top. Lift the corn sticks out of the molds with a small knife or spatula and place in a napkin-lined basket to serve.

MAKES 14 CORN STICKS

PER CORN STICK: 108 *calories, 26% calories from fat, 3.1 g fat, 22.2 mg cholesterol, 184 mg sodium, 0.95 g dietary fiber*

Caraway Tea Bread

Spread with Neufchâtel cheese and jam, this simple, cakelike bread is perfect for teatime.

- 1 tablespoon caraway seeds
- 3 cups all-purpose flour
- 3 teaspoons baking powder
- $\frac{1}{2}$ teaspoon salt
- $\frac{3}{4}$ cup sugar
- 6 tablespoons ($\frac{3}{4}$ stick) unsalted butter, at room temperature
- $\frac{3}{4}$ cup skim milk
- 1 large egg, lightly beaten

Preheat the oven to 375°F. Lightly grease a 9 × 5-inch loaf pan or coat with nonstick spray.

Put the caraway seeds into a small skillet and toast over medium heat for 2 to 3 minutes, until they become aromatic. Grind the caraway seeds in a small food chopper, with a mortar and pestle, or in a coffee grinder. Combine with the flour, baking powder, salt, and sugar in a mixing bowl. Add the butter and mix with an electric mixer until the butter is completely blended into the flour mixture. Blend in the milk and egg until well mixed, then turn out onto a lightly floured board and knead just until the dough forms a smooth ball. Gently shape into a loaf and place into the prepared pan. Bake for 60 minutes, or until a wooden skewer inserted into the center of the loaf comes out clean and dry.

MAKES 1 LOAF (16 SLICES)

PER SLICE: *164 calories, 27% calories from fat, 4.92 g fat, 25.1 mg cholesterol, 72.7 mg sodium, 0.66 g dietary fiber*

Irish Soda Bread

This recipe comes from a Dublin-born friend who serves it with hearty soups and stews. Although it slices the best on the second day, it is excellent hot. This bread is never made with added fat, although most buttermilk contains 1 percent fat. I often don't have buttermilk on hand but do have buttermilk powder, so I use it in this recipe.

4 cups whole wheat flour

2 cups all-purpose flour

1½ teaspoons salt

1½ teaspoons baking soda

2¼ cups water plus ½ cup plus 2 tablespoons buttermilk powder, or 2¼ cups buttermilk

Preheat the oven to 400°F. Cover a baking sheet with parchment paper or lightly grease or coat it with nonstick spray.

In a large mixing bowl, combine the flours, salt, and baking soda. Make a well in the center and add the water and buttermilk powder or the buttermilk. Stir with a wooden spoon until the dough is stiff.

Shape the dough into a ball and turn out onto a lightly floured board. Knead lightly just to make a smooth, round loaf. Place on the prepared baking sheet and flatten into a round 2 inches thick. Score a cross ½ inch deep through from edge to edge with a sharp knife. Bake for 35 to 40 minutes, until lightly browned. Remove from the pan and cool on a wire rack.

MAKES 1 LARGE LOAF (16 SLICES)

PER SLICE: *172 calories, 5% calories from fat, 0.96 g fat, 3.24 mg cholesterol, 303 mg sodium, 4.16 g dietary fiber*

Maple-Raisin Wheat Bread

This is an old, traditional American brown bread, naturally low in fat and deliciously grainy.

1½ cups low-fat buttermilk

2 tablespoons unsalted butter, melted

⅔ cup pure maple syrup

2 teaspoons baking soda

½ teaspoon salt

1⅓ cups whole wheat flour

1⅓ cups all-purpose flour

1 cup raisins

Preheat the oven to 350°F. Lightly grease or coat with nonstick spray a 9 × 5-inch loaf pan.

In a large mixing bowl, combine the buttermilk, butter, maple syrup, baking soda, salt, flours, and raisins. Stir just until all the dry ingredients are moistened. Turn the dough into the prepared pan or pans. Bake for 45 to 50 minutes or until a wooden skewer inserted in the center comes out clean. Remove from the pan and cool on a wire rack.

MAKES 1 LARGE LOAF (16 SLICES)

PER SLICE: *159 calories, 11% calories from fat, 1.97 g fat, 4.73 mg cholesterol, 197 mg sodium, 2.12 g dietary fiber*

Oat Soda Bread

I love this grainy, low-fat bread spread with whipped honey, and it is great toasted, too.

2 cups whole wheat flour

1 cup all-purpose flour

½ cup quick-cooking or old-fashioned rolled oats

1 teaspoon baking powder

1 teaspoon baking soda

½ teaspoon salt

3 tablespoons unsalted butter, melted

1½ cups buttermilk or 6 tablespoons buttermilk powder and 1½ cups water

Preheat the oven to 375°F. Cover a baking sheet with parchment paper or lightly grease or coat it with nonstick spray.

In a large mixing bowl, combine the flours and ¼ cup of the rolled oats. In another bowl, with a whisk, blend the baking powder, baking soda, and salt and add to the dry ingredients along with 2 tablespoons of the butter and the buttermilk. Stir until a stiff dough forms. Sprinkle the remaining oats on a bread board. Turn the dough out onto the board and knead for 1 minute, shaping the dough as you go into a perfectly round loaf. There should be a rather thick coating of extra oats on the outside of the loaf. Place the loaf onto the center of the baking sheet. With a sharp knife, score a cross about ½ inch deep on top of the loaf.

Bake for 35 to 40 minutes, or until a skewer inserted into the center of the loaf comes out clean and dry. Cool on a wire rack and brush with the reserved melted butter. Cool at least 4 hours before slicing.

MAKES ONE LARGE LOAF (16 SLICES)

PER SLICE: *117 calories, 21% calories from fat, 2.82 g fat, 7.77 mg cholesterol, 154 mg sodium, 2.36 g dietary fiber*

Orange-Chutney Quick Bread

This *is delicious served with fat-free Curried Cream Cheese Spread (page 152).*

2½ cups all-purpose flour

3 teaspoons baking powder

1 teaspoon salt

½ cup sugar

½ cup packed brown sugar

1 cup skim milk

¼ cup unsweetened applesauce

3 tablespoons canola oil

1 tablespoon grated orange zest

1 large egg, lightly beaten

¼ cup finely chopped walnuts

¾ cup chopped mango chutney

Preheat the oven to 350°F. Lightly oil or coat a 9 × 5-inch loaf pan with nonstick spray.

In a large mixing bowl, combine the flour, baking powder, salt, and sugars. Add the milk, applesauce, oil, orange zest, and egg and, with an electric mixer, beat at medium speed for 30 seconds, scraping the bowl often. With a wooden spoon, stir in the nuts and chutney. Pour the batter into the prepared pan.

Bake for 60 to 65 minutes, or until a wooden skewer inserted into the center of the loaf comes out clean and dry. Cool 5 minutes in the pan, then invert the loaf onto a wire rack to finish cooling.

MAKES 1 LOAF (20 SLICES)

PER SLICE: *183 calories, 16% calories from fat, 3.4 g fat, 10.9 mg cholesterol, 180 mg sodium, 0.63 g dietary fiber*

Poppy Seed and Date Bread

The crunch of poppy seeds give this bread a burst of flavor.

4 tablespoons (½ stick) unsalted butter, at room temperature

1 cup sugar

2 large eggs, lightly beaten

2½ teaspoons baking powder

½ teaspoon salt

¼ teaspoon ground nutmeg

2 cups all-purpose flour

1 cup skim milk

½ cup chopped dates

⅓ cup poppy seeds

¼ cup finely chopped walnuts

Preheat the oven to 350°F. Lightly grease a 9 × 5-inch baking pan or coat with nonstick spray.

In a large bowl, cream the butter and sugar together. Add the eggs and beat until light and fluffy. In another bowl, stir the baking powder, salt, and nutmeg into the flour, and add the mixture to the creamed ingredients along with the milk; beat until light. Fold in the dates, poppy seeds, and walnuts until evenly blended.

Pour the mixture into the prepared pan and bake for 1 hour and 10 minutes, or until a wooden skewer inserted into the center of the loaf comes out clean.

MAKES 1 LOAF (16 SLICES)

PER SLICE: *184 calories, 29% calories from fat, 6.15 g fat, 34.6 mg cholesterol, 136 mg sodium, 1.13 g dietary fiber*

Quick Banana Bread

Although I never thought my favorite banana bread was very high in fat, analysis of the recipe proved me wrong. It turned out to have 46 percent calories from fat and 8 grams of fat per slice. So I began trimming. Eliminating the nuts brought the total down to 40 percent, and replacing half the butter with applesauce brought the total down to an acceptable 26 percent, with 4 grams of fat per serving. The bread couldn't be simpler to make, though. I just throw all of the ingredients into a food processor and whirl it up.

1½ cups all-purpose flour

¾ cup sugar

1 teaspoon baking soda

½ teaspoon salt

4 tablespoons (½ stick) unsalted butter, at room temperature

½ cup unsweetened applesauce

⅓ cup skim milk

1 large egg, lightly beaten

2 medium (1 cup) bananas, sliced

1 tablespoon lemon juice

Preheat the oven to 350°F. Lightly grease or coat with nonstick spray one 9 × 5-inch or two 5 × 3-inch loaf pans.

Combine the flour, sugar, baking soda, and salt in a food processor with the metal blade in place. Process just until the dry ingredients are mixed. Add the butter, applesauce, milk, egg, bananas, and lemon juice and process just until the dry ingredients are moistened, scraping the sides of the bowl two times.

Turn the batter into the pan or pans. Bake for 1 hour for the large loaf, or 40 to 45 minutes for the small loaves, or until a wooden skewer inserted in the center of the loaf comes out clean and dry. Cool the bread in the pan for 5 minutes, then turn out onto a wire rack to finish cooling.

MAKES 1 LARGE LOAF (16 SLICES) OR 2 SMALL LOAVES

PER SLICE: *124 calories, 26% calories from fat, 3.67 g fat, 34.5 mg cholesterol, 129 mg sodium, 0.61 g dietary fiber*

Cinnamon-Sugared Rhubarb Nut Bread

A *buttery crust of cinnamon sugar and a half cupful of nuts seem like luxuries in a quick bread, but this sumptuous bread has only 29 percent calories from fat.*

1½ **cups packed brown sugar**

⅓ **cup vegetable oil**

1 **large egg, lightly beaten**

1 **cup low-fat buttermilk**

1 **teaspoon vanilla**

1 **teaspoon salt**

1 **teaspoon baking soda**

2½ **cups all-purpose flour**

1½ **cups thinly sliced fresh rhubarb**

½ **cup finely chopped walnuts**

½ **cup sugar**

2 **teaspoons cinnamon**

1 **tablespoon unsalted butter, melted**

Preheat the oven to 350°F. Lightly grease two 8½ × 4½-inch loaf pans or coat with nonstick spray.

In a large mixing bowl, combine the brown sugar, oil, and egg. Mix until well blended. Add the buttermilk, vanilla, salt, baking soda, and flour. Mix with an electric mixer until thick and light. Stir in the rhubarb and walnuts. Pour the batter into the prepared pans. Blend the sugar, cinnamon, and butter together and sprinkle over the batter.

Bake for 55 to 65 minutes, or until a wooden skewer inserted into the loaves comes out clean and dry. Let cool for 5 minutes in the pans, then turn out onto a wire rack to cool.

MAKES 2 LOAVES (16 SLICES EACH)

PER SLICE: *125 calories, 29% calories from fat, 4.09 g fat, 7.9 mg cholesterol, 107 mg sodium, 0.5 g dietary fiber*

Pumpkin–Sunflower Seed Bread

I like to make little loaves of pumpkin bread to give as gifts. This makes two large or six small loaves. My original recipe called for chopped pecans, but I found a significant fat reduction in using dry-roasted sunflower seeds. Not only do they add a wholesome, nutty flavor, but they retain the crunchy texture. If you leave out the sunflower seeds, the percentage of calories from fat drops to 27 and the grams of fat to 4, per slice.

2 cups all-purpose flour

1⅓ cups whole wheat flour

3 cups sugar

2 teaspoons baking soda

1½ teaspoons salt

1 teaspoon ground cinnamon

1 teaspoon ground nutmeg

¾ cup (1½ sticks) unsalted butter, melted

3 large eggs, lightly beaten

2 cups canned pumpkin purée

1 cup plain nonfat yogurt

½ cup dry-roasted sunflower seeds

Preheat the oven to 350°F. Coat two 9 × 5-inch loaf pans, or 6 small 5 × 3-inch pans, with nonstick spray and dust them lightly with flour.

In a large mixing bowl, stir together the flours, sugar, baking soda, salt, cinnamon, and nutmeg. In another bowl, whisk the butter, eggs, pumpkin purée, and yogurt together, and add to the dry ingredients. Add the sunflower seeds and stir with a wooden spoon just until the dry ingredients are moistened.

Divide the batter between the pans and bake for 1 hour, or until a wooden skewer inserted in the center of a loaf comes out clean and dry. Bake the small loaves for 40 to 45 minutes, or until they test done. Cool 5 minutes in the pans. Turn out onto a wire rack to finish cooling.

MAKES 2 LARGE LOAVES

(18 SLICES EACH)

PER SLICE: *182 calories, 29% calories from fat, 6.01 g fat, 31.6 mg cholesterol, 146 mg sodium, 1.27 g dietary fiber*

Icelandic Three-Grain Brown Bread

This is a delicious dark bread that is quick and easy to make and is inherently low in fat. It slices the best the day after it is baked and it is excellent toasted.

¼ cup packed brown sugar

4 tablespoons (½ stick) unsalted butter, at room temperature

½ cup quick-cooking rolled oats

½ cup dark rye flour

1 cup whole wheat flour

1 cup all-purpose flour

½ teaspoon salt

2 teaspoons baking soda

1¼ cups low-fat buttermilk

Preheat the oven to 350°F. Lightly grease one 9 × 5-inch loaf pan or coat with nonstick spray.

In a large bowl, cream the brown sugar and butter together. Combine the rolled oats, flours, salt, and baking soda into the bowl and stir until well blended. Add the buttermilk and stir with a rubber spatula until all the dry ingredients are moistened. Turn the mixture into the prepared pan and smooth the top. Bake for 1 hour, or until a wooden skewer inserted into the center of the loaf comes out clean and dry.

MAKES 1 LOAF (16 SLICES)

PER SLICE: *120 calories, 26% calories from fat, 3.52 g fat, 8.47 mg cholesterol, 192 mg sodium, 1.97 g dietary fiber*

Zucchini Loaves

I *used applesauce to replace ¾ cup of the oil in my original recipe and greatly improved the flavor of this popular bread while reducing the total fat.*

¼ cup chopped pecans
3½ cups all-purpose flour
1 teaspoon salt
1 teaspoon baking soda
1 teaspoon baking powder
1 teaspoon ground cinnamon
2 large eggs, lightly beaten
¾ cup sugar
¾ cup packed brown sugar
¼ cup canola or corn oil
2 teaspoons vanilla
¾ cup sweetened applesauce
2½ cups shredded fresh unpeeled zucchini

Preheat the oven to 350°F. Lightly grease or coat with nonstick spray four 5 × 3-inch loaf pans or two 8 × 4-inch loaf pans.

Spread the pecans on a baking sheet and toast in the oven as the oven preheats, for 5 to 6 minutes or just until aromatic; remove from the oven and cool.

In a mixing bowl, mix the flour, salt, baking soda, baking powder, and cinnamon. In another bowl, mix the eggs, sugars, oil, vanilla, and applesauce. Stir the liquid ingredients into the dry ingredients just until the dry ingredients are moistened. Fold in the shredded zucchini and the pecans.

Pour the batter into the prepared pans. Bake the small loaves for 35 to 40 minutes, and the large loaves for 55 to 60 minutes, or until a wooden skewer inserted into the center of a loaf comes out clean and dry.

Cool the loaves for 5 minutes in the pans, then turn out onto a wire rack to finish cooling.

MAKES 20 GENEROUS SLICES

PER SLICE: *156 calories, 26% calories from fat, 4.47 g fat, 21.3 mg cholesterol, 159 mg sodium, 0.97 g dietary fiber*

Fat-Free Lemon and Cheese Spread

1 (8-ounce) package fat-free cream cheese, at room temperature

1 tablespoon confectioners' sugar

1 teaspoon grated lemon zest

1 tablespoon lemon juice

In a medium mixing bowl, beat the cream cheese, confectioners' sugar, lemon zest, and lemon juice with an electric mixer until well blended and light. Turn into a serving dish.

MAKES 16 SERVINGS
(2 TABLESPOONS EACH)

PER SERVING: *18 calories, 0% calories from fat, 0 g fat, 2.53 mg cholesterol, 101 mg sodium, 0 g dietary fiber*

Curried Cream Cheese Spread

1 (8-ounce) package fat-free cream cheese, at room temperature

2 teaspoons confectioners' sugar

2 teaspoons curry powder

1 teaspoon grated orange zest

In a medium mixing bowl, beat the cream cheese, confectioners' sugar, curry powder, and orange zest with an electric mixer until well blended and light. Turn into a serving dish.

MAKES 16 SERVINGS
(2 TABLESPOONS EACH)

PER SERVING: *14.5 calories, 0% calories from fat, 0 g fat, 2.5 mg cholesterol, 85.2 mg sodium, 0 g dietary fiber*

Fat-Free Apricot Cheese Spread

1 (8-ounce) package fat-free cream cheese, at room temperature

¼ cup apricot preserves

1 teaspoon grated orange zest

In a medium mixing bowl, beat the cream cheese, apricot preserves, and orange zest with an electric mixer until well blended and light. Turn into a serving dish.

MAKES 16 SERVINGS
(2 TABLESPOONS EACH)

PER SERVING: *28.7 calories, 0% calories from fat, 0 g fat, 2.53 mg cholesterol, 102 mg sodium, 0.05 g dietary fiber*

BREAKFAST
YEAST BREADS

For breakfast, brunch, or a morning coffee get-together, these yeast-raised treats are real crowd-pleasers, although they are usually loaded with fat. My new versions minimize the fat in a variety of ways. I baked the doughnuts instead of frying them to eliminate much of the fat, and I reduced the fat in the yeast doughs, as well as in the fillings. Because nuts are high in fat, I used just enough of them in the filling for the Pecan Butter Coffee Cake to add texture.

Except for the Baked Raised Doughnuts, which taste best hot out of the oven, I like to keep coffee breads on hand in the freezer. We live "way out" in the country, and I figure that anybody who would take all that time to drive out to visit deserves to be offered coffee and a treat.

Reduced-fat yeast-raised breakfast breads will go stale quickly, so immediately after the breads have cooled, I wrap slices or individual portions in plastic and place them in a rigid plastic container to freeze. Then I can remove just as much as I want for serving. To reheat, let them stand at room temperature for about forty-five minutes, or microwave them on high power for thirty seconds at a time, turning the breads around often, or place the unwrapped breads on a cookie sheet in a 300°F. oven for ten to fifteen minutes.

For general information about yeast and yeast breads, see page 168.

Cinnamon Breakfast Rolls

Sweet yeast rolls depend more on the action of yeast for tenderness than on fat. I use all-purpose flour rather than bread flour because all-purpose flour contains more starch, yielding tenderness rather than the tougher dough structure that is necessary for most yeast breads. It is critical, however, to bake these rolls the minimum length of time, or just until they test done, to retain delicious moistness. My favorite glaze for cinnamon rolls is made with coffee and confectioners' sugar. This is a simple-to-stir-up refrigerated dough that requires no kneading. To serve for breakfast, you can shape the rolls in the evening, cover, and refrigerate them overnight.

¼ cup warm water (105°F to 115°F)

1 package or 1 tablespoon active dry yeast

½ cup sugar

1½ teaspoons salt

1 large egg, lightly beaten

3 to 3½ cups all-purpose flour

2 tablespoons unsalted butter, at room temperature

1 teaspoon ground cinnamon

GLAZE

½ cup confectioners' sugar

1 to 2 teaspoons hot strong coffee

In a large mixing bowl, combine the warm water and the yeast. Let stand until the yeast begins to foam, about 5 minutes. Add ¼ cup of the sugar, the salt, the egg, and 1½ cups of the flour. Beat until the batter is very smooth. With a wooden spoon, stir in additional flour until a soft but still sticky dough forms. Scrape the sides of the bowl clean, then cover with plastic wrap and refrigerate 4 to 24 hours.

Dust the dough lightly with flour. Scrape down the sides of the bowl again and turn the dough out onto a lightly floured surface. Roll out to make a rectangle about 12 inches square and ½ inch thick. Spread with the butter. Mix the remaining ¼ cup sugar with the cinnamon and sprinkle the mixture over the top of the dough. Roll up to form a log. Cut into twelve slices. Place into a lightly greased 9 × 13-inch baking pan. Cover and refrigerate overnight or let rise at room temperature for 1 hour, or until doubled. If the rolls are refrigerated, before baking bring them to room temperature and let rise for 45 minutes to 1 hour, or until doubled.

Preheat the oven to 375°F.

Bake the rolls for 20 to 25 minutes, or until just golden brown. Mix the confectioners' sugar and coffee to make a thin glaze. Brush the top of the hot rolls with the glaze.

MAKES 12 ROLLS

PER ROLL: *178 calories, 13% calories from fat, 2.63 g fat, 22.9 mg cholesterol, 95.4 mg sodium, 0.97 g dietary fiber*

Baked Raised Doughnuts

Raised doughnuts have been my weakness ever since I was a young teenager going to the Minnesota State Fair. The basic dough is not at all full of fat, and baking the doughnuts, instead of frying, significantly reduces the percentage of calories from fat. These doughnuts have a nice, spongy, yeast-doughnut texture, but they are missing the greasy crust. I like to enrich the dough with additional non-fat dry milk to give a more tender and spongy texture to the finished product.

1 cup skim milk

¼ cup instant nonfat dry milk

4 tablespoons (½ stick) unsalted butter, cut into pieces

2 teaspoons salt

½ teaspoon ground nutmeg

½ teaspoon grated lemon zest

1 package or 1 tablespoon active dry yeast

1 tablespoon sugar

1 cup warm water (105°F. to 115°F.)

5 to 5½ cups all-purpose flour

1 large egg, beaten

½ cup sugar

HONEY GLAZE

1 tablespoon honey

1 cup confectioners' sugar

1 to 2 tablespoons water

In a small saucepan, heat the milk over medium-high heat until tiny bubbles begin to appear at the edges. Remove from the heat.

In a large mixing bowl, combine the hot skim milk, dry milk powder, butter, salt, nutmeg, and lemon zest. Let stand until the butter is melted. Meanwhile, in a small bowl, dissolve the yeast and 1 tablespoon sugar in the warm water. Let stand 5 minutes until the yeast begins to bubble.

Add 3 cups of the flour, the yeast mixture, the egg, and the sugar to the milk mixture. Beat until smooth and satiny. Add the remaining flour, beating between each addition, until the dough is smooth but still soft. The dough will have a consistency a little stiffer than a batter bread. Cover and let rise in a warm place for 1 hour.

Cover two baking sheets with parchment paper or lightly grease or coat them with nonstick spray.

Turn the dough out onto a floured board and pat out to about ½ inch thickness. With a doughnut cutter, cut out the doughnuts and place them on the prepared baking sheets. Stretch each doughnut as you place them on the baking sheets so that the hole is at least 2 inches in diameter (if this is not done, the hole will close up during baking). Let rise until doubled, 30 to 45 minutes. You will be able to get 24 doughnuts cut out of the dough. Knead the scraps and doughnut holes together lightly and let rise for 15 minutes. Reroll the dough and cut out 12 more doughnuts.

Preheat the oven to 400°F. Bake the doughnuts for 10 minutes, or until lightly browned.

Meanwhile, heat the honey in the microwave oven until it is thin and runny, about 15 seconds at high power. Add the confectioners' sugar and mix well. Add enough water to make a thin glaze.

Place a wire rack over wax paper. Remove the hot doughnuts from the baking sheet to the wire rack. Brush with the honey glaze.

MAKES 36 DOUGHNUTS

PER DOUGHNUT: *102 calories, 14% calories from fat, 1.60 g fat, 9.56 mg cholesterol, 97.4 mg sodium, 0.52 g dietary fiber*

Pecan Butter Coffee Cake

This is so easy to make, and your guests won't believe it is low in fat, too, thanks to the "magic of yeast." The yeast batter is quick to mix, and you spoon it out onto a pecan and butter mixture in the pan.

TOPPING

3 tablespoons unsalted butter

3 tablespoons chopped pecans

½ cup sugar

2 tablespoons dark corn syrup

½ teaspoon vanilla

YEAST BATTER

2¼ cups all-purpose flour

¼ cup sugar

1 tablespoon unsalted butter, at room temperature

1 teaspoon salt

1 package or 1 tablespoon active dry or rapid-rise yeast

¾ cup very warm water (120°F to 130°F)

1 large egg, lightly beaten

Coat a 9-inch square pan with nonstick spray.

Combine the butter, pecans, sugar, and corn syrup in a small saucepan. Heat over medium-low heat and stir until the sugar is dissolved. Remove from the heat and stir in the vanilla. Pour the pecan mixture into the pan.

In a mixing bowl, combine 1¼ cups of the flour, the sugar, butter, salt, and yeast. With an electric mixer, mix 15 seconds, or until the ingredients are blended. Pour in the water and add the egg; mix at medium speed, scraping the sides of the bowl, until the batter is smooth and elastic. Stir in the remaining flour until the mixture is smooth. Spoon the batter into the pan over the pecan mixture. Cover and let rise in a warm place for 45 minutes to 1 hour, or until doubled.

Preheat the oven to 375°F.

Bake the coffee cake for 30 to 35 minutes, or until golden brown. Immediately invert the coffee cake onto a heatproof serving plate. Let the pan remain a minute or so over the coffee cake so that the topping can drizzle down over its sides.

MAKES 12 SERVINGS

PER SERVING: *190 calories, 26% calories from fat, 5.53 g fat, 28.1 mg cholesterol, 186 mg sodium, 1.02 g dietary fiber*

Braided Cardamom Bread

Perfect served warm or toasted, this bread is a standby at our house. Lately, I've started making it with nonfat milk and a little less sugar. If we have any left over, I cut it into slices, lay it on a baking sheet, and toast the slices in a medium oven (350°F) for 10 to 15 minutes, until the slices are toasted and crisp. This was my brothers' and sisters' favorite "toast" as children. We used to spread it with butter and peanut butter and eat it along with a glass of milk.

2 packages or 2 tablespoons active dry yeast

½ cup warm water (105°F. to 115°F.)

¾ cup plus 1 teaspoon sugar

1 teaspoon freshly crushed cardamom seeds

½ cup instant nonfat dry milk

1½ cups warm skim milk (105°F. to 115°F.)

2 large eggs, at room temperature

2 cups bread flour

4½ to 5 cups all-purpose flour

½ cup (1 stick) unsalted butter, at room temperature or melted

Egg glaze (see Note)

Sugar for sprinkling (optional)

In a large bowl, dissolve the yeast in the warm water; add 1 teaspoon of the sugar, stir, and let stand for 5 minutes until the yeast foams. Add the cardamom seeds, dry milk, warm skim milk, and eggs; beat well. Stir in the remaining ¾ cup sugar until it is dissolved. Stir in the bread flour and beat with a wooden spoon until the dough is smooth and shiny. Cover and let rest for 10 minutes. Beat in 2 cups of the all-purpose flour until the batter is smooth and elastic. Mix in the butter until blended. Stir in the remaining flour, ½ cup at a time, until a soft dough is formed. Scrape down the sides of the bowl well.

Sprinkle a bread board with flour and turn the dough out onto it. Knead, adding flour, if necessary, 1 tablespoon at a time, until the dough is smooth and satiny, 5 to 7 minutes. Wash the bowl, dry it, and spray with nonstick spray. Place the dough in the bowl, turning the dough to coat the top. Cover the bowl with plastic wrap. Place in a warm spot and let rise until doubled, 1 to 1½ hours.

Coat a work surface with nonstick spray and turn the dough out onto it. Knead lightly to remove air bubbles. Divide the dough into two parts. Divide each part into three parts. Roll out to make strands about 24 inches long. Make two braids, using three strands each.

Cover baking sheets with parchment paper and place loaves on them. If the baking sheets are large enough, you can bake both loaves on one; if not, bake them separately on two sheets. Cover and let rise until doubled, about 1 hour.

Preheat the oven to 375°F.

Brush the loaves with the egg glaze and sprinkle with sugar, if desired. Bake for 20 to 25 minutes, until golden, or until a wooden skewer inserted in the center of a loaf comes out clean. Remove and place the loaves on a wire rack to cool.

MAKES 2 LOAVES (20 SLICES EACH)

PER SLICE: *104 calories, 24% calories from fat, 2.73 g fat, 17.2 mg cholesterol, 13.4 mg sodium, 0.54 g dietary fiber*

NOTE: To make the egg glaze, mix together 1 large egg white and 1 tablespoon skim milk.

YEAST ROLLS
AND BUNS

As someone who lives in the proverbial boonies, I find it much quicker and simpler to make and bake fresh yeast rolls and buns than to run out to get them when I need them. Admittedly, if I had a bakery right around the corner, I probably wouldn't bother, but I don't. And I suspect lots of you don't have a bakery just around the corner, either, unless you live in a big city. Country folks need to be resourceful!

Most of the rolls can be mixed and baked rather quickly, in less than two hours from start to serving. The breads all freeze perfectly. They are low in fat, which means they will go stale and dry out rather quickly, so cool, wrap, and freeze them as soon as possible to retain freshness.

Basil Butterhorns

Stir up the dough for these light basil-scented crescent-shaped rolls and refrigerate it overnight. Chilled dough is easy to roll out and shape, and it handles best when you work with a portion of it at a time. For the most tender results, bake the rolls just until they are golden. You can freeze the unbaked rolls for up to four weeks before baking.

- 1 cup skim milk
- 1 package or 1 tablespoon regular active dry yeast (see Note)
- ¼ cup warm water (105°F. to 115°F.)
- ½ cup sugar
- 4 tablespoons (½ stick) unsalted butter, melted
- 1 teaspoon salt
- 2 large eggs, lightly beaten
- 1 tablespoon dried basil
- 4 to 4½ cups all-purpose flour

In a small saucepan, heat the milk over medium-high heat just until bubbles begin to form around the edges. Remove from the heat and let cool.

In a mixing bowl, dissolve the yeast in the warm water. Let stand 5 minutes, until the yeast begins to foam. Add the milk, sugar, 1 tablespoon of the butter, salt, eggs, and basil. Beat in 2 cups of the flour until the batter is smooth and satiny. Stir in the remaining flour ½ cup at a time until a soft and sticky dough is formed. Cover and refrigerate the dough 2 hours or overnight.

Cover two baking sheets with parchment paper or lightly grease or dust the baking sheets with nonstick spray.

Dust the refrigerated dough lightly with flour and turn it out onto a floured board. Knead briefly to shape the dough into a ball. Divide the dough into three parts. Working with one part of the dough at a time, roll it out to make a 12-inch circle. Brush with 1 tablespoon of the remaining butter. Cut the circle into twelve pie-shaped wedges and roll each up from the wide end. Turn the rolls into a crescent shape and place on the prepared baking sheet with the point down. Repeat with the remaining dough. (The rolls may be frozen at this point; see Note.) Cover and let rise in a warm place until doubled, about 45 minutes.

Preheat the oven to 375°F. Bake the rolls for 13 to 15 minutes, or just until light golden brown.

MAKES 36 ROLLS

PER ROLL: *90.5 calories, 20% calories from fat, 2.06 g fat, 27.3 mg cholesterol, 71.8 mg sodium, 0.79 g dietary fiber*

NOTE: Rapid-rise or quick-rise yeasts are not developed for refrigerated doughs, therefore I recommend using regular active dry yeast in this recipe. To freeze the rolls, place them on a baking sheet in the freezer until they are frozen solid, then place the frozen rolls into an airtight container. Remove frozen rolls and place on a baking sheet and allow to thaw and rise as directed above. Bake as directed above.

Beer Brat Buns

A dark, full-flavored beer gives these buns a hearty flavor. Simmer smoked brats in beer, too, or barbecue them. I usually use my large food processor to mix up the dough in a few seconds (see Note for alternate mixing directions).

1 package or 1 tablespoon active dry yeast

¼ cup warm water (105°F. to 115°F.)

1 (12-ounce) bottle of dark beer, warmed to 105°F. to 115°F.

1 tablespoon brown sugar

1½ teaspoons salt

1 tablespoon olive or canola oil

1 teaspoon caraway seeds

1 cup dark rye flour

2½ to 3 cups bread flour

In a large mixing bowl, dissolve the yeast in the warm water. Add the beer and brown sugar and let stand for 5 minutes, until the mixture begins to bubble. Add the salt, oil, and caraway seeds.

Stir in the flours, 1 cup at a time, mixing until a stiff dough forms. Cover and let rest for 15 minutes. Turn out onto a lightly floured board and knead until the dough is smooth and satiny, 8 to 10 minutes. Place into a lightly oiled bowl, turning to coat the top of the dough. Cover and let rise for 45 minutes to 1 hour, until doubled.

Turn out onto a lightly oiled surface. Cut the dough into eight equal parts. Shape each into a large oblong bun. Cover a baking sheet with parchment paper or coat with nonstick spray. Place the shaped buns onto the prepared baking sheet. Cover and let rise for 45 minutes, or until puffy.

Preheat the oven to 375°F.

Bake the buns for 20 minutes, or until lightly browned.

MAKES 8 BUNS

PER BUN: *225 calories, 11% calories from fat, 2.54 g fat, 0 mg cholesterol, 404 mg sodium, 3.74 g dietary fiber*

NOTE: To mix the dough in a food processor, measure all of the ingredients (using the entire 3 cups of bread flour) except for the water and beer into the work bowl of the food processor. Mix for 10 seconds. With the motor running, slowly add the water and beer, processing until the dough cleans the sides of the bowl and turns around the bowl 15 to 20 times. Proceed as directed for rising, shaping, and baking.

Grissini

These thin and crispy breadsticks make a great presentation standing up in a crock, but they won't stay there for long!

1 package or 1 tablespoon active dry or rapid-rise yeast

1½ cups warm water (105°F. to 115°F.)

½ teaspoon salt

2 tablespoons olive oil

4 to 4½ cups unbleached all-purpose flour

1 to 2 teaspoons coarse (kosher) salt

In a large mixing bowl, mix the yeast, water, salt, oil, and 2 cups of the flour; beat well. Let stand 15 minutes, until the mixture begins to bubble.

Stir in the remaining flour to make a soft dough. Turn out onto a lightly floured board and gently knead the dough until it is smooth and all of the flour has been evenly incorporated, 3 to 5 minutes.

Place the dough into a lightly oiled, clean bowl, turning to coat the top of the dough. Cover and let rise for 1 hour, or until doubled.

Coat a work surface with nonstick spray. Turn the dough out onto the work surface. With lightly oiled hands, press the dough into a flat rectangle, then roll out to ¼-inch thickness, about 24 inches by 18 to 20 inches. Sprinkle the surface with coarse salt. With a rolling pin, lightly roll the salt into the surface of the dough. With a pizza cutter or pastry wheel, cut the dough into long strips ⅜ inch wide and 18 to 20 inches long.

Coat two baking sheets with nonstick spray and place the dough strips lengthwise on the sheets. Cover and let rise until puffy, 30 to 45 minutes.

Preheat the oven to 375°F.

Bake the grissini for 15 to 20 minutes, until very crisp and golden.

MAKES ABOUT 40 GRISSINI

PER GRISSINI: 48.4 calories, 15% calories from fat, 0.79 g fat, 0 mg cholesterol, 80.3 mg sodium, 0.37 g dietary fiber

Mashed Potato Dinner Rolls

Mashed potatoes add a delicate tenderness to these rolls. Although the olive oil isn't absolutely necessary for success, it tends to give yeast breads such as this one a wonderful thin, tender, yet crisp crust.

- 1 package or 1 tablespoon active dry or rapid-rise yeast
- 1 tablespoon sugar
- ¾ cup warm water (105°F. to 115°F.)
- 1½ teaspoons salt
- 3 tablespoons olive oil
- 2 large eggs, lightly beaten
- 1 cup mashed cooked potatoes
- 4 to 4½ cups all-purpose flour

In a large mixing bowl, dissolve the yeast and the sugar in the water. Let stand until the yeast begins to foam, about 5 minutes. Whisk in the salt, oil, eggs, and potatoes. Whisk in 2 cups of the flour, 1 cup at a time, until the dough is smooth. Stir in enough of the remaining flour to make a stiff dough. Cover and let stand for 15 minutes.

Sprinkle a work surface with flour and turn the dough out onto it. Knead until smooth and elastic, about 5 minutes, adding flour as needed to prevent stickiness.

Wash the bowl, lightly oil it, then place the dough into the bowl. Turn the dough to coat the top. Cover and let rise in a warm place for 1 to 1½ hours if using regular yeast, or 30 to 45 minutes if using rapid-rise yeast.

Cover a baking sheet with parchment paper.

Punch the dough down and divide it into twelve equal pieces. Shape each piece into a smooth round ball and place on the prepared baking sheet about 2 inches apart. Cover and let rise until puffy, 15 to 30 minutes.

Preheat the oven to 375°F.

Bake the rolls for 18 to 20 minutes, or until golden brown.

MAKES 12 ROLLS

PER ROLL: *201 calories, 21% calories from fat, 4.7 g fat, 35.8 mg cholesterol, 342 mg sodium, 1.48 g dietary fiber*

Poppy Seed Onion Rolls

These are lovely, big, light, flavorful rolls that are perfect for sandwiches. This is an easy-to-mix-up batter bread with a minimum of kneading.

1 cup skim milk

2 tablespoons sugar

1 teaspoon salt

1 tablespoon olive oil

¼ cup warm water (105°F. to 115°F.)

1 package or 1 tablespoon active dry yeast

3½ cups all-purpose flour

TOPPING

2 medium onions, thinly sliced

2 teaspoons olive oil

1 large egg, lightly beaten

¼ cup nonfat sour cream

½ teaspoon salt

1 tablespoon poppy seeds

In a small saucepan, heat the milk just until bubbles form around the edge of the pan. Remove from the heat and stir in the sugar, salt, and olive oil. Cool to lukewarm, or no more than 115°F.

Pour the water into a large bowl and sprinkle the yeast over; stir until the yeast is dissolved. Stir in the milk mixture. Add 2½ cups of the flour and, with an electric mixer at medium speed, beat until smooth, about 2 minutes. Add the remaining flour and stir with a wooden spoon until smooth. Cover the bowl with a sheet of plastic wrap (without allowing the wrap to touch the dough). Let rise in a warm place until doubled, about 1 hour.

Lightly grease two baking sheets or cover with parchment paper.

For the topping, cook the onions in the 2 teaspoons oil in a small skillet until tender, about 10 minutes. Cool. In a small bowl, combine the egg, sour cream, and salt until well blended.

Turn the dough out onto a well-floured board. Coat the ball of dough with flour and knead about 10 times, until the dough is smooth. Cut into twelve pieces and roll each into a ball. Place the balls of dough onto the prepared baking sheets and press slightly with the palm of your hand to flatten. The rolls will be about 3 inches in diameter. Press the onions onto the rolls and spread with the sour cream mixture; sprinkle with poppy seeds. Let rise, uncovered, in a warm place until doubled, about 45 minutes.

Preheat the oven to 375°F.

Bake the rolls for 20 to 25 minutes, or until golden.

MAKES 12 ROLLS

PER ROLL: *174 calories, 15% calories from fat, 2.92 g fat, 19.8 mg cholesterol, 279 mg sodium, 1.36 g dietary fiber*

Sour Cream Burger Buns

Light *sour cream adds tenderness to any yeast dough. If you use all-purpose flour instead of bread flour, you may need to use a little more flour, because all-purpose flour doesn't absorb as much liquid.*

- **1 package or 1 tablespoon active dry or rapid-rise yeast**
- **1 tablespoon sugar**
- **1 cup warm water (105°F. to 115°F.)**
- **1½ teaspoons salt**
- **1 cup light sour cream**
- **4 to 4½ cups bread or unbleached all-purpose flour**

Measure the water into a large mixing bowl. Sprinkle the yeast and sugar over the water and let stand 5 minutes, until the yeast dissolves and foams. Sprinkle the salt over and mix in the sour cream.

Add the flour gradually, mixing with a wooden spoon, until the dough is stiff. Cover and let rest for 15 minutes. Sprinkle a work surface with flour and turn the dough out onto the flour. Knead for 5 minutes, or until the dough is smooth and springy. Or, if you have a mixer with a dough hook, mix up the dough in that bowl and knead with the dough hook for 5 minutes, until the dough is smooth and satiny in appearance, adding only as much flour as necessary.

Place the dough in a lightly oiled bowl, turning the dough to coat the top. Cover and let rise in a warm place until doubled, about 1 hour.

Cover a baking sheet with parchment paper or coat lightly with nonstick spray. Turn the dough out onto a lightly oiled surface. Shape into a long roll, cut into twelve equal pieces, and shape into balls. Place the balls of dough onto the baking sheet about 3 inches apart and flatten to a ½-inch thickness. Cover and let rise in a warm place for 25 minutes.

Preheat the oven to 425°F.

Bake the buns for 10 to 15 minutes, until golden brown. Slide the parchment with the buns onto the countertop to cool, or remove the buns to cool on a wire rack.

MAKES 12 BUNS

PER BUN: *176 calories, 10% calories from fat, 2.14 g fat, 3.33 mg cholesterol, 268 mg sodium, 1.46 g dietary fiber*

YEAST BREADS

All you need to make a yeast-raised bread are three ingredients: water, flour, and yeast. Salt is sometimes considered to be an essential, but all it does is control the yeast and add flavor. Sugar adds flavor to the crumb, helps to brown the crust, and feeds the yeast. Most bread recipes include salt, but not all include sugar.

Fat, shortening, butter, or oil is added in small quantities to the bread dough to tenderize the crumb and crust, to add flavor, and to keep the bread fresh longer. Fat in great quantity actually retards the growth of the yeast, so breads that have a large amount of fat also require more yeast or special handling. Therefore, most yeast bread recipes include a small amount of fat, making yeast bread a wonderful choice for a low-fat diet.

It's what we put on top of bread that makes it fattening. I have a friend who simply started eating bread with no spread at all, and by just cutting this fat from his diet he lost several pounds in a few weeks.

In this chapter are several wonderful low-fat breads that are great eaten all by themselves or spread with just enough butter to meld with the flavor of the grain. For every day, try the Basic Fat-Free White Bread. For wonderful, crunchy-crusted breads, try the European Country Bread, Hearth Bread, Sourdough Bread of the Old West, Black Currant Bread, or the Kalamata Olive Bread.

ABOUT YEAST

Yeast is a bacteria that is activated by a warm liquid. Yeast is really a live plant. All plants give off carbon dioxide when they grow. When yeast "grows" in a bread dough, the carbon dioxide gets trapped in the elastic structure created by the gluten in moistened flour. Carbon dioxide is lighter than air and makes little gas balloons in the bread dough, which causes it to rise.

Yeast is available in three forms: active dry, regular or quick-rising granules, or in a compressed cake. These yeasts are pretty much interchangeable; however, if you plan to refrigerate the dough, it is best to use regular dry yeast or compressed yeast rather than the quick-rising variety for the best results.

One package of active dry yeast, whether regular or a quick-rising variety, equals one scant tablespoon. For ease of measuring, and because I prefer to buy yeast in bulk, I call for one package or one tablespoon of active dry yeast in my recipes. If there is slightly more yeast in the mixture, it will not harm the dough at all; it just might make the dough rise more quickly.

In my recipes, I call for granular dry yeast, either regular or the quick-rising variety, although, if you prefer, you can substitute one cake of yeast for one package of active dry yeast.

Active dry or quick-rise yeast can be dissolved in warm water, no cooler than 105°F. (or it will stunt the development of the yeast) and no warmer than 115°F. (or it will kill the yeast). (Compressed yeast should be dissolved in water no warmer than 110°F.) Either type of dry granular yeast can be added to the flour mixture like any other ingredient, but then the temperature of the water or liquid should be between 120°F. and 130°F. because the flour and other ingredients provide a buffer and cool down the water rather quickly.

If you question the freshness of your yeast, you can check it by dissolving it in one quarter cup of the liquid in the recipe, warmed to 105°F. to 115°F. Add a small pinch of sugar and wait five minutes. If the yeast begins to bubble, it is alive. If not, get a new supply.

GETTING THE DOUGH TO RISE

Assuming the yeast is active, there are two basic reasons why bread might not rise: (1) the temperature of the dough is too cold (yeast is stunted) or the dough is too warm (yeast is killed) and (2) the dough is too dry (too much flour) and the yeast cannot form the little gas balloons to make the dough rise.

The ideal temperature for yeast to rise is 85°F., which is warmer than the average room temperature (70°F.). Where can you find a "warm place"?

1. A high shelf in the kitchen. Heat rises, and tops of cabinets are often warmer than counters.

2. A sunny window. To make a miniature "greenhouse," cover the bowl of dough with plastic wrap.

3. On top of the refrigerator. Most refrigerators produce heat and you can take advantage of that if there is enough clearance between the refrigerator and the cupboard above.

4. Fill the sink or a large pan with hot water and place a rack (an oven rack will do) over the top. Place the bowl of dough on the rack and cover it with a towel.

5. Turn the oven on to 300°F. for two minutes, then turn the oven off. Wrap the bowl of dough first in plastic, then with a damp towel. Place it in the oven and close the door. Let the dough rise until doubled.

6. Place the dough in an oiled glass or pottery bowl. Cover it with a well-dampened terry kitchen towel. Place it in a glass pie pan filled with warm water. Microwave on low power for five minutes at a time, feeling the dough with your hands between each five-minute interval. The dough should feel about as warm as body temperature.

If there is too much flour in the dough, cut the dough into chunks and return to the bowl, or put it into a heavy-duty mixer or food processor. Add warm water, one tablespoon at a time, and mix or process until the water is blended into the dough and it feels smooth and satiny. Let the dough rise until doubled.

Basic Fat-Free White Bread

The success of a yeast-raised loaf of bread does not depend on fat at all. The texture, flavor, and shape of the loaf are not at all affected. What is affected is the keeping quality of the bread; that is, fat-free bread will dry out more quickly than bread that has some fat in the formula. Fat-free bread does have wonderful eating qualities while it is still fresh, and the next day it makes wonderful toast for breakfast or sandwiches.

This recipe produces one perfect loaf. It's easy to handle, and you can make it four different ways: mix, knead, and shape it by hand; mix all of the ingredients in a food processor; mix all of the ingredients with a heavy-duty electric mixer; or add the ingredients to the container of a bread machine in the order in which your machine dictates—that is, either liquids first, yeast last, or vice versa. The fat in the nutritional analysis comes from the tiny amount of oil that is naturally present in any wheat flour.

- 1 package or 1 tablespoon active dry yeast (or for the bread machine, 1½ teaspoons yeast)
- 1¼ cups warm water (105°F. to 115°F.)
- 1 tablespoon sugar
- 1½ teaspoons salt
- 3 cups bread flour

In a large bowl, dissolve the yeast in the warm water and add the sugar and salt. Add the flour, a cupful at a time, beating well after each addition, until a soft but firm dough develops. Cover and let rest for 15 minutes. Turn out onto a floured board and knead until smooth and elastic, 5 to 8 minutes. Place in a clean, oiled bowl, turning to coat the top of the dough, and let rise in a warm place until doubled, about 45 minutes.

Lightly grease a 9 × 5-inch loaf pan or coat with nonstick spray. Turn the dough out onto a lightly oiled surface and knead lightly to express all the air bubbles. Shape into a loaf and place it with the smooth side up into the prepared pan. Cover and let rise in a warm place until almost doubled, about 1 hour.

Preheat the oven to 375°F.

Bake the bread until golden and a wooden skewer inserted into the center of the loaf comes out clean and dry, 25 to 30 minutes.

MAKES 1 LOAF (16 SLICES)

PER SLICE: 82.8 calories, 2% calories from fat, 0.22 g fat, 0 mg cholesterol, 201 mg sodium, 0.73 g dietary fiber

European Country Bread

Many Europeans eat as an everyday bread a standard, rough, chewy textured bread similar to this one. The only fat in this bread is the trace amount that is present naturally in the bread flour.

**2 packages or 2 tablespoons active dry
yeast**

**1½ cups warm water (105°F. to
115°F.)**

3 to 3½ cups bread flour

1½ teaspoons salt

2 teaspoons cornmeal

In a large bowl, combine the yeast, ¾ cup of the water, and 1 cup of the flour; beat until smooth and satiny. Cover and let stand in a warm place until spongy and doubled in bulk, about 30 minutes.

Stir the sponge down and add 1 cup more flour, the salt, and the remaining ¾ cup water. Add more flour, mixing until a stiff, but still soft, dough forms. Cover and let rest for 15 minutes. Turn out onto a lightly floured board and knead for 5 to 8 minutes, adding more flour if necessary to keep the dough from sticking. Or knead the dough with a heavy-duty mixer and a dough hook for 5 minutes, or put the dough into a food processor with the dough blade in place and process 1 minute.

Cut a sheet of foil about 12 inches square and sprinkle with the cornmeal. Shape the dough into a rough ball and place it onto the cornmeal-covered foil. Cover and let rise in a warm place until doubled, about 45 minutes.

Arrange the oven racks so that the top rack is in the center of the oven. Place a baking stone, if you have one, on the top rack. Place a heavy pan (such as the bottom part of the broiler pan that comes with most ovens) onto the bottom rack.

Preheat the oven to 450°F.

Transfer the loaf, still on the foil, onto the preheated baking stone or a baking sheet. Pour 1 cup water into the preheated pan on the lower oven rack. (This should create a burst of steam.) Close the oven door and bake for about 20 minutes, or until the loaf is browned, firm, and hollow-sounding when thumped. Remove from the oven and transfer onto a wire rack to cool.

MAKES 1 LOAF (16 SLICES)

PER SLICE: *121 calories, 2% calories from fat, 0.29 g fat, 0 mg cholesterol, 268 mg sodium, 1.58 g dietary fiber*

Hearth Bread

This rustic, plain white bread is easy to make. I shape it into a free-form round loaf on a baking sheet. When it is hot from the oven, I don't feel the need for any kind of spread.

- **1 cup skim milk**
- **1 package or 1 tablespoon active dry yeast**
- **¼ cup warm water (105°F. to 115°F.)**
- **1 tablespoon sugar**
- **1 teaspoon salt**
- **2 tablespoons olive oil**
- **3 to 3½ cups bread flour or unbleached all-purpose flour**

In a small saucepan, heat the milk over medium-high heat until bubbles begin to form around the edges. Remove from the heat and cool.

In a large mixing bowl, sprinkle the yeast over the warm water. Add the sugar and let stand 5 minutes, until the yeast begins to foam. Stir in the cooled milk, salt, and oil.

Beat in 1 cup of the flour until the mixture is smooth. Add more flour, a little at a time, until a stiff dough forms. Cover and let rest 15 minutes.

Turn the dough out onto a lightly floured board and knead until the dough is soft and springy, adding flour, if necessary, to keep the dough from being sticky. When the dough is sufficiently kneaded and the surface appears to have small blisters on it, place it in a clean, lightly oiled bowl. Cover with a towel and let rise for 1 hour in a warm place.

Punch the dough down and turn out onto a lightly oiled surface. Knead 30 seconds to squeeze out air bubbles. Shape the dough into a large round loaf. Lightly grease a baking sheet and place the loaf onto the sheet with the smooth side up. Cover with a towel and let rise until almost doubled, about 1 hour.

Preheat the oven to 375°F.

Brush the loaf with water and sprinkle with flour. Slash in three or four places using a sharp knife.

Bake for 20 to 25 minutes, or until the loaf sounds hollow when tapped on the bottom. Remove from the pan and cool on a wire rack.

MAKES 1 LOAF (ABOUT 15 SLICES)

PER SLICE: *114 calories, 17% calories from fat, 2.08 g fat, 0.27 mg cholesterol, 9.15 mg sodium, 0.83 g dietary fiber*

Sourdough Bread of the Old West

When the pioneers trudged westward with their covered wagons, they carried with them a pouch of sourdough starter. Today, sourdough bread has become a symbol of the West, but it's popular all over the country.

Sourdough bread is a simple mixture of starter, flour, and salt and has no fat added to it. Three percent of the calories are from fat, however; that is because the natural composition of wheat-based all-purpose flour has some vegetable fat along with carbohydrate and protein in its makeup.

Over the years, I've kept a starter going, which I started by setting a bowl of milk out in the open to "catch" wild yeast and then mixing it with flour and letting it stand until it was bubbly. This method is chancy, but when you get a good starter, the bread is fabulous. The classic way to save the starter is to mix the starter into a fresh batch of bread dough, then save back about a cupful, to use as yeast for the next baking. I have worked out the following method for making sourdough starter and it works well. But it takes many bakings to develop a rich sourdough flavor.

The starter needs to be made 12 to 15 hours ahead of time, so plan accordingly. For a wonderful crust on the bread and a light and airy texture, I recommend two techniques: bake the risen loaf on a preheated baking stone or tiles, and create steam in the oven by pouring water into a preheated pan placed on an oven rack beneath the tile-lined rack.

SOURDOUGH STARTER

1 package or 1 tablespoon active dry yeast

1½ cups warm water (105°F. to 115°F.)

2 cups unbleached all-purpose flour

BREAD DOUGH

4½ to 5 cups bread flour, plus 1 cup additional bread flour to replenish starter

1 cup warm water (105°F. to 115°F.)

2 teaspoons salt

To make the sourdough starter, in a large bowl (ideally a large plastic bowl that has a tight-fitting lid), dissolve the yeast in the warm water. Let stand for 5 minutes, until the yeast bubbles. Gradually stir in the 2 cups of flour, beating until the mixture is smooth and satiny. Cover and let stand at room temperature for 12 to 15 hours.

To make the bread dough, stir 1 cup of the bread flour, the warm water, and the salt into the starter. Add more flour until the dough is very stiff. Turn out onto a floured board and knead until the dough is smooth and elastic, adding flour as needed to keep the dough from being sticky. Or turn the dough into the bowl of a heavy-duty mixer with a dough hook and knead for 8 to 10 minutes, until the dough is smooth and elastic.

Wash the mixing bowl and lightly oil it. Return the dough to the bowl and cover. Coat the dough with nonstick spray. Let rise in a warm place until the dough is doubled, about 2 hours.

Turn the dough out onto a floured surface and reserve about 1 cup of the dough for your next baking. Place it into a large resealable plastic bag or a bowl or jar with a lid. Pour 1½ cups water over the reserved dough, add 1 cup bread flour, cover, and allow to bubble up again. Refrigerate until you are ready to bake again. For subsequent bakings, begin with the directions to make the bread dough.

Cut a 12-inch-square piece of foil.

Shape the remaining dough into a round loaf about 2½ inches thick. Place it on top of the foil with the smooth side up. Cover with a towel and let rise until doubled in volume, about 1 hour. With a sharp knife, slash the loaf across the top three or four times.

Position the oven racks so that one is in the center position and the other is in the bottom position. Place a baking stone or 4 (6- to 8-inch) unglazed tiles onto the center of the upper rack. Place a rimmed heavy baking pan or broiler pan (without its top) on the bottom rack.

Preheat the oven to 450°F. for 15 to 20 minutes.

Use a baker's peel or a rimless baking sheet as a tool to pick up the bread by sliding it under the foil. Slide the loaf on the foil onto the hot baking stone or tiles. Pour 1 cup of water into the heated pan on the lower oven shelf. Bake for 20 to 25 minutes, or until the loaf is golden. Remove to a rack and let cool.

MAKES 1 LARGE LOAF (18 SLICES)

Per slice: *115 calories, 3% calories from fat, 0.31 g fat, 0 mg cholesterol, 238 mg sodium, 0.97 g dietary fat*

Dill Batter Bread

The *cottage cheese lightens this very simple bread.*

1 package or 1 tablespoon active dry yeast

2 tablespoons sugar

½ cup warm water (105°F. to 115°F.)

2 cups nonfat cottage cheese, at room temperature

1 large egg, lightly beaten

1 tablespoon minced dry onion

1 tablespoon dill seed

1 teaspoon salt

3 cups bread flour

In a large mixing bowl, combine the yeast, sugar, water, cottage cheese, egg, onion, dill seed, and salt. Stir with a whisk until all the ingredients are well mixed.

With an electric mixer, beat in the flour ½ cup at a time until the batter is elastic. Cover and let rise in a warm place until doubled in bulk, about 1 hour.

Coat a 1½-quart round casserole dish or a 9-inch square pan with nonstick spray and dust with flour.

Stir the batter down and turn into the prepared dish. Let rise until the batter has almost doubled, about 30 to 45 minutes.

Preheat the oven to 350°F.

Bake the bread for 40 to 50 minutes, or until golden brown and a wooden skewer inserted through the bread comes out clean and dry.

MAKES 1 LOAF (16 SLICES)

Per slice: *113 calories, 5% calories from fat, 0.63 g fat, 14.6 mg cholesterol, 140 mg sodium, 0.79 g dietary fiber*

Herb Bread

You can mix this bread in a food processor without predissolving the yeast and let the dough rise in the work bowl. Instructions for making this in a bread machine also are provided. No matter how you make it, this bread is incredibly easy and is wonderful hot out of the oven drizzled with just a bit of extra-virgin olive oil.

3 cups all-purpose flour

1 package or 1 tablespoon active dry yeast

1 tablespoon sugar

1 teaspoon salt

2 teaspoons celery seed

2 teaspoons chopped fresh sage or 1 teaspoon dried sage

1 tablespoon olive oil

1 cup very warm water (130°F.)

Combine the flour, yeast, sugar, salt, celery seed, sage, and olive oil in the work bowl of a food processor with the dough blade in place. Turn the processor on and slowly add the water through the feed tube, processing until the dough comes together and forms a ball. Open the processor and pinch the dough. If the dough is very firm, add 1 to 2 tablespoons additional water and process again until the dough has absorbed the water and feels soft but not sticky. Cover and let rise for 45 minutes to 1 hour, or until doubled.

If you prefer to use a heavy-duty mixer with a dough hook, measure all of the ingredients into the bowl of the mixer. Turn the mixer on and mix until the dough is elastic and smooth. Cover and let rise until doubled.

To make this bread in a bread machine, pour the water into the bottom of the bread pan and measure the remaining ingredients into the pan, but add the yeast last. Program the machine to make dough, or to bake white bread. Check the dough during the kneading process; if it seems to be dry, add 1 to 2 tablespoons additional water.

Turn the risen dough out onto a lightly oiled work surface. Shape the dough into a smooth, round ball. Place in a greased round pan. Cover and let rise in a warm place, about 30 minutes, until almost doubled.

Preheat the oven to 375°F.

Bake the bread for 25 to 30 minutes, or until the loaf sounds hollow when tapped and a wooden skewer inserted through the center of the loaf comes out clean and dry.

For a crusty loaf: Place the shaped loaf on a 10-inch-square piece of foil to rise. Place a baking stone or a square of unglazed tiles onto the center oven rack. Place a heavy, flat pan (such as the base of a broiler pan) on the rack below the stone-topped rack. Preheat the oven to 475°F. Slash the risen loaf once or twice. Using a baker's peel or a rimless baking sheet, transfer the loaf (with the foil) onto the pre-heated stone. Pour about 1 cupful of water into the preheated pan below. This should create a burst of steam. Bake for 15 to 20 minutes, or until the loaf is crusty and golden.

MAKES 1 LOAF (16 SLICES)

PER SLICE: *91.3 calories, 11% calories from fat, 1.13 g fat, 0 mg cholesterol, 134 mg sodium, 0.76 g dietary fiber*

Sage Batter Bread

The inspiration for this bread is a sage batter cake described by Giuliano Bugialli that, though delicious, is more of a spoon bread, made with no yeast and lots of whole eggs. I loved the idea of sage in a batter bread and came up with this variation. And, as Giuliano describes for his batter cake, it is irresistible cut into squares and served with grated Parmesan cheese and sage leaves sprinkled all over it.

- **1 package or 1 tablespoon active dry yeast**
- **1 cup warm skim milk (105°F to 115°F)**
- **2 teaspoons sugar**
- **½ cup freshly grated Parmesan cheese**
- **1 teaspoon salt**
- **½ teaspoon coarsely ground black pepper**
- **1 large egg, lightly beaten**
- **3 cups all-purpose flour**
- **4 teaspoons chopped fresh sage or 2 teaspoons dried sage**
- **Additional Parmesan cheese and fresh sage leaves for serving (optional)**

In a large mixing bowl, mix the yeast, milk, sugar, Parmesan, salt, pepper, and egg. Let stand 5 minutes, until the yeast bubbles.

Beat in the flour ½ cup at a time until the mixture makes a stiff dough. Beat in the sage leaves until evenly mixed into the dough. Cover and let rise in a warm place until doubled, about 1 hour. Coat a 9-inch square baking pan with nonstick spray and dust with flour. Beat the batter down and pour into the pan. (You need not try to spread the batter into the corners because in rising it will spread out.)

Let the batter rise until almost doubled, about 30 minutes, in a warm place.

Preheat the oven to 350°F.

Bake the bread until a wooden skewer inserted in the center comes out clean and dry, about 40 to 45 minutes. Remove from the oven and cool on a wire rack.

Serve warm, cut into squares sprinkled with Parmesan cheese and chopped sage leaves, if desired.

MAKES 16 SERVINGS

PER SERVING: *103 calories, 12% calories from fat, 1.32 g fat, 15.5 mg cholesterol, 193 mg sodium, 0.73 g dietary fiber*

Milk and Honey Bread

A basic versatile bread, great for toasting, sand-wiches, or to serve with any meal. Shape it into an oblong loaf and bake it in a standard bread pan, or shape it into a round, a braid, or individual buns.

- **2½ cups skim milk**
- **1 package or 1 tablespoon active dry yeast**
- **1 teaspoon sugar**
- **1 tablespoon vinegar or lemon juice**
- **2 tablespoons olive or canola oil**
- **3 tablespoons honey**
- **2½ teaspoons salt**
- **5½ to 6 cups bread flour**

Heat the milk in a small saucepan over medium-high heat until bubbles begin to form around the edges. Remove from the heat and cool.

In a large bowl, dissolve the yeast and sugar in the warm milk. Let stand until foamy, about 10 minutes.

Add the vinegar, oil, honey, salt, and 2 cups of the flour. Beat well, until the mixture is smooth. Add the remaining flour ½ cup at a time, beating to keep the mixture smooth. When the dough is soft but will hold its shape, turn out onto a lightly floured board. Cover and let rest for 5 to 10 minutes.

Knead, adding flour 1 tablespoon at a time, for about 5 minutes, until the dough is smooth and satiny. Place in a clean, lightly greased bowl, turn to grease the top, and cover with a towel or plastic wrap.

Let rise until doubled in bulk, about 1 to 1½ hours. Turn the dough out onto a lightly oiled surface and knead to press out air bubbles. Divide the dough into two equal portions. Form into round or oblong loaves and place into lightly greased baking pans. Or divide the dough into three parts, roll into strands 20 inches long, and braid the three strands together to make a braided loaf. Place on a baking sheet covered with parchment paper. Cover with a towel and let rise in a warm place for 30 to 45 minutes, or until doubled in bulk.

Preheat the oven to 375°F. Bake the loaves for 30 to 35 minutes, or until a wooden skewer inserted into the center of a loaf comes out clean and dry. Remove from the pans and cool on a wire rack.

MAKES 2 LOAVES (20 SLICES EACH)

PER SLICE: *74.7 calories, 11% calories from fat, 0.87 g fat, 0.25 mg cholesterol, 142 mg sodium, 0.48 g dietary fiber*

Hungarian Fennel Bread

Fennel seeds speckle this simple white bread and add a faint licoricelike flavor. This recipe comes from a second-generation Hungarian friend, a great cook and baker. A thick slice of hot fennel bread and a bowl of hot vegetable soup is my idea of a perfect autumn lunch!

2 packages or 2 tablespoons active dry yeast

2 teaspoons sugar

2 teaspoons salt

1½ tablespoons fennel seeds

2 cups warm water (105°F. to 115°F.)

2 tablespoons unsalted butter, at room temperature

4 to 5 cups bread flour

Cornmeal for sprinkling

GLAZE

1 large egg white

2 teaspoons skim milk

In a large bowl, combine the yeast, sugar, salt, half of the fennel seeds, and warm water. Stir until the yeast is dissolved. Let stand until the yeast begins to bubble.

Add the butter and 2 cups of the flour. Beat with an electric mixer at medium speed or by hand for 2 minutes, until the batter is smooth and glossy. Stir in additional flour to make a soft dough. Turn out onto a floured board and knead until the dough is smooth and elastic, 5 to 10 minutes. Or knead in an electric mixer with the dough hook for 5 minutes.

Place the dough in a lightly greased bowl and cover. Let rise in a warm place until doubled, about 30 minutes. Cover a baking sheet with parchment paper or lightly grease or coat with nonstick spray. Sprinkle the surface with cornmeal.

Punch the dough down. Turn out onto a lightly oiled board. Divide in half and form into round balls. Place the loaves one at each end of the prepared baking sheet. Cover and let rise until almost doubled, about 30 minutes.

Preheat the oven to 400°F.

Mix the egg white and skim milk and brush over the loaves. Sprinkle the remaining fennel seeds on the loaves. Bake for 30 to 35 minutes, or until a wooden skewer inserted into the center of the loaves comes out clean and dry. Remove from the baking sheet and cool on a wire rack.

MAKES 2 LOAVES (12 SLICES EACH)

PER SLICE: *92.5 calories, 14% calories from fat, 1.39 g fat, 11.5 mg cholesterol, 179 mg sodium, 0.78 g dietary fiber*

Pumpkin Monkey Bread

This spectacular break-apart bread is perfect for a holiday buffet, especially with a lot of people. Seasoned with pumpkin and spices, baked in a fancy tube mold (I use a Bundt pan), it's delicious served with citrus-cured olive oil for dipping (see page 186).

3 teaspoons mixed pumpkin pie spice

1 cup sugar, divided

1 package or 1 tablespoon active dry yeast

1 cup warm water (105°F. to 115°F.)

1 tablespoon extra-virgin olive oil

1 teaspoon salt

½ cup instant nonfat dry milk

1 cup cooked puréed or canned pumpkin

4½ to 5 cups bread flour

In a small bowl, mix 1 teaspoon of the pumpkin pie spice with ½ cup of the sugar. Set aside.

In a mixing bowl, dissolve the yeast in the water. Stir in the remaining ½ cup sugar, the 2 teaspoons pumpkin pie spice, the olive oil, salt, dry milk, and pumpkin. Add 2 cups of the flour and, with an electric mixer, beat until the mixture is smooth and satiny. Stir in enough of the remaining flour to make a stiff but smooth dough. Cover and let rest for 15 minutes.

Sprinkle a board with flour and knead the dough for about 5 minutes, until the dough is smooth and springy. Place the dough into a clean, lightly oiled bowl. Cover and let rise for about 1 hour, until doubled.

Lightly grease a 10-inch tube pan or coat it with nonstick spray and dust lightly with flour. Punch the dough down and divide into three parts. Divide each of the parts into quarters, then divide the quarters into four parts each. Shape into balls and roll in the reserved spiced sugar. Place into the prepared pan so that the pan is evenly filled with dough. Cover and let rise in a warm place for 45 minutes, or until almost doubled.

Preheat the oven to 325°F.

Bake for 1 hour and 10 minutes, or until the bread is golden brown and a wooden skewer inserted into the center comes out clean and dry. Cool on a wire rack for 5 minutes, then invert onto a serving plate. Serve warm. To serve, pull the buns apart with forks.

MAKES 48 SPICED BUNS

PER BUN: *67.1 calories, 6% calories from fat, 0.43 g fat, 0.13 mg cholesterol, 49 mg sodium, less than 0.48 g dietary fiber*

Black Currant Bread

Each bite of this crusty bread is flecked with wine-soaked dried currants.

½ **cup port wine**

1 **cup dried black currants**

2 **packages or 2 tablespoons active dry yeast**

1½ **cups warm water (105°F to 115°F)**

3 to 3½ **cups bread flour**

1½ **teaspoons salt**

2 **teaspoons cornmeal**

Measure the wine into a saucepan and add the currants. Place over medium heat until hot and the currants are plumped. Remove from the heat and let stand 15 minutes, or until cooled. Drain and reserve the currants.

In a large bowl, combine the yeast, ¾ cup of the water, and 1 cup of the flour; beat until smooth and satiny. Cover and let stand in a warm place until spongy and doubled in bulk, about 30 minutes.

Stir the sponge down and add 1 cup more flour, the salt, and the remaining ¾ cup water. Add more flour, mixing until a stiff but still soft dough forms. Cover and let rest for 15 minutes. Turn out onto a lightly floured board and knead for 5 to 8 minutes, adding more flour if necessary to keep the dough from sticking. Or knead the dough with a heavy-duty mixer and a dough hook for 5 minutes, or put the dough into a food processor with the dough blade in place and process 1 minute. Knead in the drained plumped currants.

Cut a sheet of foil about 12 inches square and sprinkle with the cornmeal. Shape the dough into a rough ball and place it onto the cornmeal-covered foil. Cover and let rise in a warm place until doubled, about 45 minutes.

Arrange the oven racks so that the top rack is in the center of the oven. Place a baking stone, if you have one, on the top rack. Place a heavy pan (such as the bottom part of the broiler pan that comes with most ovens) onto the bottom rack.

Preheat the oven to 450°F.

Transfer the loaf, still on the foil, onto the preheated baking stone or a baking sheet. Pour 1 cup water into the preheated pan on the lower oven rack. (This should create a burst of steam.) Close the oven door and bake for about 20 minutes, or until the loaf is browned, firm, and hollow-sounding when tapped. Remove from the oven and transfer onto a wire rack to cool.

MAKES 1 LOAF (16 SLICES)

PER SLICE: *121 calories, 2% calories from fat, 0.29 g fat, 0 mg cholesterol, 268 mg sodium, 1.58 g dietary fiber*

High-Fiber Spa Bread

This is adapted from a wonderful bread I enjoyed at the Cal-a-Vie Spa in California. Sliced thin, toasted, and cut into triangles, it's great served in place of crackers with soup or salad.

- ½ cup seven-grain cereal or bulgur wheat
- 1 cup boiling water
- 1 package or 1 tablespoon active dry yeast
- 1½ cups warm water (105°F. to 115°F.)
- ½ cup light molasses
- 2 tablespoons honey
- 2 tablespoons canola or olive oil
- 1 cup quick-cooking rolled oats
- 1 cup unprocessed wheat bran
- 3 cups whole wheat bread flour
- ½ cup poppy seeds
- ½ cup sesame seeds
- ½ cup dry-roasted sunflower seeds
- 1 teaspoon salt
- 1 to 1½ cups bread flour

In a large mixing bowl, combine the cereal with the boiling water. Let stand until cooled, about 30 minutes. Sprinkle the yeast over the top of the cereal mixture and add the warm water. Let stand for 5 minutes, until the yeast begins to bubble. Stir in the molasses, honey, and oil. Add the oats, wheat bran, and whole wheat bread flour. Beat vigorously until the mixture is very smooth. Stir in the poppy seeds, sesame seeds, sunflower seeds, and salt.

Add the bread flour to make a stiff dough. Cover and let stand for 1 hour, or until the mixture has doubled.

Turn out onto a floured surface and knead until the dough feels elastic, adding just enough flour to keep the dough from being sticky. Scrape the surface clean and coat it with nonstick spray. Knead the dough on the sprayed surface just until it makes a smooth, round ball. Divide into two parts. Shape each part into an oblong loaf. Coat two 9 × 5-inch loaf pans with nonstick spray. Place the loaves into the pans and let rise in a warm place, covered, until almost doubled, about 1 hour.

Preheat the oven to 350°F.

Bake the loaves for 45 to 50 minutes, or until a wooden skewer inserted in the center of a loaf comes out clean and dry. Remove from the pans and cool on a wire rack.

MAKES 2 LOAVES (16 SLICES EACH)

PER SLICE: *138 calories, 28% calories from fat, 4.48 g fat, 0 mg cholesterol, 52.9 mg sodium, 3.37 g dietary fiber*

Kalamata Olive Bread

The purple-black kalamata olives often are slit to allow the wine-vinegar marinade in which they are soaked to penetrate the flesh of the olives themselves. Select the type that is packed in vinegar rather than olive oil. The olives speckle this irresistible coarse-textured, thick-crusted bread, which is incredibly simple to make.

2 packages or 2 tablespoons active dry yeast

1½ cups warm water (105°F. to 115°F.)

3 to 3½ cups bread flour

1½ teaspoons salt

1 cup pitted, well drained, coarsely chopped kalamata or black olives

2 teaspoons cornmeal

In a large bowl, combine the yeast, ¾ cup of the water, and 1 cup of the flour; beat until smooth and satiny. Cover and let stand in a warm place until spongy and doubled in bulk, about 30 minutes.

Stir the sponge down and add 1 cup more flour, the salt, and the remaining ¾ cup water. Add more flour, mixing until a stiff but still soft dough forms. Cover and let rest for 15 minutes. Turn out onto a lightly floured board and knead for 5 to 8 minutes, adding more flour if necessary to keep the dough from sticking. Or, knead the dough with a heavy-duty mixer and a dough hook for 5 minutes, or put the dough into a food processor with the dough blade in place and process 1 minute. Knead in the olives.

Cut a sheet of foil about 12 inches square and sprinkle with the cornmeal. Shape the dough into a rough ball and place it onto the cornmeal-covered foil. Cover and let rise in a warm place until doubled, about 45 minutes.

Arrange the oven racks so that the top rack is in the center of the oven. Place a baking stone, if you have one, on the top rack. Place a heavy pan (such as the bottom part of the broiler pan that comes with most ovens) onto the bottom rack.

Preheat the oven to 450°F.

Transfer the loaf, still on the foil, onto the preheated baking stone or a baking sheet. Pour 1 cup water into the preheated pan on the lower oven rack. (This should create a burst of steam.) Close the oven door and bake for about 20 minutes, or until the loaf is browned, firm, and hollow-sounding when tapped. Remove from the oven and transfer onto a wire rack to cool.

MAKES 1 LOAF (16 SLICES)

PER SLICE: 105 calories, 10% calories from fat, 1.17 g fat, 0 mg cholesterol, 341 mg sodium, 1.33 g dietary fiber

Walnut-Pecan Wild Rice and Raisin Bread

While this absolutely irresistible loaf is great for a holiday meal, you shouldn't wait for a special occasion to make it.

2 packages or 2 tablespoons active dry yeast

1½ cups warm water (105°F. to 115°F.)

3 to 3½ cups bread flour

1½ teaspoons salt

1 cup cooked wild rice, well drained

¼ cup chopped walnuts

¼ cup chopped pecans

½ cup raisins

2 teaspoons cornmeal

In a large bowl, combine the yeast, ¾ cup of the water, and 1 cup of the flour; beat until smooth and satiny. Cover and let stand in a warm place until spongy and doubled in bulk, about 30 minutes.

Stir the sponge down and add 1 cup more flour, the salt, and the remaining ¾ cup water. Add more flour, mixing until a stiff but still soft dough forms. Cover and let rest for 15 minutes. Turn out onto a lightly floured board and knead for 5 to 8 minutes, adding more flour if necessary to keep the dough from sticking. Or knead the dough with a heavy-duty mixer and a dough hook for 5 minutes, or put the dough into a food processor with the dough blade in place and process 1 minute. Mix in the wild rice, nuts, and raisins.

Cut a sheet of foil about 12 inches square and sprinkle with the cornmeal. Shape the dough into a rough ball and place it onto the cornmeal-covered foil. Cover and let rise in a warm place until doubled, about 45 minutes.

Arrange the oven racks so that the top rack is in the center of the oven. Place a baking stone, if you have one, on the top rack. Place a heavy pan (such as the bottom part of the broiler pan that comes with most ovens) onto the bottom rack.

Preheat the oven to 450°F.

Transfer the loaf, still on the foil, onto the preheated baking stone or a baking sheet. Pour 1 cup water into the preheated pan on the lower oven rack. (This should create a burst of steam.) Close the oven door and bake for about 20 minutes, or until the loaf is browned, firm, and hollow-sounding when tapped. Remove from the oven and transfer onto a wire rack to cool.

MAKES 1 LOAF (16 SLICES)

PER SLICE: *158 calories, 17% calories from fat, 2.88 g fat, 0 mg cholesterol, 268 mg sodium, 1.66 g dietary fiber*

Whole Wheat Sun-Dried Tomato and Rosemary Baguette

This is a real favorite of my family's. The flavors of tomato and rosemary are perfect with almost any meal. If there is any left over, I like to slice the baguettes on the diagonal about ¼ inch thick and dry them in a low oven until they are crisp and use them for crostini.

8 dry-packed sun-dried tomatoes

1 package or 1 tablespoon active dry yeast

1 cup warm water (105°F. to 115°F.)

1 teaspoon sugar or honey

1 teaspoon salt

1 tablespoon olive oil

1 cup whole wheat bread flour

1½ to 2 cups bread flour

1 tablespoon freshly grated Parmesan cheese

1 tablespoon fresh rosemary leaves, chopped

½ teaspoon red pepper flakes

In a small bowl, cover the tomatoes with warm water; set aside to soak for 10 to 15 minutes, until softened. Drain and reserve the tomatoes.

In a large bowl, dissolve the yeast in the warm water, add the sugar, and let stand for 5 minutes, until the yeast begins to foam up. Add the salt and oil. Mix in the whole wheat flour and beat well. Add the bread flour to make a stiff dough. Turn out onto a lightly floured surface and knead, adding flour, if necessary, until smooth and elastic. Place the dough in an oiled bowl, cover, and let rise in a warm place until doubled, about 1 hour.

Turn out onto a lightly oiled surface and knead in the Parmesan, rosemary, and red pepper flakes. Chop the sun-dried tomatoes and knead them into the dough.

Divide the dough into four parts. Shape each portion into a 12-inch-long baguette. Leave the loaves right on the oiled surface, covered with a towel, to rise, about 45 minutes.

Place one oven rack in the center of the oven and cover it with unglazed tiles or a baking stone, if you have one. Place a heavy, shallow pan on the bottom rack.

Preheat the oven to 450°F.

With a sharp knife, make three or four parallel diagonal slashes about ⅛ inch deep on each loaf. Pick up the loaves with both hands (one at a time) and place onto the preheated tiles in the oven or transfer them to the oven on a baking sheet.

Pour 1 cup water into the preheated pan in the oven. This should create a burst of steam. Close the door immediately to enclose the steam in the oven.

Bake for 15 to 20 minutes, until the loaves are crusty and golden and sound hollow when tapped or until a wooden skewer inserted through a loaf comes out clean and dry. Remove the loaves from the oven and cool on a wire rack.

MAKES 8 SERVINGS

PER SERVING: 197 calories, 12% calories from fat, 2.74 g fat, 1.19 mg cholesterol, 298 mg sodium, 3.34 g dietary fiber

Sweet Potato Yeast Bread

Sweet potatoes give this bread an appealing golden color and a delicate crumb. When I was in Hawaii recently, a baker at one of the large hotels made a sweet potato bread using native purple sweet potatoes. It had a purplish color and a wonderful sweet potato flavor. Once home, I began experimenting and came up with my own version of the bread, equally delicious and tender. This is especially delicious dipped in citrus-cured olive oil (see Note).

1 package or 1 tablespoon active dry yeast

¼ cup warm water (105°F. to 115°F.)

1 cup cooked, mashed sweet potatoes

⅔ cup sugar

⅔ cup instant nonfat dry milk

3 large eggs, lightly beaten

2 tablespoons canola or olive oil

1 teaspoon salt

4½ to 5 cups bread flour

In the large bowl of a heavy-duty mixer, dissolve the yeast in the warm water. Add the sweet potatoes, sugar, dry milk, eggs, oil, and salt. Slowly mix in 4 cups of the bread flour and beat for 5 minutes, until the dough is very smooth and satiny, scraping the sides of the bowl often.

Add ½ cup more flour and beat for 5 minutes longer, until the flour is thoroughly incorporated into the dough. Add more flour, if necessary, and mix until the dough is smooth again.

Dust a surface with a little of the remaining flour and turn the dough out onto it. Knead lightly for about 1 minute, until the dough

forms a smooth ball. Place the dough into a clean, lightly oiled bowl, cover, and let rise in a warm place for 1½ hours, or until doubled.

Turn the dough out onto a lightly oiled surface and divide into two parts. Shape each part into a round loaf with a smooth top. Place in two lightly greased 8- or 9-inch round cake pans. Cover and let rise in a warm place until doubled, about 45 minutes.

Preheat the oven to 350°F.

Brush the tops of the loaves with water and dust lightly with flour. With a sharp serrated knife, score the loaves decoratively. Bake for 25 to 30 minutes, until golden. Remove from the pans and cool on a wire rack.

MAKES 2 LOAVES (16 SLICES EACH)

PER SLICE: *123 calories, 12% calories from fat, 1.56 g fat, 20.2 mg cholesterol, 89.2 mg sodium, 0.95 g dietary fiber*

NOTE: To make citrus-cured olive oil, with a potato peeler, remove a 3-inch length of zest from one lemon, one lime, one grapefruit, and one orange. Place in a bowl and cover with olive oil. Heat in the microwave oven for 1 minute at high power. Cool. Turn into a 1-pint jar. Add enough olive oil to fill the jar. Let stand, covered, for three to four days before serving. Makes 2 cups of olive oil for dipping. To serve, pour a tablespoonful or two of the oil into a small dish or onto a plate. Dip pieces of bread into the olive oil as desired.

WHOLE-GRAIN BREADS

Whole-grain breads add nutrition, fiber, and bulk to the diet without straining the dietary fat budget. Whole-grain breads are loaded not only with complex carbohydrates but also with B vitamins and iron.

Most whole-grain bread recipes call for no more than 50 percent whole grain. Use bread flour for the other 50 percent because it has more of the protein gluten, which is the necessary ingredient to develop the meshwork within the dough that will capture the carbon dioxide given off by the yeast and cause the dough to rise.

When you are mixing up whole-grain breads, expect the dough to feel "tackier" or stickier than a white-bread dough. There is a great temptation to add more flour than is necessary to a whole-grain bread dough. This is the reason why I hear so many complaints from home bakers that they are making "doorstops."

It is helpful to have at least one "rest period" while mixing and kneading whole-grain yeast doughs. My recipes usually call for a fifteen-minute rest before the kneading begins.

How can you tell when the dough is kneaded enough? In spite of the tackiness, the dough should have "spring," and it should not have lumps of unmixed ingredients. Even though it feels a bit sticky, when it has been kneaded enough it will feel smooth. I often coat the surface of the countertop and my fingers with a squirt of nonstick spray. Then I knead the dough just to check its "feel." As my mother always says, "It's better to leave the dough a little wet than get it too dry."

BUYING WHOLE GRAINS AND WHOLE-GRAIN FLOURS

Depending on the area of the country in which you live, you can buy whole-grain flours at the supermarket. Where I live I can buy light and dark rye, cornmeal, rolled oats, seven-grain cereal, whole wheat, bread, and all-purpose flours. For all other whole grains, I shop at our local whole-foods cooperative.

Unless I'm planning to do extensive baking, I find it practical to buy five-pound packages of a variety of whole-grain flours and keep them in the refrigerator. Whole grains contain more natural oils and can become rancid at warm temperatures. Be sure to bring refrigerated flours to room temperature before you use them.

Depending on the time of year, flour can absorb moisture from the atmosphere, which can alter the amount you use in any bread recipe. In the summertime, when the air in our area is warm and moist, bread recipes can take up to a cup more flour (based on a two-loaf batch) than in the winter, when the air is very dry.

Storing Whole-Grain Breads

As with all baked goods, be sure to cool the bread completely before wrapping. If you plan to freeze the bread, wrap it well in plastic or put it into a plastic freezer bag and seal it well.

If you have a small household, it is handy to slice the bread before you freeze it so that you can remove just what you need and keep the rest frozen. Baked bread, well wrapped, keeps well up to three months. Let frozen bread thaw in its wrapper, and if you want to serve it hot, simply heat in a 350°F. oven for fifteen to thirty minutes before serving. Frozen sliced bread can be thawed at room temperature in just a few minutes. We often toast it for breakfast.

Cinnamon Swirl Wheat and Oat Bread

This is a bread sure to please the hungry after-school crowd.

1 package or 1 tablespoon active dry yeast

1½ cups warm water (105°F. to 115°F.)

2 tablespoons light molasses

1 tablespoon unsalted butter, melted

1 teaspoon salt

½ cup dark raisins

¾ cup quick-cooking or old-fashioned rolled oats

1 cup whole wheat flour

2 to 2½ cups bread flour

CINNAMON SWIRL

¼ cup sugar

1 teaspoon ground cinnamon

In a large mixing bowl, dissolve the yeast in the warm water; let stand 5 minutes, until the yeast bubbles. Add the molasses, butter, salt, raisins, and rolled oats. Stir in the whole wheat flour. Add the bread flour, ½ cup at a time, to make a stiff dough. Let rest for 15 minutes. Turn out onto a lightly floured board and knead until smooth and elastic, 5 to 8 minutes.

Place the dough in a clean, lightly oiled bowl. Cover and let rise in a warm place until doubled, about 1 hour. Turn the dough out onto a lightly oiled surface and pat or roll the dough out to make a rectangle about 8 inches wide and 12 inches long. Lightly grease or coat a 9 × 5-inch loaf pan with nonstick spray.

Mix the sugar and cinnamon. Sprinkle the mixture evenly over the dough. Starting from a narrow end, roll the dough up tightly. Place the loaf with the seam side down in the prepared pan. Cover and let rise in a warm place for 35 to 45 minutes, or until the loaf has almost doubled. With a sharp knife, slash the top of the loaf diagonally in three places, making the cuts about ¼ inch deep.

Preheat the oven to 375°F.

Bake the bread for 30 to 35 minutes, or until golden and a wooden skewer inserted into the center of the bread comes out clean and dry. Remove from the baking pan and cool on a wire rack.

MAKES 1 LOAF (16 SLICES)

PER SLICE: *126 calories, 8% calories from fat, 1.18 g fat, 1.94 mg cholesterol, 135 mg sodium, 1.38 g dietary fiber*

Coconut Granola Bread

This makes a tightly textured but very tasty bread that's great cut into thin slices for breakfast as well as for tea or coffee breaks. I use low-fat granola, which you can find in the cereal section of the supermarket.

1 package or 1 tablespoon active dry yeast

1 cup warm water (105°F. to 115°F.)

1 teaspoon sugar

3 tablespoons instant nonfat dry milk

$\frac{1}{2}$ cup honey

$\frac{1}{4}$ cup shredded coconut

$\frac{1}{4}$ cup chopped dates

1 teaspoon salt

2 large egg whites

$\frac{1}{2}$ cup whole wheat flour

1 cup low-fat granola cereal

$2\frac{1}{2}$ cups bread flour

In a large mixing bowl, dissolve the yeast in the warm water and add the sugar. Stir and let stand for 5 minutes, until the yeast begins to bubble. Add the dry milk, honey, coconut, dates, salt, egg whites, whole wheat flour, and granola cereal. Stir until well mixed.

Stir in bread flour gradually until the dough is stiff but still sticky. Cover the bowl and let the dough stand for 15 minutes.

Turn the dough out onto a lightly floured board. Shape into a ball and knead for 5 to 6 minutes. Wash the bowl and oil it. Place the ball of dough in the oiled bowl and turn the dough over to oil the top. Cover and let rise in a warm place until doubled, $1\frac{1}{2}$ to 2 hours.

Cover a baking sheet with parchment paper or coat with nonstick spray. Punch the dough down and turn out onto a lightly floured board. Shape into a fat loaf. Place the loaf with the smooth side up onto the center of the baking sheet. With a sharp knife, score the top of the loaf. Cover and let rise in a warm place for about 1 hour, or until almost doubled.

Preheat the oven to 350°F.

Bake the bread for 45 minutes, or until a wooden skewer inserted into the center of the loaf comes out clean and dry. Remove from the pan and cool on a wire rack.

MAKES 1 LOAF (16 SLICES)

PER SLICE: 164 calories, 11% calories from fat, 2.01 g fat, 0.14 mg cholesterol, 164 mg sodium, 2.21 g dietary fiber

Country Grain Bread

Whole grains such as wheat, rye, buckwheat, and oats add flavor and texture to homemade bread. Potato water (the broth in which potatoes were cooked) gives the yeast a boost to make the loaf high and light.

- **2 packages or 2 tablespoons active dry yeast**
- **2 cups warm water (105°F. to 115°F.), preferably from cooking potatoes**
- **¼ cup honey**
- **¼ cup molasses**
- **3 tablespoons olive or canola oil**
- **1 tablespoon salt**
- **¼ cup wheat bran**
- **¼ cup quick-cooking or old-fashioned rolled oats**
- **1 cup stone-ground whole wheat flour**
- **1 cup stone-ground rye flour**
- **3½ to 4 cups bread flour**
- **Rolled oats for sprinkling**

In a large bowl, dissolve the yeast in the warm water. Add the honey, molasses, oil, salt, bran, and rolled oats. Let stand in a warm place for 15 minutes, until the mixture bubbles.

Stir in the whole wheat and rye flours, and beat well with a wooden spoon. Gradually stir in the bread flour, ½ cup at a time, until a soft dough is formed.

Turn out onto a lightly floured surface and knead to form a soft, springy, yet slightly "tacky" dough, about 5 to 7 minutes, adding flour 1 tablespoon at a time if necessary.

Place the dough in a lightly greased bowl and turn to coat the top with oil. Cover with plastic wrap and let rise in a warm place until doubled, about 1½ hours.

Cover a baking sheet or baker's peel with rolled oats. Turn the dough out onto a lightly oiled surface and knead to remove air bubbles. Shape the dough into a round loaf and place on the prepared baking sheet with the seam side down. Cover with a towel and let rise at room temperature for 20 to 30 minutes.

Preheat the oven to 425°F. for 20 minutes.

Place a baking stone or unglazed tiles, if you have them, onto the center rack of the oven. Place a shallow pan on a rack below. Dust the top of the loaf with bread flour. Slash the top of the loaf decoratively using a sharp knife.

Slide the loaf onto the hot stone or place the loaf on the baking sheet into the oven. Pour a cupful of water into the pan on the rack below. Close the oven and bake for 25 to 30 minutes, or until the loaf is browned and a wooden skewer inserted into the center of the loaf comes out clean and dry. Remove from the oven and cool on a wire rack.

MAKES 1 LARGE LOAF
(18 THICK SLICES)

PER SLICE: *188 calories, 14% calories from fat, 2.93 g fat, 0 mg cholesterol, 358 g sodium, 3.24 g dietary fiber*

Honey–Whole Wheat–Raisin Bread

Honey brings out the grainy flavor of whole wheat. This is a wonderful bread for lunch box sandwiches, and we especially love it hot out of the oven along with a hearty vegetable stew.

2 packages or 2 tablespoons active dry yeast

2½ cups warm water (105°F. to 115°F.)

¾ cup honey

3 tablespoons olive or canola oil

2½ teaspoons salt

3 cups stone-ground whole wheat flour

4½ to 5 cups bread flour

1 cup raisins

In a large bowl, dissolve the yeast in the warm water. Add the honey, oil, and salt. Let stand in a warm place for 5 minutes, until the mixture bubbles.

Stir in the whole wheat flour and beat well with a wooden spoon. Gradually stir in the bread flour, 1 cup at a time, until a soft dough is formed. Turn out onto a lightly floured surface and knead to form a soft, springy, yet slightly "tacky" dough, about 5 to 7 minutes, adding flour 1 tablespoon at a time if necessary. Or mix with an electric mixer using the dough hook until the dough is stiff but still tacky. Mix in the raisins.

Place the dough in a lightly greased bowl and turn to coat the top with oil. Cover with plastic wrap and let rise in a warm place until doubled, about 1½ hours.

Lightly grease two 9 × 5-inch baking pans or coat with nonstick spray. Turn the dough out onto a lightly oiled surface and knead to remove air bubbles. Divide the dough into two parts and shape each into an oblong loaf; place the loaves in the prepared pans. Cover and let rise at room temperature for 20 to 30 minutes, or until almost doubled.

Preheat the oven to 375°F.

Bake the bread for 25 to 30 minutes, or until a wooden skewer inserted into the center of a loaf comes out clean and dry. Remove the loaves from the pans and cool them on a wire rack.

MAKES 2 LARGE LOAVES (20 SLICES)

PER SLICE: *125 calories, 9% calories from fat, 1.35 g fat, 0 mg cholesterol, 162 mg sodium, 1.88 g dietary fiber*

Molasses Oat Loaf

This is a unique and handy refrigerator method for making a crusty, moist round loaf. After you mix the dough, it goes in a pan, then into the refrigerator for a slow rise. Bake it the next day, after it has risen.

- **1 package or 1 tablespoon active dry yeast**
- **1¼ cups warm water (105°F. to 115°F.)**
- **2 tablespoons light molasses**
- **1 tablespoon unsalted butter, melted**
- **1 teaspoon salt**
- **½ cup dark raisins**
- **¾ cup quick-cooking or old-fashioned rolled oats**
- **½ cup whole wheat flour**
- **2 to 2½ cups bread flour**

GLAZE

- **1 large egg white, lightly beaten**
- **2 to 3 tablespoons rolled oats**

In a large mixing bowl, dissolve the yeast in the warm water; let stand 5 minutes, until the yeast bubbles. Add the molasses, butter, salt, raisins, and rolled oats. Stir in the whole wheat flour. Add the bread flour, ½ cup at a time, to make a stiff dough. Let the dough rest for 15 minutes. Turn out onto a lightly floured board and knead until smooth and elastic, 5 to 8 minutes.

Lightly grease an 8- or 9-inch round cake pan or coat with nonstick spray. Shape the dough into a round loaf, place it in the pan, cover it with plastic wrap, or seal it in a large resealable plastic bag, and refrigerate for 8 to 24 hours. Uncover the dough and let stand for 30 minutes to 1 hour, until the dough has come to room temperature.

Preheat the oven to 375°F.

Brush the loaf with the egg white and sprinkle with the rolled oats. Bake for 30 to 35 minutes, or until golden and a wooden skewer inserted into the center of the loaf comes out clean and dry. Remove from the baking pan and cool on a wire rack.

MAKES 1 LOAF (12 THICK SLICES)

PER SLICE: *144 calories, 10% calories from fat, 1.6 g fat, 2.59 mg cholesterol, 180 mg sodium, 2.3 g dietary fiber*

Seven-Grain Bread

So hearty and healthy tasting, perfect for serious sandwiches, this is a fabulous homemade bread. I buy seven-grain cereal, a mixture that looks a lot like cracked wheat, at the local whole-foods cooperative. If you have trouble finding a multi-grain cereal, you can substitute couscous, bulgur wheat, or even an old-fashioned cooked breakfast cereal, such as Wheatena or Maltex.

1 cup seven-grain cereal, uncooked

1/2 cup boiling water

1 package or 1 tablespoon active dry yeast

2 tablespoons brown sugar

1 1/4 cups warm water (105°F. to 115°F.)

2 teaspoons salt

1 tablespoon canola or corn oil

1 cup whole wheat flour

2 to 2 1/2 cups bread flour

1/2 cup dry-roasted sunflower seeds

In a small bowl, mix the cereal and boiling water and let stand 10 minutes. In a large bowl, dissolve the yeast and the brown sugar in the warm water. Let stand 5 minutes, until the yeast begins to bubble. Add the salt, oil, and whole wheat flour and mix until blended. Stir in 1 cup of the bread flour and the soaked cereal. Slowly stir in additional bread flour until the dough is stiff but still slightly soft. Cover and let stand for 15 minutes.

Sprinkle flour on a work surface and turn the dough out onto it. Knead for 5 minutes, adding flour as necessary to handle the dough. Be careful not to add more than 2 1/2 cups bread flour in all. The dough will still be slightly "tacky." If you wish, you can place the mixed dough into a food processor with the dough blade in place. Process until the dough is smooth and comes away from the sides of the work bowl.

Place the kneaded dough into a clean, lightly oiled bowl. Sprinkle with the sunflower seeds. Cover and let rise for 1 hour, or until doubled. Cover a baking sheet with parchment paper or coat lightly with nonstick spray.

Punch the dough down and knead for a few turns, working the sunflower seeds into the dough. Cut the dough into two parts. Shape each into an 8-inch oval loaf. Place the loaves on the prepared baking sheet. Cover and let rise in a warm place for 45 minutes, or until almost doubled.

Preheat the oven to 375°F.

Slash the tops of the loaves with a sharp knife or with a razor blade. Bake for 25 to 35 minutes, or until a wooden skewer inserted into the center of a loaf comes out clean and dry.

MAKES 2 LOAVES (12 SLICES EACH)

PER SLICE: *90.8 calories, 12% calories from fat, 2.13 g fat, 0 mg cholesterol, 178 mg sodium, 1.58 g dietary fiber*

Swedish Onion-Rye Bread

The flavors of onion and caraway seeds go well with cheese and cold cuts, making this bread perfect for sandwiches. It is typically baked in a round loaf, but it can be baked in an oblong loaf pan or shaped into buns.

- **1 package or 1 tablespoon active dry yeast**
- **2 cups warm water (105°F. to 115°F.)**
- **½ cup instant nonfat dry milk**
- **1 tablespoon unsalted butter**
- **1 tablespoon sugar**
- **1 teaspoon salt**
- **¾ cup finely minced fresh onion**
- **¼ cup caraway seeds**
- **2 cups light or medium rye flour**
- **3½ to 4 cups bread flour**

In a large bowl, dissolve the yeast in the warm water; add the dry milk, butter, sugar, salt, onion, and caraway seeds. Let the mixture stand until the yeast begins to bubble.

Stir in the rye flour; beat well. Stir in the bread flour ½ cup at a time, beating after each addition, until the mixture makes a stiff but soft dough. Cover and let rest for 15 minutes.

Sprinkle the work surface with flour. Turn the dough out onto the work surface and knead for 5 to 10 minutes, or until the dough is smooth and springy, adding flour if necessary to prevent sticking.

Place the dough into a clean, oiled bowl. Cover and let rise for 45 minutes to 1 hour, until doubled.

Turn the dough out onto a very lightly oiled work surface. Divide into two parts. Shape each part into a ball. Lightly grease two 8- or 9-inch round cake pans or coat with nonstick spray. Place a ball of dough with the smooth side up in each of the pans. Press the dough down slightly to flatten the loaf a little. Cover and let rise in a warm place until almost doubled, about 45 minutes.

Preheat the oven to 375°F.

Bake the loaves for 30 to 35 minutes, or until a wooden skewer inserted into the center of the bread comes out clean and dry. Take the loaves out of the oven, and remove loaves from the pans. Turn out onto on a wire rack to cool.

MAKES 2 LOAVES (16 SLICES EACH)

PER SLICE: *82.5 calories, 8% calories from fat, 0.74 g fat, 1.16 mg cholesterol, 73.3 mg sodium, 1.57 g dietary fiber*

Three-Grain Wild Rice Bread with Sunflower Seeds

Whole grains along with cooked wild rice add flavor and texture to this wholesome bread. The original recipe included a half cup of shortening, which I reduced to 3 tablespoons of olive or canola oil. Both of these oils give breads a tender crust and texture. Without any oil at all, the bread develops a chewy, firm crust in baking—which also makes a good bread, especially if it will be consumed while it is still warm.

2 packages or 2 tablespoons active dry yeast

2 cups warm water (105°F. to 115°F.)

½ cup instant nonfat dry milk

½ cup honey

3 tablespoons olive or canola oil

1 tablespoon salt

½ cup rolled oats

½ cup gluten flour

1 cup stone-ground whole wheat flour

1 cup stone-ground rye flour

1 cup cooked, well-drained wild rice

3½ to 4 cups bread flour

1 large egg, beaten

¼ cup salted, toasted sunflower seeds

In a large bowl, dissolve the yeast in the warm water. Add the dry milk, honey, oil, salt, and rolled oats. Let stand in a warm place for 15 minutes, until the mixture bubbles.

Stir in the gluten flour, whole wheat flour, rye flour, and wild rice and beat well with a wooden spoon. Gradually stir in the bread flour, ½ cup at a time, until a soft dough is formed.

Turn out onto a lightly floured surface and knead to form a soft, springy, yet slightly "tacky" dough, about 5 to 7 minutes, adding flour 1 tablespoon at a time if necessary. Place the dough in a lightly oiled bowl and turn to coat the top with oil. Cover with plastic wrap and let rise in a warm place until doubled, about 1½ hours.

Cover a baking sheet with parchment paper or lightly grease or coat it with nonstick spray. Turn the dough out onto a lightly oiled surface and knead to remove air bubbles. Divide the dough into two parts and shape each into an oblong loaf. Place the loaves on the baking sheet with the seam sides down. Cover and let rise at room temperature for 20 to 30 minutes, or until the loaves are doubled.

Preheat the oven to 375°F.

Brush the loaves with the beaten egg and sprinkle with the sunflower seeds. Bake for 25 to 30 minutes, or until the loaves are browned and a wooden skewer inserted into the center of a loaf comes out clean and dry. Remove from the oven and cool on a wire rack.

MAKES 2 LARGE LOAVES

(18 SLICES EACH)

PER SLICE: *118 calories, 15% calories from fat, 2.07 g fat, 1.65 mg cholesterol, 66 mg sodium, 1.68 g dietary fiber*

Walnut-Rosemary Wheat Bread

Yeast breads hardly need any fat for tenderness, so we can add nuts for flavor and texture and still keep the fat ratio low. When kneading this bread after the nuts are added, try to resist the urge to add more flour. Nuts tend to break through the dough to cause stickiness, but the bread will be more delicate with less flour.

1 package or 1 tablespoon active dry
    yeast

2½ cups warm water (105°F. to
    115°F.)

1 tablespoon olive oil

¼ cup honey

2½ cups whole wheat flour

2 to 2½ cups bread flour

2 teaspoons salt

1 cup whole wheat bread flour

2 tablespoons sesame seeds

¼ cup finely chopped walnuts

1 tablespoon rosemary leaves

In a small bowl, dissolve the yeast in ½ cup of the warm water and let stand 5 minutes, until the yeast begins to foam.

In a large bowl, mix the remaining 2 cups water, olive oil, and honey. Add 1 cup of the whole wheat flour, 1 cup of the bread flour, and the salt. Beat until smooth. Add the yeast mixture and beat, using an electric mixer, until the batter is very smooth and elastic. Stir in the remaining whole wheat flour, the whole wheat bread flour, the sesame seeds, the walnuts, and the rosemary; mix well. Slowly add the remaining bread flour, stirring until a stiff dough forms. Turn the dough out onto a lightly floured board and knead lightly until smooth and elastic, being careful not to add more flour than the recipe calls for. Place the dough into a clean, oiled bowl and turn the dough to coat the top with oil. Let rise in a warm place, covered, until doubled, about 1 hour.

Cover a baking sheet with parchment paper, or lightly grease two 8 × 4-inch or 9 × 5-inch loaf pans or coat with nonstick spray. Punch the dough down and knead lightly to express all air bubbles. Divide into two parts. Shape into two round loaves and place on the baking sheet, or shape into oblong loaves and place in the loaf pans. Cover and let rise in a warm place until almost doubled in volume, about 45 minutes.

Preheat the oven to 350°F.

Bake the loaves for 25 minutes, or until a wooden skewer inserted through a loaf comes out clean and dry. Remove from the pan and cool on a wire rack.

MAKES 2 LOAVES (10 SLICES EACH)

PER SLICE: *143 calories, 16% calories from fat, 2.56 g fat, 0 mg cholesterol, 215 mg sodium, 2.58 g dietary fiber*

Wild Rice and Pecan Bread

There is no added fat in this crusty bread, so this affords the opportunity to add a rather generous amount of pecans.

2 packages or 2 tablespoons active dry yeast

2 cups warm water (105°F. to 115°F.)

2 teaspoons sugar

2 teaspoons salt

1 cup whole wheat bread flour

3 to 3½ cups bread flour

½ cup chopped pecans

1 cup cooled, cooked wild rice

In a large mixing bowl, dissolve the yeast in the water. Add the sugar and let stand for 5 minutes, until the yeast begins to foam up in the water. Add the salt, the whole wheat bread flour, 1 cup of the bread flour, the pecans, and the wild rice. Beat until the batter is smooth. Stir in enough additional bread flour to make a stiff dough. Cover and let rest for 15 minutes.

Sprinkle a work surface with flour. Turn the dough out onto the surface and knead gently, adding flour as necessary to keep the batter from being sticky, about 5 minutes. (The pecans and wild rice tend to tear through the dough and make it sticky; do not be tempted to add more flour than called for.)

Put the dough into a clean, oiled bowl, turn the dough over to oil the top, cover, and let rise until doubled, about 45 minutes.

Turn the dough out onto a lightly oiled surface. Divide the dough into two equal parts. Shape each part into an oblong or round loaf. Leave the loaves right on the oiled surface, covered with a towel, to rise, for about 45 minutes.

Place one rack in the center of the oven and cover it with unglazed tiles or a baking stone, if you have one. Place a heavy, shallow pan on the bottom rack.

Preheat the oven to 450°F.

With a sharp knife, make three or four parallel diagonal slashes about ⅛ inch deep on each loaf. Pick up the loaves with both hands (one at a time) and place onto the preheated tiles in the oven or onto a baking sheet and place in the oven.

Pour 1 cup of water onto the preheated pan in the oven. This should result in a burst of steam. Close the door immediately to enclose the steam.

Bake for 15 to 20 minutes, until the loaves are crusty and golden and sound hollow when tapped or until a wooden skewer inserted through a loaf comes out clean and dry. Remove the loaves from the oven and cool on a wire rack.

MAKES 2 LOAVES (12 SLICES EACH)

PER SLICE: *105 calories, 17% calories from fat, 1.92 g fat, 0 mg cholesterol, 179 mg sodium, 1.1 g dietary fiber*

STUFFED BREADS

I've always been fascinated by all the possibilities of both stuffed and topped breads, and lately the challenge of making them low fat. I'm pleased to say that all of the breads in this chapter are healthful and full of wonderful taste. They are all related, in a way, to the ever-popular American pizza. Made with fresh ingredients, they're nutritious and great for casual entertaining. Stuffed with vegetables, cheese, and/or meats, these breads need only a salad and dessert to make a meal. Vary the vegetables and other filling ingredients according to the season and your tastes.

You can make any of these breads ahead of time and either refrigerate or freeze them. Preheat the oven to 300°F. and warm refrigerated bread until it is heated through. Thaw frozen bread in the refrigerator overnight and then reheat.

Crab and Vegetable Torte

A simple food-processor dough makes the crust for this savory brunch or supper entrée that's low in fat and high in flavor. Surimi is imitation crabmeat made from Alaskan pollock, a variety of codfish.

1 package or 1 tablespoon active dry yeast

⅓ cup warm water (105°F. to 115°F.)

1 tablespoon sugar

2 cups all-purpose flour

½ teaspoon salt

1 tablespoon olive oil

2 large eggs, lightly beaten

CRAB FILLING

12 ounces cooked fresh crabmeat or surimi

4 ounces fat-free cream cheese

1 cup shredded Swiss cheese

1 cup chopped zucchini

½ cup chopped celery (about 1 stalk)

4 green onions (scallions), thinly sliced

2 tablespoons picante sauce or salsa

1 teaspoon salt

½ teaspoon pepper

Dash of Tabasco sauce

In a small bowl, dissolve the yeast in the warm water and add the sugar. Let stand for 5 minutes, until the yeast begins to bubble. Place the flour, salt, and olive oil into a food processor with the dough or steel blade in place. Process for 5 seconds, until mixed. Add the eggs and the yeast mixture and process until the dough cleans the sides of the bowl and spins around the bowl 20 times. Let the dough rise, covered, for 1 hour, or until doubled.

Lightly grease an 8- or 10-inch springform pan or coat with nonstick spray. Dust with flour.

To make the filling: mix the crabmeat, cheeses, zucchini, celery, green onions, picante sauce, salt, pepper, and Tabasco sauce in a medium bowl.

Stir the dough down. Turn two thirds of the dough onto a lightly floured surface. Roll into an 11-inch circle. Fit the dough into the springform pan and press it about 1½ inches up the sides. Spread the filling over the dough in the pan. Roll the remaining dough into a 9- or 10-inch circle and cut into eight wedges. Arrange the wedges over the filling in the pan, slightly overlapping the edges. Tuck the ends under. Cover and let rise in a warm place for 30 minutes.

Preheat the oven to 375°F.

Bake the torte until golden brown, 35 to 40 minutes. Cool 10 to 15 minutes before serving.

MAKES 8 SERVINGS

PER SERVING: 266 calories, 27% calories from fat, 8.01 g fat, 84.9 mg cholesterol, 440 mg sodium, 1.8 g dietary fiber

Spinach- and Ham-Stuffed Sandwich Ring

Serve slices of this handsome savory stuffed twist with flavored mustard accompanied by soup or salad. The bread dough requires no kneading.

1 package or 1 tablespoon active dry yeast

¼ cup warm water (105°F. to 115°F.)

1 cup warm skim milk (105°F. to 115°F.)

2 tablespoons sugar

3 teaspoons olive oil

1½ teaspoons salt

2 large eggs, lightly beaten

4½ cups all-purpose flour

FILLING

½ cup chopped onion

1 garlic clove, minced or pressed

1 tablespoon olive oil

2 cups chopped fresh spinach

1 cup chopped fully cooked smoked ham

1 cup shredded part-skim mozzarella cheese

In a large bowl, dissolve the yeast in the warm water. Let stand 5 minutes, until the yeast begins to bubble. Add the milk, sugar, 2 teaspoons of the olive oil, salt, and eggs and beat well. Stir in 2 cups of the flour. With an electric mixer, beat until the batter is smooth and satiny. With a wooden spoon, stir in the remaining flour and continue stirring, scraping the dough from the sides of the bowl, until a soft and sticky dough is formed. Cover and let rise in a warm place until doubled, about 1 hour.

For the filling, in a small skillet over medium heat, cook the onion and garlic in the 1 tablespoon olive oil for 2 to 3 minutes, until tender. Add the spinach and cook until it is wilted, about 3 minutes. In a bowl, mix the ham and cheese, then add the spinach mixture.

Stir the dough down and turn out onto a well-floured board. Lightly roll or pat into a rectangle 20 × 12 inches. Cut the dough into two lengthwise strips. Spread half the filling down the center of each strip. Bring the long edges over the filling to enclose it and pinch the edges to seal. Cover a baking sheet with parchment paper or lightly oil or spray it with nonstick spray. Twist the two strips together and shape them into a ring. Pinch the ends together. Cover and let rise in a warm place until doubled.

Preheat the oven to 375°F.

Brush the ring with the remaining 1 teaspoon olive oil. Bake for 45 to 50 minutes, until the bread is golden and a skewer inserted into the bread comes out clean. Transfer the ring onto a serving board or platter and cool slightly before serving.

MAKES 16 SLICES

PER SLICE: *192 calories, 21% calories from fat, 4.35 g fat, 35.4 mg cholesterol, 376 mg sodium, 1.32 g dietary fiber*

Vegetable Deep-Dish Pizza

Just a little real cheese adds richness to a deep-dish pizza that was originally loaded with fat. To keep the full flavor of the original, I use nonfat ricotta, which is high in protein and calcium, and lots of succulent vegetables. You can make the pizza and freeze it, well wrapped, for up to two months.

DEEP-DISH CRUST

1 package or 1 tablespoon active dry yeast

1 cup warm water (105°F. to 115°F.)

3 cups all-purpose flour

1 teaspoon sugar

1 teaspoon salt

1 tablespoon olive oil

VEGETABLE AND CHEESE TOPPING

2 garlic cloves, minced or pressed

1/4 cup coarsely chopped onion

1 1/2 cups sliced fresh mushrooms

1 cup nonfat ricotta cheese

1 1/4 cups (6 ounces) shredded part-skim mozzarella

4 medium tomatoes, seeded and chopped (3 1/2 cups)

1 small zucchini, coarsely chopped (1 1/4 cups)

1 tablespoon chopped fresh basil

1 tablespoon chopped fresh oregano

1/4 teaspoon fennel seed

12 large pitted ripe olives, quartered

1/3 cup chopped green bell pepper

Salt and pepper to taste

Dissolve the yeast in the warm water. Measure the flour, sugar, salt, and 2 teaspoons of the olive oil into a food processor with the dough or steel blade in place. Turn the processor on and add the yeast mixture. Process until the dough cleans the sides of the bowl, about 30 seconds. If the dough is dry and stiff, add water a tablespoon at a time until the dough is sticky but not wet.

Let the dough rest for 15 minutes. Lightly grease a 12 × 2-inch round deep-dish pizza pan or coat with nonstick spray, or grease a 13 × 9 × 2-inch rectangular cake pan.

Press the dough into the bottom and 2 inches up the sides of the prepared pan. Cover and place in a warm place while preparing the topping.

While the dough rises, combine the garlic, onion, and mushrooms in a nonstick skillet over medium-low heat and sauté until the vegetables are soft and tender and the liquid from the mushrooms has cooked away, about 8 minutes.

Preheat the oven to 500°F.

Brush the dough with the remaining teaspoon of olive oil. Spread with the ricotta and sprinkle with 1/2 cup of the shredded mozzarella. Top with the tomatoes and zucchini; the garlic, onion, and mushroom mixture; and the basil, oregano, fennel seed, olives, bell pepper, and remaining 3/4 cup mozzarella. Season with salt and pepper.

Place the pizza into the oven and reduce the temperature to 425°F. Bake for 25 to 30 minutes, or until the crust is browned and the topping is hot and bubbly.

MAKES 8 SERVINGS

PER SERVING: *293 calories, 29% calories from fat, 9.43 g fat, 23.2 mg cholesterol, 487 mg sodium, 3.12 g dietary fiber*

Vegetable Torte

Perfect for brunch, this low-fat main dish goes well with a fresh tomato salad and a platter of fresh fruit to follow.

1 package or 1 tablespoon active dry yeast

¼ cup warm water (105°F. to 115°F.)

1 tablespoon sugar

2 cups all-purpose flour

½ teaspoon salt

1 tablespoon olive oil

2 large eggs, lightly beaten

FILLING

½ cup water

1 large eggplant, chopped into ½ inch cubes

1 cup thinly sliced zucchini

½ cup chopped green bell pepper

½ small onion, sliced

1 large tomato, chopped

¼ cup chopped fresh basil leaves

Salt and freshly ground black pepper

8 ounces fat-free ricotta

¼ cup grated Parmesan cheese

4 ounces (1 cup) crumbled, cooked Italian-style bulk sausage (optional)

In a small bowl, dissolve the yeast in the warm water and add the sugar. Let stand for 5 minutes, until the yeast begins to bubble. Place the flour, salt, and olive oil into a food processor with the dough or steel blade in place. Add the eggs and the yeast mixture and process until the dough turns around the bowl 20 times. Let the dough rise, covered, for 1 hour, or until doubled.

For the filling, put the water, eggplant, zucchini, green pepper, and onion into a wok or pan. Heat to boiling; reduce the heat. Simmer for 4 to 5 minutes, or until the vegetables are tender. Drain excess liquid. Stir in the tomato and basil. Season with salt and pepper and set aside to cool.

Lightly grease an 8-inch springform pan or coat with nonstick spray. Dust with flour.

Stir the dough down. Turn two thirds of the dough onto a lightly floured surface. Roll into an 11-inch circle. Fit the dough into the springform pan, bringing it about 1½ inches up the side.

Spread half of the ricotta cheese and half of the Parmesan cheese over the dough in the pan. Spread evenly with the sausage, if using, and the vegetables, and top with the remaining ricotta and Parmesan.

Roll the remaining dough into a 9-inch circle and cut into eight wedges. Arrange the wedges over the filling in the pan, slightly overlapping the edges. Tuck the ends under. Cover and let rise for 30 minutes.

Preheat the oven to 375°F.

Bake the torte until golden brown, 35 to 40 minutes. Cool 10 to 15 minutes, remove from the pan, and serve.

MAKES 8 SERVINGS

PER SERVING: *247 calories, 28% calories from fat, 7.82 g fat, 69.3 mg cholesterol, 353 mg sodium, 3.77 g dietary fiber*

Bread Machine Breads and Doughs

When you wake up to the aroma of bread baking and coffee dripping through an automatic coffeemaker, you can almost imagine you're in Paris. Although bread machines will never replace a bakery next door, enjoying a breakfast of freshly baked bread without having to get out of your pajamas is a true pleasure.

The appeal of having a bakery in your own kitchen is in keeping with the "nesting" trend of the nineties. Automatic bread machines promise fresh bread in three steps: "toss it in, turn it on, take it out." Like the microwave and the food processor, bread machines are here to stay. And technology has reached a plateau and so many companies are making quality machines, prices have dropped considerably.

As one who does a lot of bread baking, I find the dough-making feature of the machine very useful. Because the machine mixes, kneads, and lets the dough rise at the perfect temperature, the results are great for making dough to bake conventionally. It is particularly useful during cold weather, when it is difficult to find the right room temperature, and it also makes your cleanup easier. Any bread recipe can be prepared in a bread machine as long as you follow the rules.

When you use your machine, you should adapt your recipes to three to three and a half cups of flour, because most bread machines cannot mix larger amounts efficiently. Always use bread flour because it is higher in gluten than all-purpose flour.

Read the manual before you begin, because each machine is programmed in a slightly different way, though most are not too difficult to figure out. Usually all ingredients should be at room temperature, including the liquid used in the recipe, but follow the instructions in your manual. Be sure to layer the ingredients according to the manufacturer's directions. Most machines call for adding the liquid ingredients first, followed by the dry ingredients and then the yeast. A few reverse that order.

Most bread machines have a delayed-bake option or timer that allows you to program the bread to be done so you can wake up to or come home to fresh bread. To program the machine for delayed mixing and baking, follow the manufacturer's instructions; however, be careful not to delay-start breads that have ingredients that will foster bacterial growth during the delay period. Dairy products, such as milk, sour cream, fresh cheeses, and eggs, are especially dangerous. When you program the machine for a delayed mixing also be sure that the yeast will not touch the liquid ingredients until the machine begins to mix. I usually put the yeast in a little hole I dig in the flour on top of the ingredients.

In order to produce consistent loaves, you need to use the right tools and measure accurately. This rule is most critical when you use the machine to both mix and bake the loaf. Just a tablespoon or two of extra liquid or flour can make the difference between a gorgeous loaf and a brick.

Measure liquids with a glass measuring cup. Set the measuring cup on a level surface and read it at eye level. For dry ingredients, use dry measuring cups that usually come in sets of four. Spoon rather than scoop the flour into the cup. Scooping can result in a tablespoon or two of extra flour! I usually stir the flour, then spoon it into the cup and level it off with a straight edge (I like to use a chopstick).

Read the list of handy measurements to know below for help in measuring ingredients accurately.

HANDY MEASUREMENTS TO KNOW

1½ teaspoons = ½ tablespoon

3 teaspoons = 1 tablespoon

4 tablespoons = ¼ cup

5⅓ tablespoons = ⅓ cup

16 tablespoons = 1 cup

1 stick of butter = 8 tablespoons = ½ cup = ¼ pound

1 pound of butter = 2 cups

1 large egg = scant ¼ cup liquid

1 lemon = 2 to 3 tablespoons juice

1 lemon rind = 4 teaspoons grated

1 medium orange = 6 to 8 tablespoons juice

1 medium orange = 2½ tablespoons grated rind

CHOOSING A BREAD MACHINE

I am often asked the question, "Which bread machine should I buy?" The answer depends on you. How many people are in your household? How much bread do you consume? Do you have space in your kitchen?

Bread machine loaf sizes range from 1 pound to 2½ pounds. I usually recommend buying a machine with a large pan, if your kitchen will allow it. You can always bake a small loaf in a large pan. One bread machine actually bakes two large loaves at one time, allowing you to bake two different flavors or two different sizes of loaf at once.

The shapes of the pans vary and are worth checking out. One machine makes a loaf of bread that looks like a conventional loaf because it has two paddles in the bottom of its pan.

Prices range from less than $100 to about $300. Look for features that you will actually use, because some machines will bake cakes, make jam, and cook rice, too.

Many of the machines feature specialty cycles, such as French, whole grain, sweet, and raisin (a beep tells you when to add dried fruits and nuts so they will not be mashed into the dough), as well as a choice of light, medium, or dark crust.

Most machines have a "dough cycle"; if yours does not, you can still watch the machine and remove the dough after the first rising and before baking. A "keep warm" cycle, which will keep the bread warm for an hour or longer, is another common feature.

STORING BAKED BREAD

Store cooled loaves in one- or two-gallon resealable plastic bags; press as much air out of the bag as possible before sealing. Because homemade loaves get stale more quickly in the refrigerator than at room temperature, it's best to freeze them unless you will use the bread within twenty-four hours.

Milk-and-Honey White Bread

This is great for breakfast when you program the machine for delayed mixing. Be sure to put the dry milk powder on top of the bread flour so that it will not get wet until the machine begins working.

- 1¼ cups water
- 1 tablespoon honey
- 1 teaspoon salt
- 3 cups bread flour
- ¼ cup instant nonfat dry milk
- 1½ teaspoons bread-machine or rapid-rise yeast

Measure all of the ingredients in the order in which they are listed into the mixing container of the bread machine. If your machine requires that the liquid ingredients be added last, simply reverse the order. Program the machine according to the manufacturer's directions for a basic loaf of bread, medium darkness.

MAKES 1 LOAF (1½ POUNDS, 16 SLICES)

PER SLICE: 95 calories, 2% calories from fat, 0.22 g fat, 0.19 mg cholesterol, 140 mg sodium, 0.65 g dietary fiber

Maple, Wheat, and Oat Bread

The flavor of whole grains and maple are naturally compatible. This bread is a perfect accompaniment to a bowl of hot, freshly made vegetable soup.

- 1¼ cups warm water
- 2 tablespoons maple syrup
- 2¼ cups bread flour
- ½ cup whole wheat bread flour
- ¼ cup old-fashioned rolled oats
- 1½ teaspoons salt
- 1½ teaspoons bread-machine or rapid-rise yeast

Measure all of the ingredients in the order in which they are listed into the mixing container of the bread machine. If your machine requires that the liquid ingredients be added last, simply reverse the order. Program the machine according to the manufacturer's directions for a basic loaf of bread, medium darkness.

MAKES 1 LOAF (1½ POUNDS, 16 SLICES)

PER SLICE: 88.4 calories, 3% calories from fat, 0.33 g fat, 0 mg cholesterol, 134 mg sodium, 1.16 g dietary fiber

Multi-Grain Wheat Bread

This makes a very nicely textured and flavored bread. You can use uncooked couscous or any kind of granule-style breakfast cereal that has to be cooked.

1¼ cups warm water (105°F to 115°F.)

2½ cups bread flour

⅓ cup seven-grain cereal

¼ cup whole wheat flour

1 tablespoon brown sugar

1½ teaspoons salt

1½ teaspoons bread-machine or rapid-rise yeast

Measure all of the ingredients in the order in which they are listed into the mixing container of the bread machine. If your machine requires that the liquid ingredients be added last, simply reverse the order. Program the machine according to the manufacturer's directions for a basic loaf of bread, medium darkness.

MAKES 1 LOAF (1½ POUNDS, 16 SLICES)

PER SLICE: *83.3 calories, 3% calories from fat, 0.23 g fat, 0 mg cholesterol, 201 mg sodium, 0.98 g dietary fiber*

Pumpernickel Raisin Bread

This makes a dark, rather close-textured bread that's perfect for thin-slicing. I use it as a base for open-faced Danish sandwiches.

1 cup warm water (105°F to 115°F.)

1 teaspoon fresh lemon juice

3 tablespoons dark molasses

1½ teaspoons salt

1½ teaspoons onion powder

1 tablespoon unsweetened cocoa powder

1 teaspoon instant coffee granules

1 teaspoon caraway seeds

2 cups bread flour

½ cup dark rye flour

½ cup whole wheat flour

1½ teaspoons bread-machine or rapid-rise yeast

1 cup dark raisins

Measure all of the ingredients except the raisins in the order in which they are listed into the mixing container of the bread machine. If your machine requires that the liquid ingredients be added last, simply reverse the order. Program the machine according to the manufacturer's directions for a basic loaf of bread, medium darkness. Set a timer for 22 minutes. After that time, add the raisins, or if your machine has a raisin bread setting, use that program and add the raisins at the signal.

MAKES 1 LOAF (1½ POUNDS, 16 SLICES)

PER SLICE: *121 calories, 3% calories from fat, 0.48 g fat, 0 mg cholesterol, 202 mg sodium, 2.4 g dietary fiber*

Whole Wheat and Yogurt Baguette

Yogurt adds a wonderful sourdough flavor to this bread, but for an even more intense sour flavor, drain off any separated liquid from the yogurt and use it as part of the 1 cup of water.

1 cup warm water (or a combination of drained yogurt liquid and water)

½ cup nonfat plain yogurt

1½ teaspoons salt

3 cups whole wheat flour

1 package or 1 tablespoon active dry yeast

Measure all of the ingredients in the order in which they are listed into the mixing container of the bread machine. If your machine requires that the liquid ingredients be added last, simply reverse the order. Program the machine according to the manufacturer's directions to make dough.

When the dough is ready, remove it from the machine and place on a lightly oiled work surface. Shape the dough into a long, narrow baguette. Cover and let rise in a warm place until doubled, about 45 minutes.

Arrange the oven racks so that the top rack is in the center of the oven. Place a baking stone or unglazed tiles, if you have them, on the top rack. Place a heavy pan (such as the bottom part of the broiler pan that comes with most ovens) onto the bottom rack.

Preheat the oven to 450°F.

Transfer the loaf onto the baking stone or preheated tiles, if using, or put the bread on a baking sheet and place in the oven. Pour 1 cup water into the preheated pan on the lower oven rack. (This should create a burst of steam.) Close the oven door and bake for about 20 minutes, or until the loaf is browned, firm, and hollow-sounding when tapped. Remove the loaf from the oven and transfer onto a wire rack to cool.

MAKES 1 LOAF (16 SLICES)

PER SLICE: *81.3 calories, 5% calories from fat, 0.43 g fat, 0 mg cholesterol, 136 mg sodium, 2.98 g dietary fiber*

Babka

This traditional sweet Eastern European Christmas bread is baked jelly-roll fashion in a tube pan with a cinnamon-sugar filling. I find it very helpful to mix the dough in the bread machine.

DOUGH

¼ cup water

2 large eggs, lightly beaten

¼ cup packed brown sugar

2 tablespoons unsalted butter, cut into small pieces

½ teaspoon salt

2½ cups all-purpose flour

1 package or 1 tablespoon bread-machine or rapid-rise yeast

FILLING

2 tablespoons unsalted butter, at room temperature

¼ cup dark or light raisins

½ cup sugar

1 tablespoon ground cinnamon

GLAZE

1 cup confectioners' sugar

2 to 3 teaspoons strong, hot coffee

Measure the ingredients for the dough in the order in which they are listed into the mixing container of the bread machine. If your machine requires that the liquid ingredients be added last, simply reverse the order. Program the machine according to the manufacturer's directions to make dough.

Lightly grease a 10-inch tube baking pan or coat with nonstick spray.

Remove the risen dough from the bread machine and place on a lightly greased surface. Roll out the dough into a 16-inch square. To assemble the filling, spread the dough with the butter and sprinkle with the raisins. Combine the sugar and cinnamon and sprinkle evenly over the dough. Roll up the dough jelly-roll fashion. Pinch the seam to seal. Cut the roll into 16 pieces and place them with the cut sides up very close together in the prepared pan. Cover and let rise in a warm place until doubled, about 1 hour.

Preheat the oven to 350°F.

Bake the bread for 30 to 35 minutes, or until lightly browned. Remove the bread from the pan immediately and place on a wire rack. Mix the confectioners' sugar and coffee to make a thin glaze. Drizzle the glaze over the bread. Cool.

MAKES 1 BABKA (16 SLICES)

PER SLICE: 170 *calories,* 19% *calories from fat,* 3.7 g *fat,* 34.4 *mg cholesterol,* 77.4 *mg sodium,* 0.78 g *dietary fiber*

Cinnamon Swirl Bread

What could be easier than measuring a few ingredients into the mixing container of the bread machine? And shaping the bread is a snap. There's no added fat in the bread beyond the egg. To eliminate that, simply add ¼ cup water to replace it, but note that the bread is best eaten the day it is made if you cut out the egg—it dries out quickly.

DOUGH

1 cup water

1 large egg, lightly beaten

1 tablespoon sugar

1 teaspoon salt

¼ cup instant nonfat dry milk

3 cups bread flour

1 package or 1 tablespoon active dry, rapid-rise, or bread-machine yeast

CINNAMON SWIRL

2 tablespoons sugar

2 teaspoons ground cinnamon

Measure the ingredients for the dough in the order in which they are listed into the mixing container of the bread machine. If your machine requires that the liquid ingredients be added last, simply reverse the order. Program the machine according to the manufacturer's directions to make dough.

Lightly grease a 5 × 9-inch loaf pan or coat with nonstick spray.

Remove the risen dough from the bread machine and place it on a lightly greased surface. Roll out the dough into an 8 × 16-inch rectangle. Combine the sugar and cinnamon and sprinkle evenly over the dough. Roll up jelly-roll fashion starting from a short end. Pinch the seam to seal. Place into the prepared pan with the seam side down. Cover and let rise in a warm place until almost doubled, 45 minutes to 1 hour.

Preheat the oven to 375°F.

Bake the bread for 25 to 30 minutes, or until lightly browned and a wooden skewer inserted into the center of the loaf comes out clean and dry.

MAKES 1 LOAF (16 SLICES)

PER SLICE: *104 calories, 5% calories from fat, 0.56 g fat, 13.5 mg cholesterol, 144 mg sodium, 0.28 g dietary fiber*

Finnish Rye Bread

The hearty flavor of dark rye makes this a regular bread in my house. The loaf is shaped like a big, flat round with a hole in the middle, resembling a cartwheel. And since traditionally this bread has no fat added to it, I didn't have to play with the recipe to end up with a truly irresistible loaf. The bread machine makes a dough that is just perfect for handling. To serve, cut the loaf into wedges, then split the wedges horizontally.

- 1¼ cups water
- 1 tablespoon sugar
- 1 teaspoon salt
- 2 cups bread flour
- 1¼ cups dark rye flour
- 1 package or 1 tablespoon active dry, rapid-rise, or bread-machine yeast

Measure the ingredients for the dough in the order in which they are listed into the mixing container of the bread machine. If your machine requires that the liquid ingredients be added last, simply reverse the order. Program the machine according to the manufacturer's directions to make dough.

Cut a sheet of foil about 14 inches square. Shape the dough into a rough ball and place it onto the foil. Flatten the dough out to make a flat round about 12 inches in diameter, then poke a hole in the center of the round and pull the hole open to about 3 inches in diameter. Cover and let rise in a warm place until doubled, about 45 minutes.

Arrange the oven racks so that the top rack is in the center of the oven. Place a baking stone, if you have one, on the top rack. Place a heavy shallow pan (such as the bottom part of the broiler pan that comes with most ovens) onto the bottom rack.

Preheat the oven to 450°F.

Transfer the loaf, still on the foil, onto the preheated baking stone, or place it on a baking sheet and transfer that to the oven. Pour 1 cup water into the preheated pan on the lower oven rack. (This should create a burst of steam.) Close the oven door and bake for about 20 minutes, or until the loaf is browned, firm, and hollow-sounding when tapped. Remove from the oven and transfer onto a wire rack to cool.

MAKES 1 LOAF (16 SLICES)

PER SLICE: *90.9 calories, 4% calories from fat, 0.38 g fat, 0.9 mg cholesterol, 140 mg sodium, 1.68 g dietary fiber*

Julekage

The Christmas bread of Norway and Sweden is shaped into a round loaf that's stuffed with fruit and made shiny with an egg glaze.

DOUGH

¾ cup water

1 large egg, beaten

4 tablespoons (½ stick) unsalted butter, at room temperature

¼ cup sugar

1 teaspoon freshly ground cardamom

½ teaspoon salt

⅓ cup instant nonfat dry milk

2½ cups all-purpose flour

1 package or 1 tablespoon bread-machine or rapid-rise yeast

1 cup raisins

¼ cup candied cherries, lemon peel, or orange peel

GLAZE

1 large egg yolk

2 tablespoons water

1 tablespoon Swedish pearl sugar or coarsely crushed sugar cubes

Measure all of the ingredients for the dough except the raisins and cherries in the order in which they are listed into the mixing container of the bread machine. If your machine requires that the liquid ingredients be added last, simply reverse the order. Program the machine according to the manufacturer's directions to make dough.

Lightly grease a 9-inch round cake pan or coat with nonstick spray.

Remove the dough from the bread-machine container onto a lightly oiled surface. Knead in the raisins and candied fruit. Shape the dough into a ball and place it into the prepared pan. Pat the dough down to flatten it so that it reaches the edges of the pan. Cover and let rise in a warm place until almost doubled, about 45 minutes.

Preheat the oven to 350°F.

Beat the egg yolk and water and brush the mixture over the bread. Sprinkle with the Swedish pearl sugar. Bake until lightly browned and a wooden skewer inserted into the center of the bread comes out clean and dry, about 35 to 40 minutes. Remove the bread from the pan and cool on a wire rack.

MAKES 1 LOAF (16 SLICES)

PER SLICE: *159 calories, 23% calories from fat, 4.06 g fat, 23.4 mg cholesterol, 90.8 mg sodium, 1.08 g dietary fiber*

Panettone

Panettone originated in Milan and is now a favorite holiday bread throughout Italy. Although the dough is rich with egg and butter, it comes out at 28 percent calories from fat. While I have all my ingredients out to mix up Christmas cookie doughs, I just measure the ingredients for this attractive holiday treat into the bread machine and save myself all of the "messy" work. Panettone, in its rustic paper sack, makes a lovely gift.

- ½ cup water
- 2 large eggs, lightly beaten
- ¼ cup sugar
- 4 tablespoons (½ stick) unsalted butter, at room temperature, cut up
- 1½ teaspoons anise seeds
- ½ teaspoon salt
- 3 cups all-purpose flour
- 1 package or 1 tablespoon bread-machine or rapid-rise yeast
- ¼ cup golden raisins
- ¼ cup chopped candied citron or other candied fruit
- 2 tablespoons pine nuts or slivered almonds
- 1 tablespoon confectioners' sugar

Measure all of the ingredients except the raisins, candied citron, pine nuts, and confectioners' sugar in the order in which they are listed into the mixing container of the bread machine. If your machine requires that the liquid ingredients be added last, simply reverse the order. Program the machine according to the manufacturer's directions to make dough.

Line the sides of an 8- or 9-inch diameter 3-inch-deep springform pan with brown paper and coat with nonstick spray, or fold down the edges of a paper bag, about 6 × 3 inches, to make a cuff that stands about 4 inches high. Coat the inside of the paper bag with nonstick spray.

Remove the dough from the bread machine's container and turn out onto an oiled surface. Knead in the raisins, candied citron, and pine nuts. Shape into a smooth ball and place into the prepared pan or paper bag with the smooth side up. With a sharp knife or razor blade cut a cross about ½ inch deep in the top of the loaf. Cover lightly and let rise in a warm place until almost doubled, about 1 hour.

Preheat the oven to 350°F.

Bake the bread for 35 to 40 minutes, or until a wooden skewer inserted into the center of the loaf comes out clean and dry. Cool the loaf on a wire rack and dust with the confectioners' sugar.

MAKES 1 LOAF (ABOUT 16 SLICES)

PER SLICE: *159 calories, 28% calories from fat, 4.96 g fat, 47.7 mg cholesterol, 156 mg sodium, 0.96 g dietary fiber*

Russian Kulich

This *classic Easter bread is a handsome, tall loaf that is decorated with a simple icing. The shape of the loaf as it comes out of the bread machine is perfect!*

DOUGH

1 cup water

1 large egg, lightly beaten

¼ cup sugar

1 teaspoon salt

½ teaspoon freshly ground cardamom (optional)

2 tablespoons unsalted butter, at room temperature, cut into small pieces

3 cups bread flour

⅓ cup instant nonfat dry milk

1½ teaspoons bread-machine or rapid-rise yeast

½ cup chopped blanched almonds

¼ cup golden raisins

¼ cup chopped candied orange or lemon peel or candied fruit

ICING AND DECORATION

1 cup confectioners' sugar

2 to 3 teaspoons milk or cream

3 to 4 candied cherries, cut into pieces

Measure all the ingredients for the dough, except for the nuts and fruit, in the order in which they are listed into the mixing container of the bread machine. If your machine requires that the liquid ingredients be added last, simply reverse the order. Program the machine according to the manufacturer's directions for a basic loaf of bread, light crust. After 22 minutes, or when your machine indicates it (if you have one that signals adding raisins or other fruit), add the almonds, raisins, and candied orange peel.

While the loaf bakes, mix the confectioners' sugar with enough milk to make a thin glaze. Remove the loaf from the bread machine's pan and cool on a wire rack, standing up. Drizzle with the icing and decorate with the cherries. Cool before slicing.

MAKES 1 LOAF (16 SLICES)

PER SLICE: *138 calories, 19% calories from fat, 2.98 g fat, 18.4 mg cholesterol, 143 mg sodium, 2.04 g dietary fiber*

Saint Lucia Crown

In Sweden this golden saffron-scented bread is always served on Saint Lucia's Day, December 13th. It's a pretty braid of sweet, spiced dough that, when baked, makes a perfect centerpiece for the traditional breakfast "coffee" of the day. The crown theme comes from the tradition of Saint Lucia, who wears a golden crown with lighted candles.

DOUGH

¼ cup water

⅛ teaspoon powdered saffron

2 large eggs, lightly beaten

¼ cup sugar

⅓ cup instant nonfat dry milk

1 teaspoon salt

4 tablespoons (½ stick) unsalted
    butter, at room temperature

3 cups all-purpose flour

1 package or 1 tablespoon active dry,
    rapid-rise, or bread-machine yeast

½ cup golden raisins

¼ cup chopped blanched almonds

ICING

1 cup confectioners' sugar

2 to 3 teaspoons water

½ teaspoon vanilla

Measure all of the ingredients for the dough, except for the raisins and almonds, in the order in which they are listed into the mixing container of the bread machine. If your machine requires that the liquid ingredients be added last, simply reverse the order. Program the machine according to the manufacturer's directions to make dough.

Cover a baking sheet with parchment paper or coat with nonstick spray. Turn the risen dough out onto a lightly oiled surface and knead in the raisins and almonds. Cut off about ½ cup of the dough. Divide the remaining dough into three parts. Shape each part into a strand 25 inches long. Braid the strands together and place on the prepared baking sheet in the shape of a wreath. Shape the reserved dough into a thin strand about 10 inches long. Shape into a bow and place it over the seam of the braided ring. Cover and let rise in a warm place until almost doubled, about 45 minutes.

Preheat the oven to 350°F.

Bake the loaf until lightly and evenly browned, about 25 to 30 minutes. Mix the icing ingredients to make a thin glaze. Brush over the baked bread until shiny.

MAKES 1 LARGE WREATH (16 SLICES)

PER SLICE: *163 calories, 28% calories from fat, 5.13 g fat, 47.9 mg cholesterol, 153 mg sodium, 1.27 g dietary fiber*

Sun-Dried Tomato and Pesto Bread

This is a wonderful bread hot out of the machine! Although it doesn't need a dip or a spread or any embellishment, I love it for sandwiches or to slather with a garbanzo spread with garlic and herbs and sesame seeds.

8 dry-packed sun-dried tomato halves

1 cup hot water

2 tablespoons red wine vinegar

$1/3$ cup prepared pesto sauce

2 tablespoons sugar

$1^{1}/_{2}$ teaspoons salt

3 cups bread flour

2 teaspoons bread-machine or rapid-rise yeast

Snip the sun-dried tomato halves into small pieces, then put them in a small bowl and pour the water over. Let stand for 5 minutes. Drain the liquid into a measuring cup and add water to equal 1 cup.

Measure all of the ingredients (including the water and tomatoes) in the order in which they are listed into the mixing container of the bread machine. If your machine requires that the liquid ingredients be added last, simply reverse the order. Program the machine according to the manufacturer's directions for a basic loaf of bread, medium darkness.

MAKES 1 LOAF (1 POUND, 16 SLICES)

PER SLICE: 94.1 calories, 9% calories from fat, 0.84 g fat, 0.1 mg cholesterol, 211 mg sodium, 0.84 g dietary fiber

Index

C o n v e r s i o n C h a r t

EQUIVALENT IMPERIAL AND METRIC MEASUREMENTS

American cooks use standard containers, the 8-ounce cup and a tablespoon that takes exactly 16 level fillings to fill that cup level. Measuring by cup makes it very difficult to give weight equivalents, as a cup of densely packed butter will weigh considerably more than a cup of flour. The easiest way therefore to deal with cup measurements in recipes is to take the amount by volume rather than by weight. Thus the equation reads:

$$1\,cup = 240\,ml = 8\,fl.oz. \qquad \tfrac{1}{2}\,cup = 120\,ml = 4\,fl.oz.$$

It is possible to buy a set of American cup measures in major stores around the world.

In the States, butter is often measured in sticks. One stick is the equivalent of 8 tablespoons. One tablespoon of butter is therefore the equivalent to $\tfrac{1}{2}$ ounce/15 grams.

SOLID MEASURES

U.S. and Imperial Measures		Metric Measures	
Ounces	Pounds	Grams	Kilos
1		28	
2		56	
3½		100	
4	¼	112	
5		140	
6		168	
8	½	225	
9		250	¼
12	¾	340	
16	1	450	
18		500	½
20	1¼	560	
24	1½	675	
27		750	¾
32	2	900	
36	2¼	1000	1

OVEN TEMPERATURE EQUIVALENTS

Fahrenheit	Celsius	Gas Mark	Description
250	130	½	Cool
275	140	1	Very Slow
300	150	2	
325	170	3	Slow
350	180	4	Moderate
375	190	5	
400	200	6	Moderately Hot
425	220	7	Fairly Hot
450	230	8	Hot
475	240	9	Very Hot
500	250	10	Extremely Hot

LIQUID MEASURES

Fluid Ounces	U.S.	Imperial	Milliliters
	1 teaspoon	1 teaspoon	5
¼	2 teaspoons	1 dessertspoon	10
½	1 tablespoon	1 tablespoon	14
1	2 tablespoons	2 tablespoons	28
2	¼ cup	4 tablespoons	56
4	½ cup		110
5		¼ pint/1 gill	140
8	1 cup		225
9			250, ¼ liter
10	1¼ cups	½ pint	280
15		¾ pint	420
16	2 cups		450
18	2¼ cups		500, ½ liter
20	2½ cups	1 pint	560
24	3 cups		675
25		1¼ pints	700
27	3½ cups		750
30	3¾ cups	1½ pints	840
32	4 cups	1 quart	900
36	4½ cups		1000, 1 liter
40	5 cups	2 pints/1 quart	1120

INGREDIENT EQUIVALENTS

all-purpose flour—plain flour
coarse salt—kitchen salt
confectioners' sugar—icing sugar

granulated sugar—castor sugar
half and half—12% fat milk
light cream—single cream

shortening—white fat
unbleached flour—strong, white flour
zest—rind